ST. PAUL'S CONCEPTION OF CHRIST

ST. PAUL'S CONCEPTION OF CHRIST

OR

THE DOCTRINE OF THE SECOND ADAM

The Sixteenth Series of the Cunningham Lectures

BY

DAVID SOMERVILLE, M.A.
MINISTER OF
ROSEBURN FREE CHURCH, EDINBURGH

WIPF & STOCK · Eugene, Oregon

Wipf and Stock Publishers
199 W 8th Ave, Suite 3
Eugene, OR 97401

St. Paul's Conception of Christ
or The Doctrine of the Second Adam
By Somerville, David
ISBN 13: 978-1-60608-510-3
Publication date 5/19/2009
Previously published by T. & T. Clark, 1897

TO

THE MEMORY

OF

MY FATHER

PREFACE

THE following Lectures were prepared in fulfilment of the duty laid upon me by my appointment to the *Cunningham Lectureship*. They are now published in the form in which they were delivered in March of this year, with the addition of such passages as had then to be omitted for want of time. What appears now as the Sixth of this course, on "The Eternal Nature of Christ," is additional to those that were delivered.

The Lectures attempt to deal, in part, with what is generally regarded as the leading task of Modern Theology: to recover and present anew to the faith of the Church the New Testament picture of our Lord. An American writer has remarked that "all things seem to point to the fact that the world is getting ready for a new conception of Christ."[1] If there is truth in this forecast,—if the minds of men are indeed moving on towards a conception of Christ that will relate itself in the closest way to the problems and tendencies of modern life, and by which He will make His appeal afresh to this generation,—it becomes the more necessary to renew our study of the apostolic writings which record the original impressions of His Unique Greatness. The Gospels

---

[1] G. A. Gordon in his *Christ of To-day*.

and the Christ of the Gospels must always be the basis of true thoughts regarding Him; but the faith of the apostles and their understanding of His Person and Work are also of lasting importance. The fact that the eternal significance of the life and death of Jesus for the religious life of mankind was only disclosed to those who believed in a Risen and Living Christ, warrants us in regarding the apostolic testimonies concerning the glory of their Lord as a continuation of the revelation made to us in Him of the mind and will of God. It is the more necessary to insist on this, as there is a disposition on the part of certain theologians—of whom Wendt, who has done such good service in the exposition of our Lord's teaching, may be taken as the representative—to make that teaching the one norm by which we may determine what does and what does not belong to the essence of the Christian religion.[1] This would practically rule out of court the testimony of the apostles as an independent source of truth in the construction of Christian theology. It is not likely that men will ever consent to hold so cheaply the great leading thoughts about Christ and His Work which we owe to those who stood nearest to Him, and who may reasonably be supposed to have interpreted His mind most truly, and gauged most accurately the bearing of His mission on the great questions of religion.

The Pauline intuition of Christ, which it is the object of these Lectures to expound, is indeed but one of several that are contained in the writings of the New Testament. And to some it will appear of less value than these others. There will always be persons who are drawn more power-

[1] See his *Die Norm des echten Christentums*.

fully to the Johannine mode of apprehending the Master's glory, even as there are others who will prefer the simpler and more practical teaching of St. James. But certainly none of the interpretations of the Christ that we owe to apostolic insight has been so influential as St. Paul's, at least on the religious life of the West. In any reconstruction of theology his thought must find a leading place; and any explanation of the secret of Christ's power in human lives will be entirely inadequate that overlooks those elements in the conception of Him that we owe to the genius of the great apostle to the Gentiles.

It is impossible to treat the Christology of St. Paul without reference to doctrines of the Christian faith that have received elaborate expression in the theology of the Church; and my references to them must appear very insufficient, considering the complexity of the problems that are involved. Notwithstanding, I have thought it well to touch, however lightly, on the various points that come up, so as to present a general survey of the field, though quite aware that details ought often to have been added in defence of positions laid down and in illustration of statements made.

In the Appendix I have given a few supplementary notes on matters that could not be discussed in the text without interfering with the continuity of thought which it seems desirable to preserve in a lecture. I had intended to include in these notes a translation, already prepared, of that portion of Rothe's *Ethik* in which the author works out, in his own speculative way, the conception of Christ as the Second Adam, but I found it would have added too much to the bulk of the volume. For the same reason, I have abandoned my purpose to deal with each of the Epistles separately, with the view of bringing out the contribution supplied by each to the systematic account of the apostle's thought. Those who wish to see this done at length are referred to Gess's work on the *Person and Work of Christ*, the first part of the second division of which is occupied with an examination of the passages in the Epistles that bear upon this subject. It has been done also more briefly, but very interestingly, by Schenkel, in his *Christus-Bild der Apostel*; and still more briefly by Principal Fairbairn, in his *Christ in Modern Theology*.

I have made large use of the results of the labours of those who in recent years have laboured with so much success in the field of New Testament Theology; but as regards the understanding of the mind of Paul on my subject, I do not know that there is one name more than another of which I ought to make grateful mention for help received, unless, indeed, it be that of R. Schmidt, whose *Die Paulinische Christologie*, which I read twenty years ago, first interested me in the subject, and set me on the lines of thought I have here followed. His little book, indeed, is almost entirely an exegetical treatment of leading passages. It is by no means easy reading, and some of his positions are, I think, untenable. But the thoroughness and originality of his handling of the whole subject is memorable, and subsequent writers have by no means acknowledged their full indebtedness to him.

But apart from authors whom I have consulted with advantage, I feel that I am under special obligations to Albrecht Ritschl, by whose theological method I am conscious of having been largely influenced in my treatment of the subject. It is deeply to be regretted, I think, that this great theologian has been for the most part introduced to this country in a way that hinders the appreciation of his real work in theology, and that his name has been made familiar to students chiefly in connection with errors he is supposed to have taught. His system may be assailable in many of its parts, and deserving of the criticism that has been directed against it; but the real value of his work lies not so much in his system as in his method and the principles by which he was guided. As one of his own disciples has said, "the principle is fuller and richer far than the system." His rigorous exclusion of all ideas in the interpretation of Scripture that are due to outside sources; his insistence on the Person of Christ as the centre of religious thinking, the source of Divine revelation, and the measure of all knowledge on religious subjects; the importance he attaches, for the understanding of the significance of Christ's Person, to the confession of the Christian Church as recorded in the New Testament; the emphasis he places on the ethical understanding of religious truth, and on the practical character of all vital theological thought,—these principles lead to a singularly fresh treatment of theology, and account for the remarkable impulse he has given both to theological activity and to religious life itself in his own land. Were his real work better known amongst us, one might hope to see a revival of interest in that department of study which has fallen into such deplorable neglect in the Churches of our country—I mean the study of Systematic Theology.

I have, in conclusion, to thank many friends — in

	PAGE
The ground of His Sonship in His ethical Perfection	43
Are men by nature sons of God?	44
The contrast between Christ and other "sons"	47
He is the Image of God in Humanity	48
The Pattern or Archetypal Man	50
Jewish Theology and St. Paul's doctrine of the Second Adam	51
The First Adam and the Second	52
The Incarnation the second stage of man's creation?	53
The Resurrection of Christ and the Realisation of the idea of the Second Adam	54
Christ the Ideal of Mankind, in what respect	58
The Epistles and the new type of character that Christ exemplified	61
The history, in the thought of the Church, of Paul's interpretation of the Person of Christ	63
Echoes of it in the New Testament	63
Schleiermacher and his school	64
R. Rothe's doctrine of the Second Adam	65
Its influence on Anglican Theology	67
Christ compared with Religious Leaders of the race	68

LECTURE III

CHRIST THE REDEEMER AND FOUNDER OF THE NEW HUMANITY, *pp.* 71–107

	PAGE
Christ in Pauline Epistles not merely the Pattern Man, but the Redeemer	73
The Death of Christ as the Revelation of God's love	74
Conception of God's love in Christ's teaching and Paul's	75
The Death of Christ an Accomplishment	77
Achieving forgiveness of sin	79
Connection between Christ's Death and forgiveness	79
The explanation based on Gal. iii. 13	81
The theory of Sacrifice	84
Explanation of St. Paul in Rom. v. 12–20	85
Paul's emphasis on the element of obedience in the Death of Christ	87
Why was obedience necessary?	88
Theories of theology	89
Where the real difficulty lies,—human analogies	92
Function of faith in St. Paul's scheme	94
Objection from science to validity of his reasoning in Rom. v.	95
The Death of Christ as accomplishing our death to sin and our moral renewal	98

CONTENTS xiii

	PAGE
Significance of Resurrection of Christ in this connection	101
Paul's method as a moralist	103
Objection to his idealism	105
His faith in the invincible efficacy of Christ as Redeemer	106

LECTURE IV

CHRIST THE LIFE AND THE LORD OF THE NEW HUMANITY,
pp. 109–147

The twofold activity of the Exalted Christ as Spirit and as Lord	111
Christ as Spirit or Immanent in Man	113
St. Paul's doctrine of the Spirit of God	113
His distinction between gifts and graces of the Spirit	115
The Spirit of God and Spirit of Christ	116
The Spirit and the Person of Christ	117
Relation of St. Paul's doctrine of the Spirit to the *Book of Wisdom*	118
Union between Christ and His people	121
Exposition of Gal. ii. 20	123
St. Paul's experience as pneumatic man	124
The Indwelling or Mystical Christ	126
The Mystical Body of Christ	128
The truth of Christ's immanence in the history of the Church	130
Mysticism	132
The Transcendence or Lordship of Christ	134
"Lord" ascribed to Him as Exalted	135
The issue of His life-work	136
The Lordship of Christ in the Christian life	137
Christ Lord, but subject to God	140
Identified with God in St. Paul's experience	143
Confession of His Lordship the confession of His Divinity	145
Quotation from Dr. Dale to this effect	146

LECTURE V

LATER DEVELOPMENTS: CHRIST THE FULNESS OF GOD, THE HEAD OF THE CHURCH AND OF ALL PRINCIPALITIES AND POWERS,
pp. 149–180

Contrast between later and early Epistles	151
Historical circumstances of the Church at Colosse	153
Enlargement of St. Paul's thought of Christ stimulated by these	154
Christ the "Fulness of God"	155

This the expression of a religious truth, the equivalent of the "Spiritual Man"	158
Christ the "Image of the Invisible God"	159
Bearing of these ideas on Christ's Archetypal relation to mankind	160
The Death of Christ as removing the dualism between Jew and Gentile (Eph. ii. 14-16)	163
As removing the dualism between men and angelic intelligences (Col. i. 19)	165
Christ's Exalted Glory represented under the conception of His Headship	167
Head over the Church	167
Relation of Headship to the ideas of "Spirit" and "Lord"	168
Head over "principalities and powers"	170
Value of this doctrine for us	172
Christ the Final End of Creation	176
Harmony of 1 Cor. xv. 24-29 with Col. i. 16	178
Emerson's idea that these lofty expressions applied to Christ are but "sallies of love and admiration"	179

LECTURE VI

THE ETERNAL NATURE OF CHRIST, *pp.* 181–220

References in Epistles to the Preincarnate life of Christ	183
Examination of passages	184
In particular Phil. ii. 6–9	188
Col. i. 15–18	191
The value of such statements	193
Supposed influence of the ideas of the synagogue	194
Of ideas borrowed from Greek speculation	195
Unsatisfactoriness of this view	196
Also, of the explanation of the German speculative school	197
Theories regarding Eternal Nature of Christ	199
That He pre-existed as the Heavenly Man	200
As the Second Person of the Trinity	202
Doctrines of Kenosis	204
As the Eternal God-man	209
Christology of Apollinaris	211
Harnack's identification of it with the Pauline view	212
Problem insoluble	214
Relation of earthly Form of Christ's Being to His Preincarnate indefinable	215
Equally so, the relation of the latter to His state as Exalted	217

	PAGE
On its metaphysical side, the Person of Christ a mystery	218
The real proofs of our Lord's Divinity	219

LECTURE VII

THE CHRIST OF HISTORY AND PAULINE INTERPRETATION,
pp. 221–259

The relation of the Christ of Faith to the Jesus of History	223
"Not Paul but Christ"	224
Trustworthiness of the Gospel records	225
The Messianic consciousness of Jesus	226
Agreement between Jesus' judgment about Himself and Paul's thought	229
The "Son of Man" and the "Second Adam"	230
St. Paul's representation of Christ as Son of God and the embodied Spirit of God in agreement with the Gospels	231
The meaning of Christ's Death in His teaching and St. Paul's	232
Objection to St. Paul's representation that it takes account only of the Death of Christ	234
Its one-sidedness, as ignoring Christ's work as Prophet	236
The Historical Christ in the faith of the Church	238
Emphasis in modern times on the Historical Christ	241
The plea for a Christology based on the history	242
The importance of the historical for an understanding of the religious worth of Christ	243
Depreciation of the historic picture by Dale and Weiss	246
The virtue of the Exalted Christ in Paul's Gospel	248
Van Dyke's insistence on the prophetic work of Christ in *The Gospel for an Age of Doubt*	250
The judgment of history on this view	251
Uses of the knowledge of Christ's earthly history in relation to communion with the Exalted Christ	252
Harmony of the two Pictures in Christian experience	255
Von Hofmann on St. Paul and the Gospels	257
Lasting value of St. Paul's interpretation	258

APPENDIX

LECTURE	I. Note A. St. Paul and the Historical Christ	263
"	" B. St. Paul's idea of the Christ before his Conversion	265

CONTENTS

			PAGE
LECTURE I.	Note C.	The Conception of Christ in the Pastoral Epistles	267
LECTURE II.	Note A.	St. Paul and the Supernatural Birth of Christ	271
,,	,,	B. Gore on the Gradual Apprehension of the Christian Ideal . . .	274
LECTURE III.	Note A.	The Revelation of God's Love in the Death of Christ and the Resurrection	276
,,	,,	B. The Sacrificial Language in St. Paul's Epistles	277
,,	,,	C. The Meaning of 2 Cor. v. 21 . .	278
,,	,,	D. Rom. iii. 23–26	280
,,	,,	E. Whether Christ suffered Spiritual Death	282
,,	,,	F. Owen on the Atoning Element in the Death of Christ	284
,,	,,	G. Häring on the Death of Christ as a Demonstration of the Evil of Sin .	286
,,	,,	H. On the Doctrine of the Fall in Jewish Literature	287
,,	,,	I. St. Paul and the *Imitatio Christi* . .	289
LECTURE IV.	Note A.	The Difference between St. Paul's Doctrine of the Spirit and that of the *Book of Wisdom* . . .	292
,,	,,	B. Recent Literature on the Pauline Phrase ἐν Χριστῷ	293
,,	,,	C. The use of term Κύριος in the Septuagint	295
LECTURE V.	Note A.	On the Angelology of St. Paul . .	297
,,	,,	B. Beck on Truth and Life . . .	303
LECTURE VI.		Different Forms of the Theory of the Pre-existent God-manhood of Christ	305
LECTURE VII.	Note A.	Dorner on the Idea of Christ in the Middle Ages	307
,,	,,	B. The Historical and Exalted Christ .	308
,,	,,	C. The Christology of Ritschl and his School	309
,,	,,	D. Beck on Intercourse with the Christ of the Gospels	323
ERRATA	. . . .		331

I

THE GENESIS AND CHARACTERISTICS OF ST. PAUL'S CONCEPTION OF CHRIST

ST. PAUL'S CONCEPTION OF CHRIST

LECTURE I

THE GENESIS AND CHARACTERISTICS OF ST. PAUL'S CONCEPTION OF CHRIST

I PROPOSE in the lectures which I am to have the privilege of delivering, to offer a contribution toward the understanding of Paul's conception of Christ. The most notable feature of modern theological thought is the revived interest in Christological inquiry that characterises it. In the life of the Church Christ is Supreme; and there is a widespread feeling that in the theology of the Church ampler justice must be done to the supreme significance of His Person for the scheme of Christian truth, and that renewed effort is needed to unfold, with due regard to simplicity and fidelity to fact, the contents of His Person in their bearing on the life of faith. Dissatisfaction is felt and expressed with forms of thought that have become the traditional modes of apprehending the distinctive Greatness of the Church's Lord; and a longing is entertained for simpler and more living apprehensions of the Jesus who of old won the love and confidence of men. What is spoken of as the theological reconstruction that is going on around us has for its watchword the familiar, though somewhat hackneyed cry, Back to Christ: let us, if it is at all possible, overleap the centuries, and go behind the systems and dogmas that have served to obscure rather than to reveal the living form of the Lord, that we may see Him

> "As He lived and loved sublimely mild,
> A Spirit without spot."

Every movement of reform within the Church in the past has originated in the impulse received from such a renewed acquaintance with Christ at first hand. And it seems to me that we have everything to hope for the revivifying of theology and Christian faith from the fresh contact of men's spirits with Christ in His human grace, disengaged from all that time and the fancies of men have done to hide Him from our eyes. Only we must take no narrow view of this return to Christ. There are those who look for its accomplishment exclusively to the success of the efforts that are made in these days to recall the figure of the Prophet of Nazareth by the help of the abundant light that is thrown by modern research and reflection on the scenery and surroundings of His life, on the wisdom of His teachings, and the perfection of His human character. And to them a study of Paul's thought of Christ does not promise much, for Paul was not a historian, but a prophet; and it is not so much the Jesus of history he brings before us as the Christ of faith, and that, it may be said, is no direct or immediate vision of Him at all. The New Testament can scarcely, however, be regarded as recognising this distinction, at least in the sharpness with which it is often made, for it is with the eye of faith that even the historians of our Lord's life look at the picture they set before us. It is a judgment of faith they habitually apply to the interpretation of it. But in so far as the distinction is real (and there is a manifest difference between the Gospels that describe the Christ whom men saw and heard and the Epistles that speak of Him after He had become in a peculiar sense the object of faith), the contrast that is founded on it is an imaginary one; and it is begging the question to infer that the picture we owe to the Epistles must be less real or less in accordance with fact than the other. The circumstance that it brings Christ before us, not in historical situations, but in His spiritual relations to men, will excite the suspicion of its truthfulness only with those who maintain that when Jesus died He passed for ever out of all connection with the human race; but the presupposition, I need hardly say, of the New Testament is that He died in order to rise again and live in the hearts of men, and to carry on an unseen ministry on their behalf. And on this understanding, a picture of Him that draws its colours from intercourse with the Invisible and Heavenly Christ, and from the experience of the influence of His personality on the inner life, may be as true as that which is constructed out of the bare facts of history.

All this will fall to be more fully considered in the course of these lectures. At the present stage it need only be added that we must not prejudge the question, or fancy that in trying to recover the image of the Christ we are free to use only such materials as are contained in the historic records of His life. If He is to retain His place in the faith of men as the Christ of God, as not merely the subject but also the object of religion, as the Author of religious benefits to the human spirit, and the Divine Answer to its cry for a light and peace and strength it has not in itself,—the return to Him that men crave must mean not only the fresh study of His incomparable greatness as a Prophet and religious Hero, but also the living apprehension of Him as He is presented in the thoughts of those who had believing fellowship with Him. They attained to an understanding of Him that sprang from the experience of His benefits; and, if they have little to say of His earthly life, they have a great deal to tell us of the religious significance of that life and of the moral and spiritual contents of His Person.

Such a view of Him as is given to us in the words of those who have inwardly appropriated the message they have read in His life and death need not be antagonistic to anything recorded to have been done and said by the historic Christ, while it will possess a value to all who are in quest of religious certainty, additional to that which can be claimed for the picture that is taken wholly from historical material. It is the Christ of faith, present often when the sublime figure of the Gospels could only be discerned through a distorting medium, that has proved a living power in the hearts and lives of men. My meaning will become more apparent if we devote this lecture to some introductory remarks on the general character of Paul's conception of Christ, the genesis of it in his personal experience, its relation to other Christological conceptions in the New Testament that have a similar origin, and also to the dogmatic conception that has been evolved in the course of theological thought; and the result will bring out more clearly the scope of this inquiry, and the course that is to be followed.

I

In taking a general survey of the Epistles of Paul with a view to gathering up the scattered information they contain of the historical Christ, we cannot help being struck by the poverty of detail that characterises them. When we remember that at the time Paul wrote the generation had not passed away that had seen and heard Jesus, and when we consider that the recollections of Him must have formed the most precious legacy of believers, we might have expected to find frequent allusions in the writings of the apostle to the gracious acts and words of the Lord Jesus; but in this expectation we are disappointed. Paul frequently

GENESIS OF ST. PAUL'S CONCEPTION OF CHRIST   7

appeals to the Old Testament,[1] but his references to the teachings of his Master are exceedingly scanty, and do not bear on the great principles of religion so much as on matters that are of comparatively trifling import.[2] And while he does give great prominence to the death and resurrection of Christ, and mentions one or two incidents, such as the institution of the Lord's Supper, in connection with these events, there is a quite remarkable silence as to the life and ministry of Christ as a whole, and as to scenes and incidents that might well have been appealed to in illustration of the grace of Jesus and of those features of character in which He is an example to His people. It is possible of course to exaggerate this characteristic of the Epistles; and good service has been done by writers who have investigated very carefully the various allusions to the gospel history, and have been able to show that a firm historical basis for the life and ministry of Jesus of Nazareth can be constructed from the writings of Paul.[3]

---

[1] In the Epistle to the Galatians there are ten quotations from the O. T., in Romans about fifty.

[2] See *e.g.* 1 Cor. vii. 10 (comp. Mark x. 12); ix. 14 (comp. Matt. x. 10). The Lord's words are quoted in these passages in a free way, showing that Paul took them in the spirit rather than in the letter. In 1 Cor. xi. 23 we are not required to believe that he received the words of the institution direct from the Lord. He wishes to trace the institution back to Christ Himself; but he does not mean that the words that follow were put into his mouth by Christ; they were received by the apostle doubtless through tradition. In 1 Thess. iv. 15 the reference may be to some saying of Christ's that is not contained in the Gospels. Paret, in accounting for the absence in Paul of details of Christ's teaching, urges first, that had he indulged in such details he would thereby have been following the practice of the Pharisaic Scholasticism of his day, which adduced in order quotations from the sayings of the ancient Rabbis; and second, that in the principles and inward spirit of his teaching he was conscious that he was in perfect harmony with the mind of Christ, so that he did not need support or proof from individual quotations (*Jahr. f. Deuts. Theol.* III. i. p. 45).

[3] This has been done by Dr. Matheson in a series of articles in the *Expositor* (Second Series, vols. i. and ii.) on "The Historical Christ of St. Paul." The author has gone over the allusions in the Pauline

Still, the fact remains that there is a surprising dearth of detail, and that a very few sentences would embody all that we are expressly told by the apostle of the historic life of Jesus. How is this to be accounted for?

The supposition of ignorance cannot, it seems to me, be seriously entertained. Some knowledge of the earthly career of Jesus must have been possessed by Paul, even before his conversion; we cannot imagine him undergoing so radical a change in the absence of all impressions of Jesus' personality and in ignorance of the truths He was reported to have taught. Impressions of the life and teaching of Jesus of Nazareth were widespread in Jewish society at the time, and Paul must have shared them. And on that occasion to which he refers in the Epistle to the Galatians, when, after his conversion, he went to Jerusalem on a visit to the apostles, and remained with them fifteen days, he had the opportunity of making himself acquainted with the course and incidents of our Lord's life, and the principles of His teaching. He seems, moreover, to have had access to sources of information about the historical Christ apart from the common tradition, which probably owed its origin to apostolic circles; for once he quoted a saying of Jesus' that is not recorded in the Gospels (Acts xx. 35). But if we are right in supposing on Paul's part an intimate knowledge of the human life of Jesus, the difficulty seems all the greater of explaining the fact that the image of Him that was most vital to the apostle's faith,

Epistles, both in thought and language, to the earthly life of Jesus, and out of these has constructed a life-portrait of the historical Christ that is identical with that in the Gospels. His conclusion is: "In the light of St. Paul's Epistles the facts recorded in these Gospels are proved beyond a shadow of doubt not merely to belong to the first Christian century, but to be the product of the first Christian age and the objects of implicit belief with the first Christian converts." Dr. Matheson is sometimes fanciful, but his argument on the whole is well put, and is valuable from an apologetic point of view. See Note A on Paul and the Historical Christ.

and that is stamped most unmistakably on his letters, is not made up of historical reminiscences, is not drawn from the tradition of the earthly life and teaching of Jesus, is not taken directly from history, but from a different source altogether.

There is no evidence, it must be borne in mind, that Paul ever met Jesus in the flesh,[1] or that he had personal associations of a human sort with Him such as the other apostles had. We may speculate as to what might have happened if he had come under the personal influence of Jesus in His lifetime. It is hard to think that, bigoted though he was in his Pharisaism, he would have resisted the impression which Jesus made on all noble-hearted men who thirsted, as Paul must ever have done, after a perfection which was above them. Be that as it may, the fact is that he first came to know Jesus and to believe in Him, on the way to Damascus, after He had Risen from the dead and had been Exalted, so that his direct knowledge of Him began where that of the other disciples ended; and the knowledge that dates from that period, and was derived from the impressions of the Saviour thus apprehended as the Lord, who was Spirit, retained to the end the character thus given to it at the first. It is always of the Exalted Jesus Paul speaks, of whom he predicates what he believes to be true regarding Him. The supreme worth of Christ for Paul was one that belonged to Him in His present and invisible heavenly life. In his view, the Christhood of Jesus was not an accomplished fact till He had risen from the dead and had entered on the higher stage of Being and Activity that followed. The historic Jesus alone was no Messiah to Paul. His earthly career, with all that distinguished it, was simply a preparation for, and a prelude to, a fuller life

---

[1] In 1 Cor. ix. 1 Paul asks: "Have I not seen Jesus Christ our Lord?" but this reference must be to the appearing to him of the Risen Christ on his way to Damascus. This constituted him a witness to the Resurrection.

and a vaster progress in the souls of men that was to reveal Him in His true proportions as the Divine Christ. The knowledge of the Risen Lord then was to him the essential thing in the understanding of Christ.[1] And since only they who knew Him as Glorified, knew Him as the Christ of God, understood the real significance of His mission, and shared in the blessings that He had come to give to men, we can see how natural it was for Paul to pass by the memories of Christ's earthly course in his anxiety to set forth the greater glories of the Risen Lord. There is a disposition among popular writers on theological subjects to exalt Christ at the expense of Paul. They dwell on the superiority of the teaching of the former to that of the latter, and limit the acceptance of Paul's authority to those doctrines of his that are found as well in the teachings of his Master. But Christ and Paul were not rival teachers; and, before we criticise the apostle, it is necessary that we should understand him and the precise relation in which he stood to the Lord. He does not come before us as a commentator, or an interpreter of the words of Christ, but as an interpreter of Christ Himself, and of the relation of His death and Risen Life to the religious wants of men. Jesus' own work was primarily not to teach, but to live the Life; not to say something, but to be and do something.[2] And

---

[1] In this connection the infrequency of the name of "Jesus" alone (the earthly designation), in the Epistles of Paul, may be noted. In Colossians it does not occur at all; in Galatians, Philippians, 1 Corinthians, only once; in 1 Thessalonians twice; in Romans three times; in 2 Corinthians twice. The formula "The Lord Jesus Christ," occurs in the undisputed Epistles seventy-three times; the "Lord Jesus" alone a little over a dozen times; Κύριος alone, where the reference is to Christ, is found about one hundred and thirty, "Christ" alone one hundred and eighty times.

[2] Strong (*Christian Ethics*, Bampton Lecture, 1895) observes that there is "extraordinarily little of positive moral exhortation in the Gospels" (p. 48); and that "the important element in the Gospels is the life historically described rather than the moral precepts which emerged in the course of it" (p. 50).

Paul recognised it as his task not to expound or enforce the doctrines of his Master, but to open up the message of His life and death. Men who do great deeds do not speak about them. "Heroes," as one has said, "are not their own heralds." Christ was not His own apostle or interpreter. It was given to Paul to tell men what Christ in His real nature was, and what was the significance of His life and death for mankind. If we hear from him scarcely any echo of the utterances of the historic Christ, the reason is, that it had not been the surpassing beauty or wisdom of the teaching of the Prophet of Galilee that had led him to accept Jesus as the Messiah, but the power and grace of the Risen and Glorified One; and hence it is round the latter that all his testimony turns. Not that he disparaged the historic tradition; the memories of Jesus remained a precious heritage, for they were memories of Him who was the same in heaven that He had been on earth, and who was known in His Eternal Nature by the things He had done and said in time. But they were inferior in value to the personal knowledge of a living Christ, and we cannot wonder that the interest that belonged to the earthly Son of Man was for him overshadowed by the grandeur and the power of the conception he derived from intercourse with the Risen and Glorified Son of God.[1]

II

And this brings us to the inquiry, what that conception was that Paul owed to his knowledge of and fellowship

---

[1] We are also to bear in mind in this connection the vividness with which the apostle looked forward to the coming in the near future of the Glorified Christ, and his intense interest in the salvation presently to be revealed, which must have withdrawn his thoughts from the past "days of the Son of Man." We now look back upon that life, and every word and incident of the historical Christ is of profound interest to us; Paul looked forward to the Christ to come, "forgetting the things that were behind" in his anticipation of the glory to follow.

with the Risen Christ. Fundamental to it, of course, was the belief common to Paul with the primitive Church, that Jesus, the historic Jesus, was indeed the Christ, the Chosen of God, Supreme over all. This truth, which he had struggled against and had refused for long to admit, he accepted at once as soon as he was convinced by supernatural means that Jesus was alive, and that in having been raised from the dead He had received the seal of His Messiahship. From that moment he transferred to Jesus who had suffered and died on the Cross all those ideas of sovereignty, universal Lordship, and judicial authority which the Jews associated with the office and Person of the Messiah, recognising in Him who had died a death of shame in love to men, One who embodied these ideas in their truth and purity. In the meek and lowly Jesus, crowned with glory, He now saw the fulfilment of the Messianic ideal. It is difficult for us to appreciate the vastness of the change, intellectual and religious, which was involved in this faith. To confess One as the Christ and God-sent King of men, who had lived in poverty as Jesus had done, and who, dishonoured by men, had died a malefactor's death, meant the complete surrender of all preconceived ideas, and the acceptance of an entirely new conception of what was worthy of God and man.[1] Nothing was more repellent both to the Greek and the Jewish mind, than the notion that One who had been in His earthly appearance the very embodiment of human weakness and helplessness, could either truly represent the character of God or exhibit the highest conception of human worth. The Messiahship of Jesus was the apotheosis of meekness, humility, patient self-sacrificing love; and to recognise the moral beauty of this Ideal, and the Divinity and claim to universal Lordship of One who had realised it as Jesus had done, was an act of faith so great, so completely in defiance

---

[1] See Note B on Paul's Idea of the "Christ" before his Conversion.

of the accepted dogma about the Christ, so revolutionary in its effects on the character of the believer, that it was viewed as springing from Divine inspiration. "No man," said Paul in writing to the Corinthians, "can say that Jesus is Lord, but by the Holy Spirit."[1]

The conviction, however, that Jesus was the Christ, while the turning point in the religious history of Paul, was the common conviction of all believers in the apostolic age. And proceeding to inquire into what was distinctive in the Christological thought of the apostle, we must now consider the fruit of that conviction in his inner life and experience. Here we must take into account the extraordinary personality of the man, and the influence of natural genius in shaping his religious life and colouring his apprehension of Christian truth. We know him indeed only through his Epistles, but we cannot fail to be impressed with the evidence these afford of his extraordinary fitness, by natural endowment and psychological characteristics, to be the instrument by whom a spiritual understanding or interpretation of the Christ of history was to be conveyed to the Church. It is not only his amazing grasp of mind and capacity for dealing with principles of truth that strike one, it is, above all, the firmness and delicacy of his spiritual touch, his power of concentration on the problems of religion and life, his vivid understanding of, and keen sympathy with, the conflict of humanity torn by the contending forces of good and evil; all this marked him out as pre-eminently fitted to discover for himself and tell to others what the living Christ is, and can do as the

---

[1] 1 Cor. xii. 3. Stanton (*Jewish and Christian Messiah*, p. 122) shows that the idea of a suffering Messiah was contrary to prevailing Jewish beliefs. Drummond, also, in his *The Jewish Messiah* (p. 358), says that "there was no anticipation that the Messiah must submit to pain and dishonour." See also Schürer (II. ii. p. 186), and Baldensperger (*Das Selbstbewusstsein Jesu*, p. 145).

Redeemer from sin and death and all that hinders the Perfection of man.

From the moment he was laid hold of by the Lord on the way to Damascus, and had surrendered himself to Him, he found himself in possession of a new life, in which Christ was everything to him—the Revealer of God's grace, opening up a way of acceptance and pardon, irrespective of his own doings, as well as the Pattern and the Power of an obedience to the Divine Will that flowed from the springs of affection and sentiment. In fellowship with Him he stepped into a wonderful experience of life. The consciousness of Sonship to God, and of spiritual freedom, of separation from all that had dragged him down, and union with and hopeful effort after the loftiest ideals of life and conduct that had hitherto moved him only to despair, a sense of peace and moral power,—these and other such elements, testifying to the new creative force under which his inner life had come, entered into the experience that finds such abundant expression in the Epistles in which he poured out his heart to the Churches. That new force was the Spirit of God infusing into his soul a passion of love for the Personal Christ that was henceforth the dominant note of his life; and that experience received its specific character from the many-sided Good which he found in Christ, the fulness of Blessing to his whole nature that proceeded from Him. Now it is here, in the consciousness of what the Glorified Christ was to him in his personal life, that we are to look for the genesis of Paul's Christology. The conception of Christ's nature that was vital to him was derived from the experience of the new life. He saw Christ through the medium of all that wealth of religious benefit that flowed from living union with his Lord. The Christ of Paul, in a word, is the Christ of his experience, Christ interpreted to him by his vivid consciousness of the Divine life which he owed to

Him. His Christology is the account of that experience in the terms suggested by thought and reflection upon it. It is a judgment or series of judgments regarding Christ that are based on the impressions of Him received in the life of faith.

It is this feature, its being borrowed from his own religious experience, that distinguishes Paul's idea of Christ from a philosophical conception. There are those who account for the apostle's Christology on the supposition that, once convinced that Jesus was the Messiah, he proceeded to draw on his acquaintance with the doctrines of the Jewish schools, and constructed by a process of reasoning a Christ who answered to the theological ideas of the age. On this view, the Christ of Paul would be a purely ideal creation and destitute of objective reality. The question how far and to what extent Paul was influenced in his Christian thinking by the current ideas of the age, and by the intellectual training he had received in the schools of the Rabbis, and whether his teaching is encrusted with elements of error and imperfection from that source, which must be disengaged from the rest in estimating what is of permanent value in his representation of the truth, is a question that has to do with Paul's apprehension of Christianity as a whole, and which I do not feel called upon to discuss at large in dealing with a particular aspect of his theology. It will come up again and again in the course of these lectures in its bearing on particular aspects of our subject, as points occur that suggest the inquiry whether Paul transferred to his thought about Christ ideas that are traceable to outside sources, and therefore I need not dwell upon it now.

Meanwhile it is only fair to bear in mind his own account of the origin of his beliefs, and he tells us expressly that he owed them to the "revelation of Jesus Christ"[1] It was not then that he, Paul, clothed Jesus with ideas of Christhood

[1] Gal. i. 12.

that he got elsewhere; but Christ Himself, through all that wealth of moral and religious good which He communicated to His servant and made part of his inmost possession, supplied Paul with the ideas under which the latter regarded the Lord.[1] It was no mere intellectual conception that ruled the apostle's mind, no philosophical theorem resting on the authority of the schools. It was a conception of His nature that was most intimately related to his own experience of the redeeming power of Christ, and was as certain to him as were the facts of his own soul, its truth resting on the imperial authority inherent in every proposition regarding realities that are accessible to human experience.

The Christ of experience whom Paul brings before us, is at the same time connected in the closest possible way with the historic Personality of Jesus. It is true, indeed, that he takes account of only one event in the Gospel history, viewing, as Baur says,[2] the life of Jesus entirely in the light of the Death on the Cross. That event, however, had for the apostle a supreme significance,[3] for it communicated to the Heavenly activity of the Risen Christ its power to save men from sin and death. His Christology is accordingly an interpretation of the historic Jesus, and more particularly of His Death, from the view-point of one who believed that He had not only died, but had risen

---

[1] We are not to infer, however, that this "revelation of Jesus Christ" was equivalent to the communication to the mind of the apostle of the articles of the Christian faith. These were the result of reflection, but the material of his reflection was the impressions received in the life of faith. "It is manifest," says Paret, "that in his doctrinal conceptions Paul in the main elaborates the experience of his own inner life. His doctrine is a part of his person."

[2] Baur's *Paulus*, p. 290.

[3] This point of view is taken by all writers of the N. T.; it is shared by the evangelists themselves who narrate the story of Christ's life. How otherwise can we account for the length and particularity of the narrative of the passion and death of Christ, compared with the brief outline of the life they give, except on the supposition that the Death was in their view the supremely important event in Christ's course?

again, and who had entered on the experience of a Life that flowed from the Crucified and Risen One. The Resurrection was to Paul the disclosure of the nature of Christ. It was not only the crowning stage in the development of the Life that had been lived on earth, its natural consummation, but as such it was also the revelation of the inner nature of Christ and of the forces of His personal life that were concealed, as well as hindered in their proper exercise on others, as long as He was in the flesh. He came forth when He rose again, revealed in His proper Being, and freed from all that had prevented the universal significance and worth of His Person being seen and recognised.[1] It is, therefore, when viewed as Risen and Glorified that Jesus is properly understood, and His worth for the human race estimated aright. The nature of a thing, as Aristotle reminds us, is understood only when its process of development is over; and on this principle Paul habitually takes his stand on the Resurrection of Christ, where the last stage in that wonderful history was reached, and shows us from the light that thence falls on what went before, what it all means, what the issue of it all was for Christ and the work He had come into the world to do. Not till He had passed through death to the Resurrection-life was He fitted to become the Redeemer and Restorer of man to his ideal state, a Second Adam to the human race, the Power of a new life, moral and spiritual, to His brethren.

The conception of Christ as the Second Adam which is the nerve of the Pauline Christology, possesses this

[1] "Weil sich das wahre göttliche Wesen Jesu erst durch den Tod und die auferstehung vollkommen offenbarte, so hebt auch erst mit diesen Thatsachen und durch sie eine tiefere Erkenntniss des Wesens Christi an. Die Synoptiker, welche die Grenze und Schranke ihrer Darstellung an diesen Begebenheiten haben, haben eben damit auch die Schranke ihrer Lehre von dem Wesen Christi. Es ist Christi ewiges Wesen verhüllt vom Fleisch, von der σαρξ: der Menschensohn verdeckt den Gottessohn" (Grau, *Entwickelungs-Geschichte der N. Tlichen. Schrifthums*, ii. 14).

peculiarity that it is, as Sabatier puts it, "a blending of history and faith"; it is an interpretation of the historic Jesus from the view-point of the Resurrection, and drawn from the apostle's own experience of the working of the Spirit of the Risen Christ on his inner life. And the object of these lectures will be to expound this interpretation, to exhibit the significance to the apostle of the Person of Christ in the light of this conception of the Second Adam, to the truth of which his experience as a Christian man bore witness. But before entering on our task, it may be useful in what remains of this lecture to distinguish this from other Christological conceptions that we owe to apostolic inspiration, as well as from that which is the product of dogmatic theology.

III

In the New Testament we find other two classic interpretations of the historic Jesus besides that of Paul, other two leading types of Christological doctrine. In the Epistle to the Hebrews, Christ is presented to us as the Eternal High Priest of the human race, who is sat down at the Right Hand of God, reigning in His Glorified manhood. The standpoint of the author is the Exaltation of Christ; it is the theology of the Ascension and Exaltation that he sets forth. He wrote to Christians who had been brought up Jews, and who had associated the stability of their Christian standing and their freedom of access to God with the permanence of the temple service, and the stated performance of the offices of the Levitical Priesthood. When they perceived these institutions passing away, they naturally enough fell into doubt as to there being now any legitimate way of approach to God, any certainty that God had fellowship with them or they with God. The author writes to point them to Christ and His Glorified Humanity as the new and living way to the Father, to assure them of an access to God in prayer and worship that is of a nature fitted to inspire perfect confidence in the worshipper. There seems to be little or nothing in the outward events of Jesus' life on earth to suggest the work or office of a priest, or to warrant the author conceiving of Christ under this scheme of thought. But with great skill and tenderness he dwells on the temptation and sufferings of Jesus as intended to perfect Him in the qualities of character needed in One, who, after death, was to reign over men and to act on their behalf as their High Priest and Representative in the presence of God. This truth, then, that Christ is the Eternal High Priest of men, is the contribution which the author of the Epistle to the Hebrews makes to the Christ-idea; it is a truth that sets in a light of its own the perfection of the religious state and standing of believers, and the correspondence between Christ and what He is become, on the one hand, and the needs of human nature, on the other. It is a truth which, while religious in its character, is based on historic fact, and is an interpretation of the historic Christ seen with the eye of faith in His relation to human need.

And so with the Johannine view of the Person of Christ. The Gospel of John, whatever of historical value it may possess, is strictly speaking a doctrinal treatise; it is history written to illustrate a truth of faith, the truth that in Christ we have the Perfect and Final Revelation of God. The point of view here is neither the *Resurrection*, as with Paul, nor the *Ascension*, as with the author of the Hebrews, but the *Incarnation*. John is the theologian of the Incarnation; his concern is to show that Jesus is the Word or Logos of God, the perfect embodiment of the Divine mind and character; and for this purpose he sets Jesus before us as He walked about among men in Jerusalem and Galilee, and bids us mark that this highest and best of men is the Son of God, and His character the revelation of the perfections of the Heavenly Father.

These are the leading ideas of the Christ of the apostles; He is the Second Adam, the true High Priest, and the Logos—the Redeemer of men, the Fulfiller of all symbolic worship, the Revealer of God. As the Second Adam, He is the Christ of sinful mortal men, and appeals to the universal need, moral and spiritual, of the human race, in contrast to the National Deliverer that answered to the Jewish ideal of Messiahship. As the High Priest after the order of Melchisedec, He is declared to be the true abiding Representative of Man in the Heavenly Places, clothed with a function that is in vivid antithesis to the temporary and imperfect priesthood of those who, under provisional systems of worship, acted with God for their fellowmen. While as the Logos He is the manifestation of the Father in a human life and history, satisfying the desire for a true and living knowledge of God in a way that was impossible under systems of speculation in which the Logos was no more than an abstract idea. In this threefold conception, as Redeemer, Perfecter, Revealer, we have a presentation of the Person of Christ that is liberated from all admixture of particularistic elements which betrayed the radical imperfection of the Jewish, Hebrew, and Greek ideas of Christhood, and that commends Him to our faith, as able out of the riches of His life to meet the various needs of men as religious beings.

It is, moreover, to be observed that while each is distinct from the others, all three alike are based on history, and while, strictly speaking, religious conceptions, they are interpretations of the historic Christ. They are, in short, different aspects of the one Christ interpreted by the Christian consciousness, and by the experience of the Good it finds in Him. Apostolic Christology, then, is the doctrine of the Person of Jesus as understood and interpreted by the needs, aspirations, hopes, of the human soul. We can know Him only through the impressions His exalted Personality makes upon us when it is brought into connection with the deeper elements of our nature. The truth thus known is eternal, as all truths of faith are, and independent of the details or circumstances of His earthly life, but, at the same time, it is truth that rests on history; it is truth respecting Him in those deeper relations and wider aspects which the study of every great historical character more or less reveals, when, abstracting from outward details, we grasp its idea or spiritual content.

In this respect all the three forms of Christological doctrine in the New Testament differ from the Christology that has been formed by the application of human thought to the subject of the Person of Christ; and it is necessary to emphasise the distinction between the religious conception that we find in the New Testament and the intellectual or dogmatic one that is the product of ecclesiastical theology. At an early period in the history of the Church, the necessity arose for safeguarding its faith from the inroads of error. To preserve the truth of the revelation that had come through Christ, the Church was compelled to give intellectual expression to its faith, and to state in the terms which were current at the time, and were supplied by the Greek philosophy, which then moulded the thinking of men on the highest subjects, what it believed to be true regarding the different aspects of the Person of Christ, as these became matters of debate in the conflict with heresy. Now it was the reality of the Divine Factor in the Personal Christ that was endangered by speculation, now it was the truth of His humanity; again, it was the integrity and reality of the union between the Divine and the Human. Error on these matters was serious; religious interests were at stake; the issue was, had men really in Christ the salvation they believed they had, a real revelation of God expressed in the terms of a genuine human Life? Accordingly, the Church was occupied during the early centuries of our era in defining its faith against false opinion. And as the monument of the gigantic labour spent upon this task, we have the great Dogmatic decisions of the Councils on the Person of Christ, culminating in the formula of the Council of Chalcedon of "the two natures in one Person."[1] The work had to be done, and it is not easy to see how it could have been better done. But the result was by no means an unmixed gain. The faith was cast into the mould of intellectual formulæ that really added nothing to the knowledge of Christ, and were never intended to add to it, their sole purpose being to fence round the knowledge of faith so as to protect it from error. But it was inevitable that men who were so much occupied in defining should attach to the definition the importance that belonged to the truth itself.[2] It became to them the equivalent of the latter. The intellectual conception thrust into the background the religious, and belief in the dogma was substituted for the faith that rests on intuition. That this has indeed been the result we may see from the answer to the one question in our own Shorter Catechism that deals with the Person of Christ, "Who is the only Redeemer of God's elect?" "The only Redeemer is the Lord Jesus Christ, Who, being the Eternal Son of God, became man, and so was and continueth

---

[1] Properly speaking, of course, the last stage of the development of the dogma was not reached till, as the result of the Monothelite controversy, the doctrine of the Two Wills in the Person of Christ was affirmed by the Sixth General Council more than two hundred years after that of Chalcedon. This doctrinal finding, by which the last effort of the Monophysites to make good the unity of the personal life of our Lord was overcome, brought out into clear light the contradictions contained in the formula of Chalcedon, for two wills means two subjects, or egos, in which they reside, and thus we are landed at once in a double personality. The unity was reduced to a mere abstraction.

[2] See Fairbairn, *Christ in Modern Theology*, p. 89, and Gore's *Dissertations*, p. 173.

to be both God and man in two distinct natures, and one Person for ever,"—where the dogmatic definition, the result of the evolution of centuries of theological thought, which was originally intended to serve as a bulwark of the faith against error, is represented as the very truth of the faith itself. By being thus treated as sources of information about Christ, the dogmatic statements absorbed the interest that was properly due to the Christ of history and Christian experience. In the final form given to them, they made the understanding of the historic Christ an impossibility, for the Divine element in His Person had been defined in a way that when applied to the interpretation of the historic Christ, involved the sacrifice of the human element, and destroyed the naturalness of the Picture in the Gospels. That injury has been inflicted on the life of the Church by the tendency of dogma to emphasise the Divine at the expense of the Human in men's thoughts about Christ, is admitted even by those who naturally are disposed to attach the highest importance to the dogmas of the ancient Church. "There is no doubt, I think," says Gore, "that the genuine teaching of the Catholic Church for many centuries about our Lord has removed Him very far from human sympathies, very much farther than the Christ of the New Testament."[1]

It was to be expected that as soon as an interest in historic inquiry arose, and men sought, unfettered by theological opinion, to reconstruct from the Gospels the image of the historic Christ, that they would discover the inadequacy of the formulated dogma of the Church, and would either reject it altogether, and along with it the faith which had been translated into the creed, or they would endeavour so to modify the dogma as to leave room for the understanding of the Jesus of history and the maintenance of the faith that had been based upon Him. And this is just what has happened. In modern

[1] *Dissertations*, pp. 205, 206.

times the growth of the historic spirit has led to an amount of attention being given to the study of the records of Christ's earthly life and of His human Personality that has greatly enriched our knowledge. But the result has been to confirm the impression of the insufficiency of the Christological dogma. Some proclaim the hopeless variance between the Jesus of history and the Christ of dogma, and, accepting the purely humanitarian position, ignore the religious significance of the Person of our Lord. Others continue to maintain the old faith of the Church in Him as the Divine Christ, but frankly admit that the dogmatic statements in which that faith has been set forth call for revision or modification, and that something is needed to bring into harmony the findings of faith and the facts of the evangelical narrative. This is the object of the labours of the many students who have in recent years done good work in this department of theological research. One serious attempt has been made, and it is the most notable result of the Christological movement in modern theology, to develop the dogma of the ancient Church so as to leave room for the understanding in a human way of the life of Jesus. I refer to the theories of Kenosis, which under various forms of statement agree in regarding the Divine nature in the Person of our Lord as having in the Incarnation undergone a change resulting in its being contracted within the limits of humanity, and in the suspense of those Divine attributes whose presence and exercise are incompatible with a genuine human consciousness.

These theories are deserving of our earnest sympathy, for they are the efforts of believing men who aim, in consistency with their faith in the Higher Nature of Christ, at doing justice to the condescension of Divine Grace in the assumption of our human nature. And theologians of this school do succeed in presenting to us a Picture of Jesus that is distinguished by its fidelity to the record.[1] The serious difficulties, however, connected with nearly every form in which the theory of the Kenosis has been advocated by modern theologians, have prevented its general acceptance as a satisfactory solution of the problem. It is at least doubtful whether instead of being a development of the ancient dogma it is not an entire subversion of it. Few readers of the article in his *Dissertations*, in which Mr. Gore espouses the theory and compares it with the opinions of the Greek Fathers, will regard him as successful in the endeavour to show its harmony with the dogma as formulated by them, or with the theoretic presuppositions on which they work. And the fresh speculation to which we are driven to make out the consistency of such a doctrine of the Person of Christ with the Catholic dogma, speculation in a region where all is so uncertain, points to the wisdom of suspending our judgment on the matter in dispute. But if we are not satisfied with the last effort to save the old Christology, what is there left to us but to return to the New Testament and recover if possible the intuition of the apostles? Giving up the attempt to construct an intellectual conception of the Person of Christ that will satisfy speculation, we must learn to content ourselves with the understanding of His religious significance, and the knowledge of His nature that is gathered from the life of faith. On this view the Personality of Christ will come before us, not so much as a problem to be solved, as a fact to be apprehended and interpreted; and this happily is the attitude that serious-minded men in our generation are disposed to take toward the subject under discussion. They are less interested in the explanation of the Person of Christ than in the interpretation of It. How is He to be understood? What is

[1] For a fine instance of this, see Gess' *Christi Person u. Werk*, vol. iii. pp. 10–43.

the significance of His work for men? What is the place that belongs to Him in our own life and in the life of the world? These are the questions that are of interest to us, that must determine the method in which we approach the study of the subject, and to which an answer is found in the representation of those who, like Paul, depict the Christ of faith.

The Christology that will then fall to be considered embraces, it must be evident, more than is included under the term in dogmatic theology, where a rigid distinction is observed between the Person and work of the Redeemer. The nature of the Person is indeed only revealed in the experience of the peculiar effects that proceed from Him on the life and character, in the specific influence that He exerts on those who yield themselves to His sway. There is thus the closest and most vital connection between the doctrine of the Person and the doctrine of the Work of Christ; and the terms in which we express our Christological beliefs will be determined by our Soteriological experiences, that is, by the conception we have formed to ourselves of the Redemption of Christ.[1]

---

[1] R. Schmidt (*Die Paulinische Christologie*, 1870) insists that the understanding of Paul's doctrine of the nature of Christ depends on our understanding of his distinctive doctrine of the significance of Christ's redemption, and that every genuine insight of the person of Christ includes the knowledge of the worth of His salvation (pp. 4, 5). Similarly, Baur (*NTliche Theol.*) says, "The view of the Person of Christ is always conditioned by the view of His work. Christ can neither have done anything for, nor communicated anything to, men, except what was in Himself in principle (auf principielle Weise)." It is a position common to theologians of the school of Ritschl that the consideration of what Christ does in the experience of the life of faith must precede the understanding of what He is in His own Person. And it is significant that Gess, the orthodox opponent of Ritschl, reverses the usual order of treatment in his constructive book on the *Person and Work of Christ*, and begins with the discussion of His Work. "To proceed from the work to the Person," he says, "is the way to a living knowledge." "It is only real insight into Jesus' work that opens up to view the heights and depths of the Being that is able to do this work" (vol. iii. p. 7).

The inquiry, then, into the thought that at once regulated and expressed Paul's faith regarding Christ must take the form as well of an inquiry into the apostle's experience of the Good which he found in Him. The Person is made known in what He does for us, and the consciousness of what He does helps in turn to the understanding of who and what He is. Keeping this in view, I propose in my next lecture to consider Paul's interpretation of the Person of Christ, furnished to him by that specific experience of His influence which reveals Him as the Pattern or Archetypal Man; and in the lecture that follows, his interpretation of the death of Christ, in which He is viewed as the Redeemer from sin and the Founder of a new humanity. In the fourth lecture we will go on to consider the significance of the Resurrection-life of Christ, His present activity, on the one hand as *Spirit*, and on the other as *Lord*, by which He continues to carry on His work as the Second Head of the Human Race. We will thus have gone over the main truths asserted of Christ when He is designated the Second Adam. Three things are predicated of Him in this connection; first, that He is the Pattern Man; second, that He is the new Representative of the human race; and third, that He is the Power of a new and Divine life within humanity itself, reproducing and perpetuating His own Manhood. We will then proceed to the exposition of the development of these leading ideas in the later Epistles, what are known, from the prominence in them of the thought of Christ, as the Christological Epistles. The sixth lecture will deal with those passages in his writings generally that bear on the Pre-existence and Eternal Nature of Christ, His transcendental relations to God and Humanity. And in the closing lecture we will compare the Christ thus depicted in the apostle's writings with the picture of the historic Christ in the Synoptic Gospels, adding such reflections as are suggested by this study as to the relation of the one to the other, and the place that belongs to the Pauline Christ in the life and teaching of the Church.

With regard to the sources of information from which we are to draw for this study, it is enough to say that I accept as Pauline and available for use in the exposition of his teaching not only the four leading Epistles whose genuineness is almost universally recognised, but also what are known as the Epistles of the imprisonment. For, however unlike in certain particulars the latter may be to the former, the peculiarities do not seem to be such as to require us to refer them to a different authorship. The most recent opinion as to the authorship of the Epistles to the Colossians and Ephesians, coming from a school that cannot be charged with any championship of orthodoxy in criticism, is that the doubts which, in the view of many, attach to their Pauline authorship, are not insuperable. We are not likely, then, to go far wrong in proceeding on the tradition that refers them to Paul.[1] The authorship of the Pastoral Epistles constitutes a different problem. But as the material they offer for our present purpose is inconsiderable, the propriety of their use for the understanding of the apostle's doctrine on the subject on hand need not be discussed.[2]

Let me ask your indulgence in carrying out the task I have set before me. To re-think the thoughts of Paul is no easy work, and in no part of his teaching is one more frequently baffled in the attempt to penetrate the meaning of his words than when his theme is Christ, and what Christ is to the human spirit. It is not only that his language is cramped, and that in some of the most important passages we must remain in doubt as to which of several meanings that suggest themselves we are to accept as the intended

---

[1] Jülicher, *Einleitung in das N.T.*, pp. 84–97.
[2] See Note C on the Conception of Christ in the Pastoral Epistles.

one.[1] Nor is it merely that the intellectual atmosphere Paul breathed was so different from ours, and current ideas to which reference is made are so little understood by us; and his arguments, owing to his training in the Rabbinic schools, are so difficult for us to fit in to our logical forms; but, being the language of experience and the reproduction in human modes of thought of the facts of his inner life,—an inner life fused in so wonderful a way with the life and spirit of his Master,—it seems to demand an experience sympathetic with his, as rich, as full, and as subtle in its apprehension of spiritual things; and also a soul magnetised, if one may be allowed the expression, as his was with the love of Christ, in order that a true account may be given of who and what he believed Christ to be. "Where lives the Christian," exclaims Herrmann,[2] "who could with truth presume to say that he treasures the thoughts of Paul as his very own? Surely all of us read the apostle with the feeling that he has a different measure and a different energy of faith from ours." There is truth in the remark. It is but a feeble echo at the most that one can hope to catch of the grand strain of Christological thought that sounds through the apostle's writings, and which, stirring the deepest feelings of his heart, so often rises into the exultant language of a hymn. But since it has pleased God to reveal the truth of His Son, and of His salvation through the medium of a life and of experiences that bear witness to His commanding power over the human will, and to the satisfaction to all that is deepest in man that flows

---

[1] Holtzmann speaks of the following passages as "die sieben vornehmsten cruces interpretum": Rom. v. 12, viii. 3, ix. 5; 1 Cor. xv. 45; 2 Cor. v. 3; Gal. iii. 20; Phil. ii. 6; and, he adds, "aber der Stellen sind unsäglich viele, die sich aller hermeneutischen Kunst so unzugänglich erweisen, dass auch eine so methodisch als möglich geübte Exegese immer noch einen Rest von Zweifel übrig behält" (*Lehrbuch der Neutest. Theologie*, p. 204).

[2] *Intercourse with God*, p. 186.

from the voluntary surrender to that power, it is our duty to renew the endeavour to look with the eyes of this great interpreter of Christ at the picture of the Risen Glory of the Lord. We may cherish the hope that some features, at least, of that picture will be disclosed to the honest student, and that the vision, however partial it may be, will reward the effort to get it.

II

CHRIST THE ARCHETYPE OF HUMANITY

LECTURE II

CHRIST THE ARCHETYPE OF HUMANITY

In my opening lecture I aimed at showing that if we would be guided aright in our inquiry regarding Paul's thought of Christ, we must interrogate his inner life and experience as formed in union with the Risen Lord. It was the consciousness of the Power of Christ on his personal life that led him into that understanding of his Master, "for whose excellency he counted all things loss."[1] His Christology was in this way the product of his experience, the expression of what he had found Christ to be in his deepest life. There is in friendship such a thing as a union between two of so intimate a character that the inner forces that mould the life of the one pass into and become factors in the personal life of the other, and by their effects on his experience disclose to him the inmost nature of the man who has thus entered his personality to possess and dominate it. Now, from the moment that Paul was arrested by the Risen Lord on the way to Damascus and surrendered himself to Him, his whole soul was thrown wide open to His influence, to receive impressions that resulted in the communication to him of what was most distinctive in the personal life of his Master, and in the forming within him of an experience, with features of its own, that in its turn shed light on the nature of the Heavenly Being with whom he had been brought into so intimate a fellowship. The new elements that enriched his personal life, and that were

[1] Phil. iii. 8.

due to the influence of the Exalted Christ, supplied him with the means of construing to his thought the nature of that wonderful Personality that had made all things new within him.

His Epistles contain the record of that experience;[1] and from them we learn that in its essential features it was, on the one hand, a consciousness of new moral power identified by him with the power of the Holy Spirit of God, and, on the other hand, a consciousness of religious satisfaction rooting itself in reconciliation or sonship to God. He was conscious, in short, from the outset of his connection with Christ, of power proceeding from Him that was the power of the Holy Spirit, for by it that which was spiritual in him regained its supremacy over the flesh. And He who shed that influence on his inner life was thus revealed to him as a Being whose nature was Spirit, a Man distinguished from and contrasted with all others in this, that the Spirit of God was the indwelling Power of His personal life. Again, in communion with Christ, the old Judaic feeling of legalism and estrangement in his relation to God had given place to the consciousness of forgiveness and sonship; and this too, derived from Christ, pointed back to Him as the Son of God, differing from all others in the reality and power of His Divine Sonship and in His perfect oneness with God, constituting Him the Source to all who believed in Him of the Standing, Spirit, and Character of the children of God.

We have here the root conception of Christ in the

[1] "Im Epistolaren," says Auerbach in his *Auf der Höhe*, "ist personliche Gegenwart des Schreibenden: der Brief hat noch Stimme." It has often been pointed out how well fitted this form of literary expression is to be the medium by which truth that is personal and subjective in its character is conveyed. Of Paul's Epistles, Ewald says, "Es gibt in alter Zeiten und Völker Schriftthum sehr wenige Schriftsteller, deren Werke ein so unverkennbares, festes und gewaltiges Gepräge ihres eigenthümlichen Geistes tragen" (*Sendschr. des Apostel Paulus*, p. 2).

mind of the apostle. He is at once the PNEUMATIC or SPIRITUAL MAN, in whom the Holy Spirit of God is operative as the very principle of His Personality; and the MAN who is the SON OF GOD, the embodiment through His full participation of the life of the Father of the filial relation of Man to God.

This, in a single sentence, is the interpretation of the Person of Christ that we find in his writings, and that evidently dominated his thoughts; it is a religious interpretation, and takes account not of the metaphysical nature of Christ's Person, but of His significance for the moral and religious life of man. And in what follows it will be my object to expound this interpretation in its bearing on the fitness of Christ to occupy the central place assigned to Him in Paul's writings in relation to the human race as the Second Adam or Archetypal Man, adding a brief account of the history of this interpretation in the thought of the Church.

I

1. The one element in the conception of Christ that ruled the thoughts of the apostle was that of Spirituality. Christ is the SPIRITUAL MAN in whom the old antagonism in human nature between flesh and spirit has been overcome. It is the Exalted Christ to whom the apostle always refers; and it is of Him that this description holds in its absolute truth; but it holds also of the historic Jesus and of His state of humiliation, and we must look at it as the account of what He was when on earth in order to understand the full significance of it as the account of His glorified Person.

The supremacy of Christ as the Spiritual Man is best understood when we bear in mind what Paul's doctrine of human nature is. He regards man in his ideal constitution as made up of two parts, spirit and flesh. This is, of course, not a metaphysical definition, it is a religious account of the matter. It has respect to man as a religious being, having a nature that connects him with God and the spiritual world, as well as one that connects him with the world of sense and the material order of things. In virtue of his power of choice, man may determine himself either in the one direction or the other; he may obey the higher law of his being, or he may surrender himself to the desire and impulse of his sensuous nature; and, according to the choice he makes, he becomes either a spiritual or a carnal man. In point of fact he has made his choice in favour of the flesh, and this choice is repeated in every member of the human race, so that owing to the preponderating influence of the appetites and desires that have their seat in the material part of us, we are now carnal in character and mind, conformed to the principle of the flesh. Paul denies to human nature in its actual condition the possession of the Spirit of God.[1] He recognises, of course, the presence and working in human nature

---

[1] "Not till faith with its consequences begins," says Holtzmann in expounding the doctrine of Paul, "does the transcendent Spirit become an immanent principle in man." But it is going too far to assert, as he does, that the spiritual is the exclusive attribute of God, and is, "apart from our renewal by Christ, which is essentially our elevation to a higher stage of being, alien to the nature of man" (*N.T. Theol.* p. 16). Gloel is more cautious: "If the apostle nowhere expressly mentions the spirit of man when he speaks of our carnal state, the reason is that in his view man's 'spirit' does not unfold itself in its religious susceptibility and religious self-activity till it comes into contact with the Divine Spirit" (*Der Heilige Geist*, p. 80). The spirituality of man's nature even as fallen is demonstrated by the activity of the nous or faculty of moral cognition and will (practical reason) which is the organ of the Spirit of God, by which the latter finds access, under the Gospel, to the springs of our being to renew us in knowledge and reinforce our wills (Rom. xii. 2; Eph. iv. 23). These and other points relating to the *psychologia sacra* of the apostle are well put in the useful monograph of Simon on *Die Psychologie des Ap. Paulus*, 1897.

of spiritual elements, the activity of the nous, or mind, with its perception of a law that coerces the animal nature, the existence, in short, of an Inner Man that responds to the voice of God and duty. But when he speaks of Spirit, there is present to his mind the idea of power, energy, a principle of life and activity, and there is no such principle in man's nature. We are "without strength,"[1] though we strive after the Ideal we cannot reach it. The flesh is supreme, and if elements that are spiritual are still found in us, we are without the Spirit of God whose energy is needed to make them vital and dominant. Without this indwelling of God man is now a moral failure, and the highest capacities of his nature remain undeveloped.

In contrast is Jesus Christ, the Man in whom God is Immanent, and who, in consequence, realises the Ideal of our being. In Him also were Spirit and Flesh, but related to each other as they ought to be—the Spirit of God controlling the flesh and determining all the activities of the personal life, so that He became the Type of the Spiritual Man. To this peculiarity in the Person of Christ, the indwelling of the Spirit of God, is to be referred the fact, so fundamental in Paul's thought of Christ, of His personal holiness and entire freedom from sin. What distinguished Christ from all other men in the view of the apostle, and constituted the secret of His power to save, was His sinlessness. And in referring this exceptional position of Christ in humanity to His supernatural endowment by the Spirit of God, we are not to understand him as implying that it was not also the personal attainment of Christ. The apostle, indeed, says nothing explicit as to the process by which Christ achieved holiness, but that the latter was in no sense a ready-made virtue, or the result of a natural and necessary process, may, I think,

[1] Rom. v. 6.

be inferred from the fact that the apostle asserts the solidarity of Christ with mankind in sharing with them the flesh or material nature, with its weakness for good, its openness to temptation, its mortality.[1]

I can refer only in passing to the controversy on which so much has been written as to what precisely is meant by the term "flesh" in Paul's writings. A certain class of writers maintain that he was influenced in his use of the term by the usage of Greek philosophy, and that he held the essential evil of matter. According to them, his teaching is that the flesh, in virtue of its being material, is in itself evil, and that assumed by Christ it was in Him, as in us all, the seat of sinful passions and desires; His personal sinlessness being conserved by the admission that while it was an objective reality in His flesh it never became sin subjectively, or His own personal act, having been kept from passing into an act of will by the opposite principle of the Spirit. There is no proof, however, that Paul used the term in this metaphysical sense, while the strong probability is that he held the Old Testament view of the historical connection between the flesh and sin. The two things are separable in idea, although in concrete experience and in the life of the race the flesh is sinful; but the distinction leaves us free to hold that the flesh of Christ was that of unfallen human nature. It is another question whether it really was so. The doctrine that Christ was not born by ordinary generation seems to secure for Him a participation of flesh

---

[1] Rothe has discussed the process by which Christ achieved holiness in his speculative construction of the idea of the Second Adam in his *Ethik* (iii. pp. 135–170). But there is much force in Kähler's remarks on attempts to explain this matter: "The inner course of a sinless development is as inconceivable to us as life on the Sandwich Islands is to a Laplander. How can we, who are so different from Him in the very roots of our being that we need to undergo a new birth in order to acquire an element of likeness to Him, pretend to apply human measures to His development, its stages and course?" (*Der Sogenannte Historische Jesu*, 1896, pp. 53, 54).

exempt from sin. But whatever Paul's view was concerning the supernatural origin of Christ's life, this doctrine was not taught by him, and we can scarcely proceed upon it in the interpretation of his language on the subject under consideration.[1] Some accordingly have held, not on speculative grounds but on grounds of Scripture, and what appear to them the necessities of the case, that the flesh attributed by the apostle to our Lord in His humiliation was in itself, and apart from His personal will, identical with ours,— convinced that unless we take this view we cannot hold that His temptations were ours, or that His victory over evil is available for us. On the other hand, we have statements of the apostle's that make us pause before we go so far. We are told that "Christ knew no sin";[2] and such an aloofness of it from His very consciousness is scarcely consistent with its presence as an active principle or power in His material frame. Again, we read that He came in the "likeness of sinful flesh,"[3] a phrase that seems to have been chosen to guard against the idea of a perfect identity between the flesh of Christ and that of ordinary men. Two things may be like without being the very same. And the similarity between Christ's flesh and our own may well have been accompanied by a difference affecting the experience of the moral life, when we remember the strength of the Divine consciousness in Him. At the same time, the dissimilarity must not be pressed. The likeness was real enough to involve Him in a conflict with sin in the flesh that called forth His active "condemnation"[4] of it. For whatever else the apostle may mean to imply by that expression, he points to a dealing on the part of Christ with sin, in which he practically denied its right to rule in human nature, and demonstrated that a man who has the Holy Spirit for his life and strength is superior to

---

[1] See Note A on St. Paul and the Supernatural Birth of Christ.
[2] 2 Cor. v. 21.   [3] Rom. viii. 3.   [4] Rom. viii. 3.

the flesh, and need not succumb to its weakness. And this practical condemnation of sin in the flesh involved a continual resistance to it in its manifold approaches and forms of assault on His integrity, that establishes a community of feeling and experience between the sinless One and His brethren of a very real description.

If the flesh of Christ was not in itself sinful, the being in the flesh was nevertheless a humiliation to Him, and marked a lower stage in His history compared with that which followed. The flesh is a hindrance to the full unimpeded activity of the Spirit; it is weak, mortal, perishable, and the death of Christ is spoken of as significant of a new and higher step in the development of His Person; for, rising again, He became wholly spiritual, filled and pervaded by the unbounded power of the Spirit of God, which, although given to Him without measure when He was in the world, was then restrained by the material conditions of His earthly life, and could not till death took place glorify every part of His humanity. He became, then, in the fullest sense a Spiritual Man, so identified with the Spirit of God indeed that He is called Spirit. "The Lord is the Spirit."[1] It was as Spirit that Christ was first known to Paul, and it was the impression of Him as thus apprehended that ruled his thought of Christ to the end. Not that there is intended any negation of body. Paul does not conceive of Spirit apart from corporeity. He refers to the "Body of Glory"[2] in which the Risen One is clothed. Nor is the manhood lost sight of in his conception of the Exalted One. It is noticeable that he often applies to Him the name of Jesus, redolent of earth and of human memories. But withal, Christ as Exalted is in His very nature in a pre-eminent sense Spirit, free from the limitations of sense and flesh, the " Life-

[1] 2 Cor. iii. 17. [2] Phil. iii. 21.

Giving Spirit,"[1] or Dispenser of Spiritual Energy to men. Moreover, in His Glory as Spiritual Man He is the Forerunner of His brethren, who, with the laying aside of the flesh, are destined to enter on a similar form of life and activity. Perfected in their spiritual nature they will then receive bodies 'like unto His Body of Glory."[2]

To sum up then under this head: in the Risen Christ the apostle sees the triumph of the principle of Spirituality in Man. He beholds a manhood dwelt in by the Spirit of God and reaching its true end in the sinless perfection of its powers and in the attainment of eternal Life. Thus is Christ, Risen and Glorified, the realisation of the true idea of our nature,—Man, drawing his life from the Holy Spirit of God, become thereby holy and immortal.

2. But to Paul Christ was more than the Spiritual Man. He was also the SON OF GOD, the Original of that sonship that is a primary fact of Christian consciousness, the Man in whom the filial relationship was embodied in its absolute truth. The intimate connection between the Divine Sonship of Christ and the indwelling in Him of the Divine Spirit is set forth in the opening of the great Epistle to the Romans, where Paul speaks of the subject of the Gospel as being "God's Son, Jesus Christ our Lord, who was made of the seed of David according to the flesh, and marked out as, or appointed[3] to be, Son of God, with

[1] 1 Cor. xv. 45.
[2] Phil. iii. 21; Rom. viii. 12; 1 Cor. xv. 49; Eph. i. 18–20. "Glory" ($δόξη$) is almost a technical expression in Paul's writings. It is the characteristic of all that belongs to the world of heavenly reality. There belongs to everything that has its origin in heaven a "glory." It is the full manifestation of the "Spiritual." When all hindrances to the perfected activity of "Spirit" are removed, it appears as "glory." What is outwardly $δόξα$ is inwardly $πνεῦμα$. Christ is called the "Lord of glory" (1 Cor. ii. 8). He is also called the "Lord of the spirit" (2 Cor. iii. 18). These are like the reverse and obverse sides of a coin, the outward and inward aspects of the Exalted Christ.
[3] Weizäcker, in his version of the N. T., has it "Gesetzt zum Sohn Gottes mit-Macht." In their Commentary on Romans, Sanday

power according to the Spirit of Holiness by (or in consequence of) His resurrection from the dead."¹ Two things are to be noticed here.

On the one hand, we have the statement of the two factors of Christ's Person, the Flesh and the Spirit, and of the relations arising out of these to men and to God. As regards the flesh, He was a Jew and the Son of David. He is declared here and elsewhere² to be a Man of a particular nationality, having in His veins the blood of the Royal House of Judah. The Davidic descent of Christ was after all a carnal distinction, and of no value in the kingdom of God, and it surprises us to find the apostle who is so strenuous an opponent of all inequalities among men that arise out of the flesh, taking account of this accident of Christ's birth. Possibly it was his object to commend the gospel thereby to the Jewish section of his readers, who from this description of Christ would recognise Him as the Messiah promised to their fathers. Or he may have wished, in condescending to particularise His nationality, to make broad and plain the fact that He was a true Man.³ But the real importance of the words quoted attaches to the account they contain of what Christ is in reference to the Spirit that constituted His higher Nature—" appointed to be the Son of God in power, according to the Spirit of

---

and Headlam render it "designated." But this rather misses the meaning: we want a word to express the truth, that while He had been a Son before, Christ at the resurrection became a Son of God in *power*, "passed into a form of human life in which He had power over that which formerly had power over Him" (Hofmann, *in loco*).

¹ Rom. i. 4.   ² Rom. ix. 5.

³ This is Dr. Bruce's explanation of the apparent importance Paul attached to the Davidic descent of Jesus (*Paul's Conception of Christianity*, pp. 332-334). In his *Pastor Pastorum*, Latham remarks on the fact that Jesus Himself carefully abstained from basing His claim to be the Sent of God on His royal ancestry : " He never proclaims Himself the Jewish Messiah. No Greek or Roman would have listened for a moment to one who declared himself the special Prophet of the

Holiness." The ground of His Glorified Sonship is said to be the Indwelling in Him of the Holy Spirit of God;[1] and we gather that the Sonship itself is a union with God that is ethical in its character and manifestation, consisting in a community of mind and spirit with God, an identity with Him in moral feature and purpose. It is a relationship in which, as a man, Christ stands to God. By the perfection of His filial Spirit and life He fulfils the idea of our humanity, and is thus qualified to be the First-born of many brethren and the Author of Sonship in His people. Inasmuch as it is a relationship which He graciously shares with us, it is plain that it is as a man, the Man in whom the Divine Life was found in its fulness, and who in His human excellences altogether resembled God, that He is called His Son. What deeper significance the term has in Paul's writings when applied to Christ will appear in another lecture; but there is no doubt it is as a human Son of God we are to think of Him when He is so called, His pre-eminence being not that He is God's Son, while all others are, and can only be, sons of men, but that He is what He is, in distinction from all others, God's Son, in order to share His glory with us, to invest us in His own Sonship, and so to raise us to the dignity and power of true manhood.[2]

Jews. Though of the House and Family of David (Matt. xxii. 43, 44; Mark xii. 35–37; Luke xx. 41), He will accept no advantage on this score. He repudiates for the Saviour of the world the title of the 'Son of David,' which from its nature was based on legitimacy and must rest on the veracity of genealogical rolls. The apostles were to divine the nature of His Personality by long and close intercourse with Him, more than by canvassing claims or interpreting texts" (p. 415).

[1] "The ground and cause of His Sonship-in-power was that the Spirit that ruled His life was a Spirit of Holiness, that His life was a holy one" (Hofmann).

[2] The identity of Christ's Sonship with that of His people was the point in dispute in the Adoptianist controversy in the eighth century. It was maintained, by those who were strenuous in holding by the

The other thing we learn from the opening words of the Epistle to the Romans is, that it was when He rose again from the dead that Jesus entered on His full glory as the Son of God. He was appointed, or determined, to be the "Son of God with power in consequence of His resurrection from the dead." The meaning is not that Jesus then first became Son of God, but that the glory of His Sonship, which was obscured before, was then manifested, and the full power that belonged to it entered upon. His Messiahship became an accomplished fact. His distinction from all others, as a Man who had lived a human life under

reality of Christ's human nature, that unless Christ was the human Son of God, the sonship of believers must be wholly different from His. Accordingly, besides His sonship by nature as God, the Adoptianists predicated of Him a sonship as man by grace. In this latter sense He was the Son of God by *adoption*, as we are; and under this scheme of thought justice was done to the truth of Christ as the Firstborn of many brethren. This doctrine, however, was condemned on the ground of its involving a double personality in Christ. After this abortive attempt to rescue the humanity of Christ, the reign of Greek orthodoxy continued undisturbed till the Reformation. A remarkable effort has been made in modern times by Dr. Candlish (Cunningham Lecture, First Series, On the Fatherhood of God) to base the identity of the Sonship of Christ with that of believers on their participation of the eternal Sonship of Christ as God. He avoids the dualism of the Adoptianist view by holding that the Sonship of Christ as God and His Sonship as Man are one and the same. He regards the eternal filial relationship of Christ as separable from His Divine nature, and capable of being communicated to men; and he maintains that in Christ's human Person humanity becomes partaker in His filial relationship as God. Immense ingenuity is expended on the exposition of this view; but it cannot be denied that there is involved in it, first, a Doketic understanding of the Humanity of Christ, for He cannot be a man as we are men if the basis of His Humanity is not such a relation of man to God as is proper to the creature, but one that is proper to Him as the second Person of the Trinity; and second, the Deification of humanity, for must not this follow if man is made partaker of a relationship proper to the Son of God as God? The speculation, formed in the interest of religious truth, is another instance of the extreme difficulty of doing justice to the religious view of the Person of Christ, when we approach the subject with the mind fettered by the categories of metaphysical thought. Though advocated with great acuteness it does not seem to have had much influence on the subsequent course of theology.

our limitations, lay in this, that He was the Son of God. Paul does not allow that men in their natural state are sons of God any more than he will allow that they have the Spirit of God. And his teaching in this respect is criticised by many on the ground that it falls far behind that of his Master, who proclaimed the universal Fatherhood of God. But let us do no injustice to the apostle. He does indeed expressly say that the end of Christ's mission was that we might receive the "adoption of sons,"[1] which implies that apart from Him this is not our privilege. But in the same passage he compares Humanity, while under the law and before Christ came, to a child that is "under tutors or governors." If then the actual relation of man to God as affected by sin is that of a servant, obeying a law that is foreign to his likings, and conscious of God as Law Giver and Judge rather than as a Father, man is nevertheless a servant who is by birth a son or child of God, and is destined to receive the position and spirit that are proper to sonship. In distinguishing between the legal relation, in which man is God's servant, and the relation of grace which he owes to Christ, in which man is God's son, Paul does not deny a natural capacity for sonship in man as made in the image of God. But the apostle sets no value on metaphysical distinction; he deals with religious facts. It is enough for him that men in their actual state are at best servants, and can make no claim either to the position or character of children. While acknowledging that God is Father of all, he declines to say that all men are God's sons in any real sense; for the only sonship that is of value in his eyes is that which is accompanied with the power of sonship, with the full status before God as well as the love and devotion to Him that enter into the very idea, and that were exemplified in the life and character of Him who

[1] Gal. iv. 5.

was *the* Son of God. He alone was God's dear Child, the image of His Father, partaker with Him of a life of love and holiness.¹

At the same time, Paul teaches that as long as He was in the flesh, Jesus was the Son of God in weakness, and that it was not till He was raised from the dead that He was determined to be Son of God "in power." While He was in the flesh he was under the law, in appearance a servant rather than a son, submitting to all the legal ordinances of the Jews. Not that there was anything of the servile spirit in the obedience that was thus conditioned. As He partook of the flesh without its sin, so He was under the law without partaking of that spirit of slavish subjection which the legal system engendered in those in whom the spirit of sonship was absent.² His goodness was none the

---

¹ Three stages of Sonship are recognised in Paul's Epistles: 1. The *natural* sonship, of no account with Paul because a potentiality rather than an actual fact; 2. the *Spiritual*, or real sonship, by faith in Christ "the Son"; 3. The *perfected form* of it in *glory*. The third is so great an advance even on the second, that it is spoken of as the "adoption" (Rom. viii. 23), which we as yet "wait for." It would be wrong to infer from the last named passage that we have not already received this "adoption of children"; we know from Gal. iv. 6, 7 that we have. It would be equally wrong to infer from the passage just mentioned that we are not in a certain sense children by nature and before we believe. "Adoption" is a legal term, and is borrowed from the ceremony common among the ancient Romans and Greeks (not among the Jews) of investing in the rights or privileges of a son one who was no blood connection of the family, and might have been a slave in it. It would be wrong, however, to press the metaphor in the interpretation of the spiritual fact. "Adoption" in the kingdom of God is consistent with a previous filial relationship of an inferior sort, and means, as we see from the double "adoption" in the Christian life, the investment in fuller privileges and powers, in a sonship worthy of the name, of persons who had been sons in an imperfect degree. See the interesting paper on "Allusions to Roman Law in St. Paul's Epistles," by Ball, in *Contemporary Review*, August 1891.

² "Christ had not to make, in His own Person, the transition from His religion to that of redemption, from His relation of servant to that of Son, but without any such change He developed Himself so that God was always manifest to Him as Love, and He bore Himself ever to God

less spontaneous that it manifested itself in obedience to legal enactments. But the freedom which belongs to a spiritual Being from outward arrangements and ordinances that are carnal in their character was thereby concealed. And, moreover, He was, from His connection with the flesh, subject to weakness and death, under the power of that to which in His proper nature He was superior. Hence it was the Resurrection that manifested the real Glory and Power of Sonship. He then left behind Him all that impaired the freedom of His activity as a Son of God and the completeness of His spiritual resemblance to His Father, entering on a condition in which He was raised above weakness and death, and invested in all the prerogatives that belong to Divine Sonship in its perfected form.

According to the teaching of our apostle, then, the constitution of the Person of Christ presents a radical contrast to that of all other men, in virtue of which He occupies a position that no other can share with Him. But let us mark wherein the difference and contrast consist. It is no exact or intelligible account of it to say that "He is God and Man in two distinct natures and one Person," while we are human beings only. The antithesis between the Divine and Human that is implied in this definition of His Person is not applicable to the matter, and does not give a true account of the difference between Christ and us. For, on the one hand, He is not represented as Divine in a sense that isolates or places Him out of relation to others as One possessed of qualities that cannot be communicated or transferred to them. And in the second place, it is ascribing to those with whom He is contrasted more than is true to say that, in our natural state, we are perfect and complete men, for

as to His Father, as a trustful Son of God by means of the love imprinted on His personality from the first" (Schweizer, *Christl. Glaubenslehre*, II. i. 11).

we are defective in what constitutes proper manhood, in the higher life of the Spirit and Divine Sonship.[1] The real contrast is to be found here, that while Christ is the Spiritual Man and Son of God, we are carnal, and at best servants of God, than while He perfectly fulfils the idea of a human personality, we entirely fail, being only potentially what He was in very truth. God made man *capax Dei*, capable of His own life, and of manifesting His own perfection. But Christ alone expresses the Divine thought, and stands out in contrast to all others in the very constitution of His inner life which was determined by the Divine Spirit to be the Life of God's true Son on earth. There is then a constitutional difference between Christ and all other men; but the ground of that difference is not so much metaphysical as religious, although there is a metaphysical element in the case too, as will appear in another lecture. We are not to find His Divinity in anything outside of His human life, but in the Divine Perfection of that human life itself, in the perfection of His love and holiness. He is more than Man, He is Divine; but His Divinity, in so far as it is apprehensible by us, is that of which human nature is capable, without which it is an imperfect and fragmentary thing, and infinitely less than what God made it to be—a Divinity which He communicates to as many as receive Him and in Him become children of God.

From this peculiarity in the Person of Christ there flows a twofold distinction from others, in the light of which His supreme significance for the moral and religious life of mankind is apparent. On the one hand, He is the Image of God in humanity, the pure and perfect revelation of Divinity in a human life. We can know God only through the medium of the best and worthiest qualities of

---

[1] The incompleteness of man in his present state, compared with the completeness of Christ's being, is finely set forth in the suggestive book, *But How, if the Gospels are Historic?* (pp. 149-159).

our own nature:[1] and he who carries our humanity to its true height becomes thereby the organ by whom God can communicate Himself and reveal to us all that we are able to know of His nature. And in virtue of His human perfection Christ is to us the embodiment of the highest truth we can know about God as a spiritual Being. We learn from the goodness of Christ how we are to think of Him whose invisible qualities He translated into the language of human dispositions and actions. What of God became human in Him, was His Spiritual Being, His Love and Truth and Grace, not such natural or metaphysical attributes as His Omnipotence or Omniscience which cannot be expressed in a man. Only that can be in man and was in Christ, which man was made capable of sharing with God. This is limited to the Spiritual or Personal qualities. Christ is the Revelation of the Love and Holiness of God.[2]

It must be observed, however, that Paul does not dwell much on this aspect of Christ, on His being personally the human representation of God. In one passage,[3] indeed, he speaks of the "light of the knowledge of the glory of God" made visible in the face of Jesus Christ His Son, where it is evident that the Perfected humanity of Christ is viewed as the mirror in which we are to see reflected the glory of the Divine character.[4] And the idea of Christ's Lordship, which, as will appear more fully by and by, is so prominent in Paul's conception, is based on the truth that He is the Son of God, and as such the Revealer of His mind

[1] "For man, man alone, is the adequate medium through which God can reveal Himself" (Rothe, *Ethik*, ii. p. 140).

[2] This does not mean that Christ had not supernatural knowledge and power, but these were given to Him by God and exercised by Him as man.

[3] 2 Cor. iv. 6.

[4] In his Commentary on this passage, Calvin says: "In Christo suam justitiam, bonitatem, sapientiam, virtutem, se denique totum nobis (Deus) exhibet. Cavendum ergo, ne alibi eum quæramus; nam extra Christum, quicquid se Dei nomine venditabit, idolum erit."

and will. But while it is fundamental with the apostle that Christ is the revelation of the Grace of God, the exhibition of the Divine character, it is not so much to the personal life of Jesus that he makes his appeal in proof of this, as to the gracious ends accomplished by God through the death on the Cross. To this I shall return in my next lecture. For the present it is enough to remark, what is indeed obvious to everyone familiar with the Epistles, that the idea of Christ as personally the Image of God does not receive in the thought of the apostle anything like the place that is given to the other aspect of His Person, under which He is viewed, not in relation to God as His Image, but in relation to mankind as its Pattern or Archetype.

II

Here we come to the characteristic feature of the Christology of the apostle. In virtue of the constitution of His Person as now unfolded, Christ is the ARCHETYPAL Man, the Revelation of the Divine idea of human nature, the Second Man,[1] the Prototype of a new race differing from that descended from the first man in its realising the capacity for the Divine and Spiritual that must otherwise remain a capacity only in the nature we are born with,—a race of men who are Spiritual (κατὰ πνεῦμα) in the law of their being, children in their relation to God, immortal in their destiny, in contrast with those who have the first Adam alone for their progenitor, who are carnal (κατὰ σάρκα), under condemnation, doomed to die. As Head of a new Mankind He is called also the "Heavenly" Man[2] to describe His origin and nature. He is also called the "Last" Man,[3] to intimate that He is the perfected Form of Manhood, that nothing higher or more Divine, or more fully

---

[1] 1 Cor. xv. 47.   [2] 1 Cor. xv. 49.   [3] 1 Cor. xv. 45.

answering to the capacities of our souls can be looked for than the Christ-Type already embodied in the Risen Jesus.

Now, in the application of these terms to Christ, Paul, it is alleged by certain writers, has clothed his Christology in the garb of Jewish thought. Reference is made to Philo, whose doctrines had at this time penetrated into the schools of the Rabbis and moulded their theology. After the manner of Plato's speculations, Philo distinguishes between an "earthly" and a "heavenly" man, the latter being the pre-existent idea, the former its imperfect realisation in the individual human being. The theology of the Synagogue, combining this idea with the belief that widely prevailed that the Messiah existed in heaven until the time of His appearing on earth, conceived of the Christ to come as the Heavenly Man; and Paul, it is said, sharing this idea, transferred it to Christ, and taught that He existed as the Heavenly Man in a previous state before He was born into the world. The hinge of the question is the meaning we are to assign to 1 Cor. xv. 45–47, where he speaks of the Second Adam as "the Man who is from heaven." The passage is confessedly one of the most difficult in Paul's writings; it seems most in accordance with the context to take the words "from heaven" (ἐκ τοῦ οὐρανοῦ) as pointing to the nature and origin of the Second Adam, or rather to the nature and origin of the spiritual body with which He is now clothed, for the whole discussion in the passage has reference to His body. "The first man was of the earth"; and his body, composed of earth, was liable to death. "The Second Adam" was of a heavenly nature (ἐξ οὐρανοῦ); and His body, partaking of the same element, is immortal, and the seed of a life in believers that is immortal. Other interpreters of note, such as Gess, Hofmann, and Meyer, view the words "from heaven" as referring to the second coming of Christ in glory, when believers shall receive the resurrection body. The uncertainty of the sense of the words, and the variety of interpretation they admit of, is a valid reason for our refusing to accept as Paul's this doctrine of the pre-existent Heavenly Man, to which there is no further reference in his Epistles. It may well be that he borrowed from the systems with which he was familiar the terms in which he expressed his thought, for that thought had points of affinity with the speculations of the schools. These terms would naturally occur in thinking of the truth that was revealed in Christ. But the truth itself was not derived from these speculations. It was an intuition which he owed to his spiritual understanding of his Master. The Person of the Risen One, seen as the complete expression of the Divine idea of man, was recognised by him as that Second Adam of whom philosophy vaguely talked, as the New Spiritual Head and Progenitor of the human race, from whom was derivable all that entered into God's great gift to men of life eternal, even as sin and death had come to all from their natural Head, the first Adam.

There may seem to be, indeed, a lack of propriety in the application of the term "Second Adam" to Christ, when we think of the dissimilarity between Him and Adam.[1] They are alike, indeed, in this, that both were parents of orders of beings that take after those from whom they are severally descended. But in all other respects the parallel assumes the form of contrast, the most striking that can be

---

[1] Nösgen, indeed, thinks that the term "Second Adam" applied by Paul to Christ expresses Soteriological rather than Christological truth, that he means by it to describe simply Christ's function as the Author of eternal life in men, and not any peculiarity in His Person qualifying Him to discharge that function. (See his *Christus der Menschen u. Gottessohn*, pp. 110–115). There is nothing, however, to warrant this limitation, and we cannot separate the effect of the working of Christ from its cause in the distinctive content of Christ's Person.

imagined. The "first" man was natural; Christ is spiritual. The first was "from the earth"; Christ was "from heaven." The first was a "living soul," a being animated by a merely natural life, sensuous in his constitution; Christ is a "Life-producing" Spirit. If in spite of these differences Christ is still spoken of as a Man, the Second Man, it is to remind us that it is the spiritual that is the truly human, and that human nature is properly beheld in Him who was the Spiritual Man and Son of God, and not in the other in whom it existed only in an incomplete and imperfect form. In 1 Cor. xv. 45, 46, Paul seems to teach that there were two stages in the creation of the being that was to answer to the Divine idea. The initial stage was reached when the man stood forth, perfect in his physical organisation, with the possibilities of higher functions latent in him; the second, and final one, when he received a fresh accession of spiritual endowment for the realisation of these possibilities, and true manhood was seen to consist in union with God and in the exercise of a spiritual nature through an organ adapted to it.

Whether the ascent from the lower to the higher might have been made by man himself, and the spiritual in this way evolved by a natural process in the course of obedience to the Divine Will; or whether, even had man not fallen, the Incarnation would still have been necessary to reveal the Archetypal Man, is a question on which much has been written on both sides. Many have held strongly the latter view,—that the idea of the incarnation corresponds with the very perfection of man as he was constituted at the first, and not merely with the restoration of man who had missed his end; that even, therefore, though sin had never entered, the Son of God would have come in order to raise man to the perfection that answered to the idea of his creation in the Divine mind. There is much to be said in favour of this view, especially when account is taken of the teaching of the Epistle to the Colossians, which will be considered at a later stage.[1] Paul's Gospel, however, deals not with the ideal relations between God and man, but with the actual relations consequent on sin and death. It begins not with the Incarnation, but with the suffering and death of Jesus as necessitated by the actual condition of the race. The interest of the question is mainly speculative. The entrance of sin through our sensuous nature has rendered a normal development from the natural to the spiritual impossible; and by the supernatural act of God, a Personality has appeared who fully answers to God's idea of human nature, and who, like him who was the partial fulfilment of that idea, is a Public and Central Person, and is exalted to be the author, in all who attach themselves to Him, of a life that in its essential features and destiny answers to His own.

It is indeed a radical part of the Pauline idea of the Second Adam that it is in Christ *as Risen from the dead* it is fully realised. It is the Man that has passed victorious through death, and has entered on a new life clothed in a body that is the appropriate organ of a spiritual nature, who is to be regarded as having lived the life and fulfilled

[1] Among modern theologians who hold that the Incarnation was necessary apart from sin, may be mentioned Bishop Westcott, in his Essay on the "Gospel of Creation" in his exposition of 1 John; and Edwards (*The God-Man*, pp. 82–89); also Dorner (*Doctrine of Person of Christ*, vol. ii. p. 82, Eng. tr., and *Christian Doctrine*, ii. p. 218). Gess, on the other hand (*Christi Person u. Werk*, vol. iii. p. 476), argues strongly against this view. "The testimonies of Christ and the Apostles," he says, "tell us that the Father's love sent the Son, and that the Son was willing to be sent to seek that which was *lost*. That God's love must have sent the Son as Man even had man pursued the right path, we are unable to maintain, because we are not in a position to say that it was not possible for man by other means to have attained to the goal of his being, *i.e.* to love God with all his powers, and to render to God the service of his life." Gess has not, however, in my opinion, shaken the force of Dorner's striking argument on speculative grounds in favour of the view that the Incarnation is rooted in God's plan of creation.

the destiny of man. "If in Adam all die, while in Christ all shall be made alive,"[1] this Life-giving Power belongs to Him who rose from the dead, and who is now in possession of a humanity that has been redeemed in its integrity from sin and death, and transfigured in all its parts. He is in this way fitted to be the seed in His people of a life similarly complete in its taking up into itself all the elements of our present life, changed and transfigured, into a form that will be the counterpart of the Glorified Manhood of Christ Himself.[2]

But for another reason also, death and resurrection had to intervene before Christ could be revealed as the Second Adam. As long as He was in the flesh, this significance of His Person was concealed from men. Belonging to a particular nation, appearing at a special period in the world's history, holding definite relations as an individual Man to certain other men, manifesting Himself in special ways and forms of activity called forth by the circumstances in which He was placed, He exhibited a particularism as regards the outward aspects of His Personality that hindered men perceiving what was universal, essential, and of worldwide significance in His human nature and in the ideals that were embodied in His life. There was needed a change in the outward form of His Being; and that change came when, laying aside the flesh at death, He rose again in the power of a Glorified Humanity, and entered on those universal relations to mankind that disclosed the higher, the ideal

---

[1] 1 Cor. xv. 22.
[2] The popular idea that the resurrection body will be the same organism that the spirit of man has had during life, has no warrant in Paul's writings. The spiritual body must be wholly different. The apostle's idea of it was formed in the vision he had on the way to Damascus, when the Lord came to him from heaven—the place of light—in a body of "glory," relieved from ordinary conditions that limit our material bodies to one spot. On Paul's doctrine of the Resurrection Body see the wise and careful statement of Professor Salmond in his *Christian Doctrine of Immortality*, pp. 568–572.

truth of His Person. It is a connection with the Risen Christ on which Paul insists as alone of worth, because alone securing for us those blessings and benefits that are moral and religious in their character, and have nothing to do with distinctions that arise out of the life of sense. As belonging to the sphere of the Spirit, Christ is now loosed from those relations that are rooted in the flesh. And in union with Him all differences pertaining to the lower sphere, whether of nationality, culture, social position, sex, are seen to be only provisional and temporary, and to be now merged in the higher unity of the Spirit and of those spiritual relations that bind together into one fellowship all who share the one Perfected Humanity of Christ. "There is neither Jew nor Greek, bond nor free, male nor female, but ye are all one in Christ Jesus."[1]

The universalism of Paul's Gospel is closely connected with the significance he attaches to the Person of Christ as the Second Adam, and as forming a Type of spiritual Manhood that is universal and final. There are some, indeed, who would have it that in thus presenting the Risen Christ as the ideal for man, Paul has substituted for the Jesus of history, who is rich in human qualities of character, a bald conception of Manhood stripped of all definiteness and points of contact with reality. They criticise his conception of the Second Adam as being little more than the abstract idea of a Man who, having no longer any connection with the earth or the circumstances of an earthly life, is consequently destitute of those features of interest by which human beings are distinguished, and which are necessary to give warmth and colour to our ideas of human character. But it would be a great mistake to imagine that in placing the Risen Christ before our faith Paul has exalted a mere

[1] Gal. iii. 28.

ideal, or has sacrificed historic truth to the demands of a speculative system. Christ was in no sense whatever an abstraction to him. Some of the expressions used of Him, such as the "Son of God" and "the Power and Wisdom of God," might be familiar to Jewish ears and readers of Rabbinical theology. But to Paul Christ was no incarnation of a Divine attribute. Although He was indeed divested of those characteristics and accidents of time and place by which human personalities are marked, He remained, in the ground-work of His human character, the same that He was on earth, unaffected by the change that followed death, possessed of a Personality so intense, so vivid, as to excite the most ardent affection, for "never man," as one has said, "loved Christ with so absorbing a passion as did Paul." His love for Christ is indeed without a parallel in the history of religious emotions. He never lost the vision of Him whom he saw but once on the way to Damascus. Dedicating his whole being to the Christ "who had loved him and had given Himself for him," he had no thought but to please Christ, no aim but to advance His glory. All this is evidence that he did not regard his Master as having undergone the deprivation of those qualities that evoke the boundless love and adoration of the human soul, or as having suffered the loss of aught essential to His true humanity, when He died and rose again, to be no longer a mere individual member of the race, but invested with universal significance as the Second Adam.

The truth is, as has often been pointed out, the character of Christ as depicted in the Gospels themselves is entirely independent of those peculiarities, arising out of circumstances of time and place, that are incident to the best human characters, and prevent any one of them being typical for others. The type of excellence realised in Jesus escaped all onesidedness and taint of peculiarity that could disqualify it from being the ideal. Although set in the mould of special circumstances, the life of Jesus issued in an example of goodness that included in it every essential feature of man's nobility, and that had in it nothing national, limited, isolated, or that was adapted to certain persons more than to others.[1] It was the essence of man's moral nature embodied in a personality intensely individual, and capable of arousing the deepest affections of the soul, and at the same time free from any idiosyncrasy that could affect its universal import. And Paul, in investing the Risen Christ with the powers and prerogatives of a Second Adam, is just recognising the truth of what the records of the historical Jesus themselves bear witness to, of His possession of a humanity that was without one "transitory touch of time or kindred or aim," and is therefore of a universal significance. "If," as one has said, "the Christ of the Church is an Ideal Being, it was Jesus who made the Ideal. The Ideal in Him is simply the result of that disengagement from the earthly vestiture which death and distance work in all who live in history;" only, in the present instance, it was the Resurrection even more than the Death that revealed the inner life of the historic Jesus and illustrated His fitness to be the Second Head of the race.

But wherein does this fitness consist? Paul's designation of Christ as the Second Adam means that He is to be regarded as the true Type or Ideal of Manhood, that He is and possesses in Himself that which constitutes Him the Pattern after whom humanity is to be remodelled. And that statement calls for some explanation. There are various functions and activities of

---

[1] Bishop Westcott emphasises this point in his writings. See in particular his *The Gospel of Life*, pp. 299–301; and the *Victory of the Cross*, pp. 43–46.

human nature, and we must distinguish amongst them if we would have a clear idea of the sphere in which Christ is to be recognised as Supreme, the Ideal to be followed as a Pattern. There is the sphere of Science and that of Art; and great names might be mentioned, of whom our race is proud, who have excelled in these forms of human activity and may be regarded as having reached an ideal greatness. But we do not think of Christ as the Ideal of Knowledge or of Art, because we know He did not come either to enlarge our knowledge of the world or to furnish conceptions of beauty such as we owe to the imagination of natural genius. He came to meet the moral and religious needs of the race that are far deeper and more imperative than those to which the scientist or artist makes his appeal. And it is in this moral and religious sphere that He is to be recognised as the Ideal, who lays on every man the obligation, and inspires in every man the hope of being what He is. For, while Newton and Shakespeare and Darwin obtain our admiration, they do not make us feel it is our duty to follow them, still less do they suggest that each one of us has that capacity of thought and imagination that can ever bring us into equality with them were we to make the attempt. But to understand what Christ is, and to have our eyes opened to His greatness, is to feel at the same time, amid all that humbles us in the discovery, this is what I was made for, what I ought to be, — to love as Jesus loved, to live as Jesus lived. What we mean by Christ being the Ideal Character is that He presents to us human nature in its typical or ideal form, related to God and to men as human nature ought to be, under which He is recognised to be the law for everyone, in obedience to which everyone reaches the true end of his being. There is no human being who may not see in Him the Divine Idea and Purpose, the true conception and end of himself. He is God's truth and word to every man of himself.

And if the further question be asked, in what respect does the apostle teach us so to regard Christ, the answer is suggested by the view of the constitution of the Person of our Lord that was sketched in the beginning of this lecture. That indwelling of the Spirit of God that was the moulding principle of His Person secured that He was all that a man ought to be, both in His relation to God and to His fellow-men, both as a Son of God and a Brother to man. And accordingly we find in the letters of the apostle references to His commanding importance both as the Religious and the Moral Ideal for men.

He is the Religious Ideal. He is the Son of God; in Him we behold, in a perfect form, the true relation of man to God. Paul does not dwell on the Sonship of Christ or on its ideal character, on the trust, the childlike obedience, the humility and sincerity in which it was manifested. His Epistles seem to take for granted the readers' familiarity with the Gospel Picture, and simply refer to the Sonship of Christ as an essential part of the good that comes to believers, a religious ideal realised in Christ that it might be realised in those who connect themselves with Him—" as many as put on Christ," by faith and love, " have become sons of God."[1]

He is also the Moral Ideal. The Spirit of God, the principle of the Personality of Christ, is in fact the Spirit of Love. In asserting the supremacy in Him of the Spirit over the flesh, Paul meant that in Him the Spirit of Love was supreme. The life and character of Christ were the incarnation of grace to sinners, of sympathy, of humble, loving service. And therein is He the Ideal for us in our social relations. But neither on this does Paul enlarge. The history of Jesus was known to his readers. It was universally recognised as an imperishable memorial of pure

[1] Gal. iii. 22.

unselfish love. We are surely not wrong in supposing that the apostle was drawing from his own impressions of that wonderful history when he sang the praises of Love in 1 Cor. xiii., and outlined the character that love inspires. We learn how deeply he was impressed with the all-sufficiency of Christ as the Moral Ideal in one passage in the Epistle to Romans (xiii. 14), where, after enumerating the graces of the Christian life and the dispositions it beomes believers to manifest in their relations to one another, he sums up all and ends the discussion in these words, " Put ye on the Lord Jesus Christ, and make no provision for the flesh," intimating that in fellowship with Him they will be united with Love at its source and will be mastered by a principle of action that must issue in all goodness.

Paul makes little reference, as we saw in last lecture, to the historic Christ. But the new type of character that the historic Christ originated and exemplified is never absent from his thoughts, and the Epistles are largely occupied with its delineation, and with precept illustrative of it.[1] These writings are considered to be doctrinal by some; they are really ethical. The mind of the author is absorbed in the Heavenly Ideal of human character that had appeared on earth, and that had in it the power to create a new humanity. And where doctrine is taught it is to show how that new type of character is produced, and what motives the Christian religion can bring to bear on its production. " Paul's writings," to use the words of another, " retain their hold, not because he is thought to be inspired, nor because he was the first and greatest of the apostles, but because he held up the Ideal of renewed character with a vividness, a reality, a sense of never-ending wonder, which are always needed to express the feelings appropriate to the faith struggling up in every age towards that same Ideal to embrace and

---

[1] In the epistle of Barnabas, Christians are described as a "new type" of men, ἐποίησεν ἡμᾶς ἄλλον τύπον (chap. vi.).

possess it." It is, indeed, only in the course of the ages, and bit by bit, that the rich fulness of that Ideal is apprehended. Many degrees of religious culture are found amongst men, many varieties of mental gift and moral discernment. These differences reveal themselves in the presence of Christ, each individual, each race of mankind, each age of the world discovering in Him that virtue it is prepared specially to value, the embodiment of that idea of human worth that is peculiar to it. It has been finely said by Dean Church in his well-known sermon on "Christ's Example,"[1] "That one and the same Form has borne the eager scrutiny of each anxious and imperfect age: and each age has recognised with boundless sympathy and devotion what it missed in the world, and has found in Him what is wanted. Each age has caught in those august lineaments what most touched and swayed its heart, and as generations go on and unfold themselves, they still find that Character answering to their best thoughts and hopes: they still find in it what their predecessors had not seen or cared for: they bow down to it as their inimitable pattern, and draw comfort from a model who was plain enough and universal enough to be the Master as of rich and poor, so of the first century and the last. It has been the root of all that was great and good in our fathers. We look forward with hope to its making our children greater and better still. 'Regnum tuum regnum omnium sæculorum: et dominatio tua in omni generatione et generatione.'"[2]

What Paul has further to teach us of the Power of Christ to reproduce in others the type of character embodied in His own Person will fall to be considered in another lecture. In bringing the present one to a close, it remains that we review very briefly the history in the thought of

[1] In his *The Gifts of Civilisation*, pp. 111, 112.
[2] Ps. cxlv. 13. See Note B on The Gradual Apprehension of the Christian Ideal.

the Church of that interpretation of the Person of Christ that has occupied our attention.

III

The idea of Christ as the Archetypal Man is original to the apostle among the writers of the New Testament. We have an echo of it, indeed, in the Epistle to the Hebrews, which is not surprising if that production was written, as many think it was, by a disciple of Paul's. In the second chapter (vers. 5–10), the author in very beautiful language dwells on the contrast between man's actual condition and the Divine idea of his destiny. Called by his birthright to sovereignty, he is as yet in subjection, and so far he is a failure and a disappointment. But the writer sees Christ Sovereign over all, having passed through suffering and death to glory and honour; and Christ Exalted is to him the pattern and pledge of man's exaltation. Here there is a virtual recognition of Christ as the Ideal of humanity, the Second Adam; although it is not, as it is with Paul, because He is the Spiritual Man who is also the Son of God that the author regards Christ as the fulfilment of the Divine idea of man, but because He is Lord of all and Sovereign over the world, because He has risen by the way of sorrow to supreme Dominion. His account of the natural man differs also from Paul's. With the latter, the token of man's present inferiority is that he is of "the earth," "a living soul," ruled by the flesh instead of ruling it by the spirit; while, according to the author of Hebrews, the token is man's subjection to the angels, a description, however, which is equivalent to the statement that he is in subjection to the material order of things, and which, on this side, approaches very closely to the Pauline thought.

This is the most distinct trace of the influence of Paul's interpretation on the books of the New Testament canon.

When we pass on to the fathers of the Greek Church, we find that, in the case of the earlier of them at least, this truth met with a recognition that manifested a real sense of its importance. Passages from Irenaeus might be quoted to this effect. Among the later writers, however, it was lost sight of in the degree in which metaphysical definition took the place of earnest attempts to interpret the religious significance of the Person of Christ. And it is not till we come to the theological thought of modern times, that we find a large and fruitful appreciation of the great Pauline thought of Christ as the Archetypal Man. Nor is this confined to any one school of theologians; it is common to all, and is a characteristic feature of what may be spoken of as Modern Theology. Much is due doubtless to the influence of Schleiermacher, who set forth the religious worth of the Person of Christ in a way that proved epoch-making. The pre-eminence of His Person, this theologian showed, is to be seen in the fulness, originality, and strength in which the consciousness of God lived in Him, guaranteeing His Moral perfection, and ensuring His close fellowship with God. While a real Man, He was so penetrated and possessed with God, that He became the Creator of a new race of men, determined in their personal life, as He was, by God. Thus did He prove a Second Adam, at once the Pattern and the Power of a life and experience resembling His own, carrying in Himself the germs of a new spiritual Creation. Schleiermacher's non-recognition of the supernatural, however, lessened the value of his representation; for with him the Resurrection of Christ, that is so vital in Paul's Christology, was a non-essential of the faith. But it is scarcely possible, apart from the idea of a Risen and Living Christ, to regard the Person as possessed of creative power to reproduce in others its own fulness of religious life and truth. A certain section of Schleiermacher's followers, of whom Schweizer, Lipsius, and Pfleiderer may be named, while recognising with their master what is unique and original in the Person of Christ, accept the consequence that must follow when the supernatural is denied, and distinguish between the Person of Christ and the idea or principle it embodies. He is indeed, they say, the supreme instance in an historic individual of the religious principle, the principle of Divine sonship. But the truth or value of the principle is not dependent on the personal embodiment of it, though the latter is useful as an illustration of the former, or even as first introducing us to the experience of its truth.[1] The principle is the essential thing, and is to be accepted on the ground of its own truth irrespective of its realisation in the historic Christ. The effect of all this is to exalt the religious idea or principle at the expense of the Person, and to lessen the significance of the living Christ as a Source of Life to men. He is no more the *object* of faith, nor can He be regarded as the author of that new manhood with its Divine relationships and spiritual endowments which is our desideratum. He is simply an example of the manhood each must attain for himself by faith in the truth of the Fatherhood of God. Experience, however, is against the supposition that a mere idea can have the operative power ascribed to it under this system. Life needs life to quicken it. What is wanted is a Supreme Personality like that of the Risen Christ, who is all that we ought to be and from whom influence proceeds that can awaken in others life similar to His own. We cannot separate the Person from the idea; the idea has for us no existence, no vital force, except in the Person, and it is only faith in the Personal Christ that can ensure its realisation in us.

The treatment of the subject by Richard Rothe is free

---

[1] A good criticism of the views of this school of theologians will be found in Gess' *Christi Person u. Werk*, vol. iii. p. 254, in a chapter entitled "Modern Attempts to Explain the Work of Jesus on the Presupposition that He is Originally no more than a Man."

from the defect that I have noticed in Schleiermacher and in those who claim to be his disciples. In Rothe's scheme of thought, the Resurrection is of first importance in liberating the Person of Christ from material limits and conditions, and in affecting its complete spiritualisation. The idea of the Second Adam is fundamental in his Christology, and is expounded in one of the most interesting and original parts of his *Ethik*.[1] No one has done fuller justice to the commanding Personality of Christ as the New Beginner of the human race. An individual indeed He is, according to Rothe, but He is unlike all other individuals in His being no partial or defective realisation of human nature, but the realisation of it in the genuine union of all its special sides, related to other men as the centre is related to the different points of the circle. Not that the Second Adam exhausts in Himself the idea of humanity, but He is the principle of its realisation, inasmuch as there dwells in Him a completeness of human nature that suffices for the separate unfolding into an organic whole of the differences among the various members of the human race. He is an absolutely perfect instrument for exerting a saving, transforming influence upon the individual members of humanity, of such a kind that each man finds the fulfilment of his own separate and partial individuality by means of that which He supplies. No one has set forth more strikingly than Rothe has done in these chapters the supreme Place that Jesus occupies as the Second Adam, as the Head of a Spiritual Life that issues in the full realisation in those united to Him of the Divine Idea of humanity.[2]

---

[1] Vol. iii. pp. 135–170.

[2] The style of Rothe, which is heavy and dragging, is apt to deter one from the reading of his great work, the *Ethik* ; but the massive thought well repays the effort. There is a just characterisation of him in Lichtenberg's *History of German Thought in the Nineteenth Century*: "It might be said that in reading him one feels as if walking amidst fragments of rocks flung abroad at hazard, and that they arrest and

This Pauline conception has come much to the front in the theology of our own country in this century. Readers of F. D. Maurice's works and our own Thomas Erskine's will remember how much is made by these theologians of the idea of the Second Adam, although with their exposition of His universal significance for the higher life of man, there are combined in their writings Neo-Platonic speculations regarding the original relation of Christ to the human race which will appear to some of doubtful value. None have made a fuller use of this conception than the writers of the modern Sacramentarian School, from Canon Wilberforce, in whose work on *The Doctrine of the Incarnation* it receives a large place, to Canon Gore in our own day. Although here, too, as it appears to me, the value of their contributions is impaired by the attempt to make the Church in its ordinances, and especially in its sacramental acts, the sole channel or medium by which the supernatural Influence that flows from the new Adam or Representative of our Race, is communicated to men. Hampered by their adherence to the definitions of the Greek theologians, and understanding the life communicated by the Second Adam in a quasi-physical sense, writers of that school connect it with physical media in a way that leaves them open to the charge of taking a magical view of the operation of the grace of God in the soul.

The deep hold of the Pauline interpretation of the historic Christ on the Christian thought of the ages is a testimony to its truth and to its correspondence with the actual effect of the working of Christ on human hearts and lives. Wherever men have submitted themselves to the

wound us at every step ; yet here and there are found blocks of the purest granite, and afar off is heard the murmur of foaming cascades. And, in fact, in its substance the thought of Rothe is like granite, while his speculation produces the effect of mountain torrents, the mere sight of which refreshes and inspires power " (p. 500).

power of His Personality, the result has been the creation in them of a new type of moral and religious life, than which none higher, more fruitful of inward satisfaction, more stimulating to progress can be conceived. To awaken and sustain this new life of sonship and spirituality in men, is the Prerogative of Jesus Christ. What is wanting to the integrity of our true life can be supplied only by Him who, in His own inner life, is all that man is not. The Personal alone can heal the personal. At different periods in the world's history there have appeared men of original genius, who, in respect of the vast influence they have exerted by their lives and words on the religious destinies of their fellowmen, may be compared with Christ. The names of Paul, Augustine, St. Francis, Savonarola, Luther, Calvin, and Wesley will occur in this connection. These and such like men were endowed by nature above others with a passion for religion, an enthusiasm for God, for truth, for holiness, that accounts for their extraordinary power to impress themselves upon their fellowmen. They were in a peculiar sense organs created to influence men for God. It is part of the Divine plan to carry on the work of the Kingdom by great personalities fitted by nature for the functions they are to discharge. And Christ is sometimes mentioned in the same breath with these prophetic souls as a great religious genius, whose nature and appearance are no more mysterious than theirs. But such comparisons overlook one great point of difference. The power they exercised was derived power, and power derived from Him; His was original. They, one and all, bowed down before His supreme Personality in whom they saw the truth of religion and humanity embodied. And they recognised it as their highest, their solitary function, to interpret Him to their fellowmen. Their influence was due not to anything in or of themselves, but to the measure in which the Power and Truth and Spirit of Christ went forth through them.

Christ, on the other hand, is alone in being in His own Person the Interpretation of God, and the Fountain of a Divine Life at which all others draw their inspiration. We may speak of Him, if we choose, as a Religious Genius, if we mean by such language to emphasise the fact that, as with the others so with Him, there was an original basis of endowment and nature that explains the influence that proceeds from Him on the moral and religious life of men. But the dependence upon Him of all who have possessed a measure of His power, the fact that in all alike it is derived from Him and is proportioned to their success in assimilating the contents of His Personality, points to a peculiarity of nature that no other shares with Him, and that sets Him on a platform where He stands apart, superior, supreme. Here is not a Man merely, but the Archetypal Man, and we are forced back on the recognition of a nature in Him that is an absolutely new fact, and is identified in a special way with the life of God, on an origin that is exceptional, on a function in relation to the spiritual history of the human race that is His alone.

III

CHRIST THE REDEEMER AND FOUNDER OF THE NEW HUMANITY

LECTURE III

Christ the Redeemer and Founder of the New Humanity

THE subject of my last lecture was the Pauline Interpretation of the Person of Christ, the key to which is to be found in the apostle's consciousness of the influence of the Exalted Christ on his inner life. From this point of view He is presented to us by Paul as the Second Adam or Archetypal Man, qualified by the very constitution of His manhood and by His being the personal embodiment of the Divine idea of human nature, to be the Firstborn of many brethren, the prototype of a race after His own likeness and destined to attain to His perfection. We now proceed to the apostle's interpretation of the Death of Christ, the event in which the earthly history of Jesus is summed up by him, the one event in that history which is represented as possessing supreme worth for the religious life of man. Here, too, we shall find that the conception of the Second Adam is the regulating thought of the apostle; not so much because He is the realisation in His own Person of the true idea of man, as because of the Representative character that attaches to His personal act in dying for men, by which He determined human life and destiny toward God and Righteousness, even as the act of the first Adam had determined it towards sin and death. In the Epistles of Paul Christ is not presented simply as the typical instance of the New Humanity. Were He no more than this, no more than the Pattern Man, His personal life would have no power to redeem us from sin; contact with

Him would have no power to take us out of ourselves, would, indeed, only make us more deeply conscious of our distance from Him and from God. To the faith of the apostle, however, Christ had proved Himself to be a mighty redeeming power, the Divine instrument by whom he had been restored to fellowship with God,—the Author, in short, of a new relation to God and of a new disposition of love to His will.

Now, Christ had this significance of Redeemer to the apostle in virtue chiefly of His Death, or rather in virtue of the issues that had been wrought out by God through His Death. In order, therefore, that we may understand the supreme place he assigned to Christ as the Author of our fellowship with God, we must consider the interpretation put by him on the Death of Christ, the Divine thought he found expressed in it, and the effects on the spiritual life of mankind that he ascribed to it.

I

Now, in the first place, the death of Christ had for Paul absolute worth in relation to our salvation as the REVELATION of God's gracious love to man; and to this aspect of it is consistently referred its power to produce penitence and to awaken trust in God. Nothing could be farther from Paul's thought than the idea that the death of Christ was needed to win the love of God for us, or to overcome any reluctance in Him to show mercy to sinners. On every page of his writings we are taught that the event on Calvary, so far from begetting love in God's heart, simply revealed and put into exercise the love that was there from eternity. God is habitually set forth as the originating cause of the redemption that has come to us through the Cross, and as manifesting His love in the blessings that Christ has brought to us. "God hath set

Him forth to be the propitiation."[1] "When the fulness of the time came, God sent forth His Son, made of a woman, made under the law, to redeem them that were under the law."[2] "God was in Christ reconciling the world to Himself."[3] "God sent forth His Son to condemn sin in the flesh."[4] Words could not more emphatically proclaim that the death of Jesus was an event ordained by God for the accomplishment of His own gracious purpose towards the race. It was the deed of men, and revealed the enormity of their sin, but God was present in it as well, revealing His grace to sinners; and what followed from it in the way of blessing expressed God's love and God's purpose to bless and save us.

Paul's conception of the Divine character is sometimes contrasted unfavourably with that of his Master. Christ, it is said, taught that God is the Father of all; Paul, that God is the Judge of all and the Loving Father only of some. But this is not just to the apostle. He also teaches that God is in His very nature a gracious Being, who is impelled by His own love and pity for men to seek their recovery to Himself, and welcomes them to His Fellowship on a basis not of works but of trust in His free forgiving love. There is, however, a difference between the teaching of Jesus and Paul here. With Jesus, God's love is a truth of intuition. He sees into the heart of the Father, and beholding it written there, He proclaims it abroad that men may believe it; He makes it visible in His own gracious intercourse with sinners, that He may thus commend it to their faith. With Paul, on the other hand, the truth of God's love is partly an inference from the death of Christ, and partly an experience of the happy issues to himself of that event. He makes no reference to the teaching of Jesus on this subject, or to the instruction to

---

[1] Rom. iii. 25.   [2] Gal. iv. 4.
[3] 2 Cor. v. 19.   [4] Rom. viii. 3.

be gathered from His historic life; but arrives at the truth through the personal discovery of the gracious ends secured by the death of the Cross. Those who discard Paul for Christ, and are content to rest their faith in the love and Fatherhood of God on the authority of Christ alone, place themselves at a disadvantage in the maintenance of that faith. They not only lose the confirmation of it that comes from the Cross of Christ and the experience of salvation, but they have also to contend with the doubt, arising from the fact that Jesus died a victim to the wickedness of the world and the powers of darkness, lest He who rules the world and suffers His Dearest and Best thus to perish and yet gives no sign, should not be Love after all. Paul, viewing the Death and Resurrection as the two parts of a Divine arrangement intended to work out human redemption, is not troubled with this difficulty. The death of Christ was the very hinge on which the execution of God's redeeming purpose turned; and so far from being a stumbling-block to his faith, the Cross became the object of his glorying, for it was the supreme revelation of the infinite love of God to men. "God commendeth His own love to us," he could say, "in that, while we were yet sinners, Christ died for us."[1] It will not do to base our faith in the doctrines of Christianity on the teaching of Christ alone, and apart from the revelation of truth contained in the historic facts of the Death and Resurrection as interpreted to us in the Pauline Gospel.[2]

[1] Rom. v. 8 and Gal. vi. 14.
[2] Referring to the Death on the Cross, Gess asks, "How can one maintain that here God's love and faithfulness is revealed? Could it be more completely concealed than it was from the Friday afternoon to the Sunday morning? Only by the Resurrection was the mystery solved, and it became credible, and gradually indisputable, that what appeared the very opposite of love and faithfulness must nevertheless have been love and faithfulness" (*Christi Person u. Werk*, vol. iii. p. 263). See also extract from Häring to the same effect in Note A on the Significance of the Resurrection in Relation to the Love of God.

The peculiarity, moreover, that belongs to the apostle's presentation of the love of God as an inference from the death of Christ, suggests that in his view, that event was something more than a revelation of the love of God, it was an accomplishment as well, an offering to God, a deed that effected the redemption of men. Those who would explain the virtue of the death of Christ to save solely on the ground that it is a manifestation of the love of God that has force to draw us out of our sins and win us to His love and service, are certainly out of harmony with the apostolic thought. Love, indeed, is revealed in that deed; but, as Paul puts the matter, it is not that God reveals His love in the death of Christ, and so redeems us, but rather that God redeems us by the death of Christ, and so reveals His love.[1] Redemption is an objective benefit that has been obtained for us by the death of His Son. We are called, therefore, to consider that event as a deed, an achievement by Christ, and a factor in our redemption as much so as the love is from which it issued and to which it bears witness.[2] This is the leading point of view from which the matter is regarded by the apostle, and, accordingly, we go on now to consider the characteristic features of his teaching on this subject.

II

In approaching this theme, namely, the nature of the connection between the death of Christ and our salvation

---

[1] The difference between these two conceptions of the Death of Christ is well illustrated by Dr. Dale in his *Christian Doctrine*, pp. 219, 220.

[2] In His death Christ acts at once on God's behalf, revealing to us God's love, and on our behalf, offering to God what we ought but cannot offer. These two points of view are difficult to adjust, the one to the other; and error has arisen from theologians pressing the one to the exclusion of the other, sometimes emphasising the death of Christ as a Revelation, so that no reason can be found for it as an Offering to God; at other times exaggerating its purpose as an Offering so as to compromise its value and purpose as supreme Revelation. It is the task of theology to harmonise these two sides of truth.

viewed as a veritable ACCOMPLISHMENT on His part, it is necessary to recall what Paul's conception was of the salvation that he traces so directly to the death of Jesus. His experience, as we found, was a very rich and full one, including benefits that were both religious and moral in their character. The new life in Christ was at once a life of forgiveness, of restored fellowship with God, of sonship, and all that enters into the perfection of our religious standing; and it was a life of moral power, of deliverance from the dominion of sin, issuing in the renewal of the whole being. All this moral and religious good which formed his consciousness of salvation was connected directly with the death of Christ, and gave to that event the character of a deed possessing saving power. Now, while that good was in his experience an indivisible unity, while forgiveness is in fact inseparable from moral renewal, still the two things are separate in idea, and are dealt with separately by the apostle: and we may look at these two elements of his Christian experience as distinct effects of the death of Christ. We ask, then, what further light is shed by Paul's Epistles, first, on the connection between the death of Christ and the forgiveness of sin, or the perfection of the religious state of man? and second, on the connection between that event and freedom from sin itself, or the attainment of the moral Ideal?[1]

What is the teaching of the apostle regarding the death of Christ and its connection with the forgiveness

[1] It is one of the merits of Ritschl's treatment of Pauline doctrine that he brings out clearly that Justification does not bear directly on the ethical life, that it has to do with our relation to God and secures our *religious* perfection. Its direct consequences, falling within experience, are peace with God and the firm hope of acquittal at the last judgment, confidence in prayer, patience under the sufferings of life, trust in God's providence, mastery over the world and all the ills of life—all of them religious determinations. See his chapter on "The Religious Functions that flow from Reconciliation with God," in his great work on *Rechtfertigung u. Versöhnung*, vol. iii. pp. 575–635, third ed.

of sin, or restoration to the favour of God? That there was in his view a most intimate connection between these two things every page of his writings shows. That on the ground of what Christ did when He died for men God is now dealing with His creatures on a principle of grace, forgiving sin and receiving them into His fellowship, on the condition of their faith in Him and in the love manifested in Christ—this, in broad terms, is the tenor, not of one Epistle, but of all. Nor is this doctrine peculiar to Paul; it is the doctrine of the New Testament writers generally. The apostolic Churches with one accord attached this value to the death of their Lord. In writing to the Church at Corinth Paul reminds them that he had preached to them what he had received, and what had become part of the tradition of the Church, that "Christ died for our sins according to the Scriptures and rose again";[1] that is, that the death of Christ possesses the significance of a Deed of salvation—is the ground on which sin is forgiven. We find allusions in the New Testament to current doctrines that were subversive of the Christian faith. We do not find one that suggests the suspicion that any section of Christians denied that Christ's death was the ground of man's salvation;[2] and in this matter we are safe in saying that the teaching of Paul echoes the testimony of the entire Church.

There is more reason for hesitation as to the answer to be given to the question, what is distinctive in his doctrine here, and what explanation is contained in it of the connection, admitted by all, between the death of Christ and the forgiveness of sin? Why had Christ to die in order that sin might be forgiven? Wherein does the efficacy of that event to achieve the result consist?

---

[1] 1 Cor. xv. 3.
[2] This point is emphasised by Seeberg in his work, *Der Tod Christi in seiner Bedeutung für die Erlösung* (pp. 180, 181).

When we ask what answer Paul enables us to give to this question, it is evident, from the different interpretations which his words bearing on it have received from men at once competent and believing, that we are here on more uncertain ground, where it becomes us to proceed with caution. There are some, indeed, who despair of the attempt to harmonise the different points of view that we find in the Epistles. They hold that Paul had no consistent doctrine on the subject, and that we must be satisfied to believe that there is a connection, abandoning the hope of arriving at any reliable conclusion as to the how or why of it. One would be slow to adopt this view. It is not likely that so penetrating a mind as the apostle's would be satisfied with a belief in Christ that could not give any account of itself to his intelligence, that did not embrace in it some perception of the way in which the death of his Lord was related to so vast a change on the religious fortunes of men as he ascribed to it. It is to be expected, indeed, that some of the forms of statement used by him in this connection would be more luminous to those for whose benefit he wrote than they can be to us whose religious training differs so widely from theirs. He wrote no systematic treatise on the atonement. He never formulated his views. His utterances were on each occasion directed to meet the religious wants and difficulties of the Churches he had founded; and it is by no means easy for us to put ourselves into their mental condition and appreciate the bearing of what he says on their thoughts and feelings. On the other hand, it is easy for us to read far more into his affirmations than they really contain, and to understand him as answering our problems while in reality he is dealing with problems very different. But giving all weight to such considerations, we are prepared to find in the Epistles the outline at least of some scheme of thought on the subject that will commend itself to the Christian intelligence of all time, and that, while not satisfying our curiosity or removing all our difficulties, will fit in with the facts of our experience.

Let me, in the first place, refer to explanations that have been ascribed to Paul that do not seem to me fairly to represent his thought. On the one hand, he is made responsible for the view that Christ's death secured forgiveness in virtue of its being the vicarious endurance of the punishment that followed transgression under the law, and that would have been inflicted on us had He not, by bearing it in our room, released us from liability. Holding the view taught in the Rabbinical schools that the relation between God and man was of the nature of a legal compact under which man had contracted guilt and exposed himself to punishment, and sharing also their view that the innocent individual might take upon him the punishment that was due to the transgressor, and so deliver him from the liability to punishment,—the apostle, it is alleged, ascribed to the death of Christ efficacy to bring about the remission of sins in virtue of its having been undeserved by Him personally, and its having, consequently, power to take the place of the sinner's death and deliver him from it.[1] This is the view supposed to be set forth in Gal. iii. 12, where we read that "Christ has redeemed us from the curse of the law being made a curse for us." Now it is undoubtedly true

---

[1] According to the Pharisaic theology, forgiveness of sin was impossible without payment of the debt by some one, if not by the offender, then by another for him, who, by reason of his innocence, did not need on his own account to die the death that was the penalty of sin, whose submission to it would compensate for its remission to the guilty. An outward mechanical idea of guilt and forgiveness and religion generally underlies this scheme. We have here, too, the real root of the Catholic doctrine of the merit of the saints being available to cover the shortcomings of others. The Pharisees taught the vicarious righteousness of the patriarchs and saints of Israel. See Weber, *Altsyn. Theologie*, pp. 267-300; also *Apocal. Baruch*, xiv. 7.

that deliverance from the law, both in its condemnatory and enactive power, was one chief element in the salvation Paul owed to Christ and to His death. But in using the term law he sometimes had in view the idea of law generally, the idea of moral obligation in a preceptive categorical form which is part of our constitution as moral beings; and at other times that legal system which had been imposed by God on Israel for a temporary purpose.[1] It is with law in the latter sense—the Jewish national law—that he brings the death of Christ into connection, in the striking passage in Galatians. This he does in order to show that it had achieved the deliverance of the Jews from the consequences of their failure to keep that legal system, with all its ceremonial details, under which they had been placed for providential ends. And there arises a serious difficulty in the way of our giving a universal scope to an argument that is intended primarily to explain the deliverance of the Jews from the consequences of the transgressions of their law, and that carries on the face of it the marks of its limited significance; for the sentence which Christ is represented as bearing in the place and stead of others, the curse of transgression, "the hanging on the tree" (ver. 13), is not the sentence of death as a universal fact, but the sentence of death threatened under the special laws of the Jews.

We have, indeed, no means of determining even how Christ's bearing the curse of the law resulted in its removal from those who were under it; and questions arise here which we cannot answer with certainty. Was the deliverance itself a subjective one? Or was it more, was it

[1] Perhaps it would be more correct to say that, according to the object he has in view, Paul, in speaking of the law, thinks sometimes of the ritual aspect of it, as in his Epistle to the Galatians; at other times of its ethical aspect, as in Romans. For an instructive account of the meanings of "law" in Paul's writings, see Grafe's *Die Paulinische Lehre vom Gesetz*, 1893.

objective as well? That is, did Christ's undeserved endurance of the curse of the law at the hands of those who administered it deliver believers from the law and from the fear of its threatenings by the impression made upon their minds of the worthlessness and moral effeteness of a religious system that had culminated in such a crime? Was it that the believing Jew felt he might well afford to ignore the threatenings of a legal system that had been so blind as to inflict its heaviest curse on its own Messiah? Is that what is meant by Christ having delivered us from the curse of the law through His having submitted to be accursed for our sakes?[1] Or, if that is regarded as too modern an explanation to be attributed to Paul, and if he is to be viewed as teaching that the deliverance was objective in its nature, and that it effected a real change in the relations of God and Israel, in what way did Christ's being made a curse accomplish such a change? Was it as a substitutionary infliction on Him of the punishment which the transgressors would otherwise have borne? or was it as a moral equivalent for it? And if, as the passage shows, it was to the law regarded as a personified power that this homage was paid, in what relation does law on this view stand to God? And how is God to be conceived as affected by the surrender of His Son to the curse of the law? These are questions that are left unanswered, and till we have a satisfactory answer to them a dogmatic conclusion from the passage is unwarranted.

Nor have I been able to convince myself of the truth of

[1] This is the view advocated by Schweizer in the searching examination of this passage in his article in the *Studien u. Kritiken*, on " Paul's Doctrine of the Redemptive Death of Christ in Gal. iii. 13, 14" (1858, iii.). Dr. Fairbairn, in his *Christ in Modern Theology*, takes the same view, p. 481. "The law that thus judged Him condemned itself: by cursing Him, it became accursed." The explanation commends itself by its naturalness, substituting an historical for a dogmatic understanding of the words. But there is a doubt whether it is the explanation intended by the apostle.

the view which is at present popular amongst expounders of Paulinism, that the idea of *sacrifice*, as elaborated in the legal system of the Jews, furnishes the key to the understanding of the apostle's references to the connection between the death of Christ and the forgiveness of sins. His allusions to the Levitical cultus are exceedingly scanty. That he should borrow sacrificial language in speaking of the death of Christ is indeed what might be expected. Sacrifice among the Jews, and, indeed, in all religious systems of antiquity, was the means of reconciliation; a special virtue was ascribed to the blood of victims as the appointed means of making atonement for sin; and it was natural, when he spoke of the death of Christ in connection with our reconciliation to God, that he should make use of language that belonged to that system that made provision for the Israelites' legal approach to God. The frequent references to the "blood of Christ" may thus be accounted for; and it is to be noticed that it is not any one kind of sacrifice, such as the sin-offering, that is suggested in the use of the term "blood," but the sacrificial system generally, in which blood denoted cleansing and the impartation of new life as well as atonement. Paul is careful not to associate forgiveness of sin distinctly or exclusively with the type of the sin-offering. The nearest approach to this application of sacrificial language is in Rom. iii. 25, where we are told of Christ that "God hath set Him forth to be a propitiation through faith in His blood." The word propitiation (ἱλαστήριον) is one in regard to which a great deal of discussion has taken place; but, without entering at all on the different explanations of it, it must suffice to say that a very large consensus of opinion is in favour of its being taken as a verbal adjective. In conformity with the general usage of similar words ending in τηριος, the word would then be rendered "that which *serves the purpose* of propitiation":

and the meaning would be, God has set Him forth as a means of propitiation, available for those who put their trust in His death. In other words, God appointed Christ to die in order that all who place their confidence in Him might have, in His death, that which possesses the virtue of an expiation of sin, that which ensures the forgiveness of their sins and their admission to His fellowship.

The language, certainly, is borrowed from that ceremonial cultus that prescribed animal sacrifice as a means of propitiation; but in what way the death of Christ served this end, or possessed this efficacy, is not taught here, and is not to be inferred from the use of the word. We have no theory of sacrifice in the Bible, no explanation of the ceremonial value attached to it. And, even if we had, it would be unwarrantable to apply it to the death of Christ, for we degrade His offering by regarding it as a sacrifice of that sort. The Sacrifice of Christ was the offering of Himself to God, the sublime expression of His love to men, and was an entirely different thing from the legal sacrifices. It may throw light on them, being the very truth which they dimly shadowed forth; and the legal system of sacrifice may be interpreted by means of it. But the interpretation of the Sacrifice of Christ itself must be derived from another source. As illustrations of Gospel truth, sacrificial terms may be useful, but it is an abuse to view them as teaching or conveying that truth. The Sacrifice of Christ must be interpreted by the light which itself supplies, being the spiritual reality prefigured by the ceremonial cultus, it can reflect light on the system of animal sacrifices but can receive none from it.[1]

The real clue to the apostle's thought on this subject is to be found, as it seems to me, in the single passage where there is anything like a formal discussion or explanation of

[1] See Note B on Sacrificial Language in Paul's Epistles.

it, where he treats it as a problem that had been consciously present to his mind. I refer to the latter half of the fifth chapter of the Epistle to the Romans, in which we have the famous parallel and contrast between the two Adams—the two representatives of the human race whose acts have determined the religious histories of all severally descended from them. The human race is there conceived of as a moral unity that possesses a collective life of its own. Humanity is not an aggregate of atoms; it rather resembles a tree whose leaves are distinct, while, at the same time, they partake of the common life and the qualities of the stem with which they are organically connected. Without ceasing to be personally responsible, we are so related to the race as a whole that its sin lives in us, and involves us in consequences that are not the result of our individual actions. Not through the personal sin of each, but through the sin of one man, has death come into the world. All were included in that one; and in idea, or potentially, sinned and died in his act. "The judgment of all men was by one man to condemnation,"[1] and through the organic unity of the race, sin, thus originating, worked itself out in the actual sinning and dying of all the individual members of mankind. But Adam in this respect was a Type of the Man to come, *i.e.* of Christ.[2] In Him humanity came to possess a Second Adam, or Representative, who summed up in Himself and realised perfectly its capacities for the higher life; and in His actings He became the proper organ of the race. In His holy and sinless Person humanity was born again, as it were, abandoned its revolt against God, and returned to its proper allegiance to Him, overcame evil and lived the perfect life well pleasing to God. Christ thus begins a new period in the moral history of mankind, imparting a new element to our collective being; and for that relation

[1] Rom. v. 16.   [2] Rom. v. 14.

of "all" to Adam, which makes them, through their organic connection with him, partakers of his sin and death, there is substituted now a new relation of "all" to Christ, the Second Adam, that makes them partakers of His righteousness and life, a relation which in its ideal truth holds of mankind as a whole, and becomes a reality in those who connect themselves with Him by their personal faith, and with the new Humanity of which He is the Head.

Now our attention is specially called to the fact that it is in virtue of His death that our Second Adam has power to bring mankind into that new relation to God which is realised in His Person; and, further, that His death possesses this efficacy because of its moral value, because it was a supreme act of obedience to the will of God,—"as by one man's disobedience the many were made sinners, so by the obedience of one shall the many be made righteous."[1] As the disobedience of the first Adam brought condemnation on all, a countervailing obedience on the part of Christ secures the removal of condemnation, and establishes mankind in a relation of life and reconciliation to God. It is as a sublime act of obedience to the Divine will that the death of Christ is declared to be the ground or cause of the new footing on which we stand with God.[2]

---

[1] Rom. v. 19. When he speaks of the "obedience of Christ" and the "one righteous act," δικαίωμα (ver. 18) Paul refers doubtless to the Death of Christ, in which His obedience to the Will of God was consummated. But it would be wrong to separate the Death from the Life of Christ, and this is not intended. For inasmuch as His whole Life was animated by the Spirit of obedience, and involved submission to elements of suffering and sorrow of the same nature with those that fell to Him in an aggravated form at the close, *it* was most truly a Sacrifice as well as His Death, and possessed the same worth in relation to the forgiveness of sins that belongs to His obedience on the Cross. In reference to Christ's obedience, "which reached its highest expression and purest form in His death," Ritschl says it is "the concrete representation of the Will of God in a man" (*Die Altkath. Kirche*, p. 91).

[2] See Note C on the additional light on this subject furnished by 2 Cor. v. 21.

The further question may be asked, why was Christ's obedience to death necessary to this result? It may be doubted whether Paul has given us a definite answer to this question, or one at least that we can identify with any of the later theories of theology that profess to answer it. It does not seem to have occurred to him that there was needed an answer to the question why the Second Adam had to render an obedience to the Will of God, carried to the extent of dying, in order that communion between God and man might be restored. The necessity for this seemed to him axiomatic. Conceiving of God as not only loving and gracious, but as holy, and in His very nature opposed to sin, it seemed to him a self-evident condition of forgiveness that the death which expressed the Divine judgment upon its evil, should be borne in a spirit of obedience to the Divine Will, and that God's holiness should be thereby manifested in the very event that revealed His love.[1] And the wonderfulness of God's grace was beheld in that arrangement under which humanity, in the Person of its one perfect Member, in whom the moral life of the race was concentrated, rendered that obedience, and was thus in Him restored, in a way consistent with holiness, to the favour and fellowship of God.[2]

[1] See Note D on Rom. iii. 23-26, where the Death of Christ is represented as manifesting the Righteousness of God.

[2] Paul's view of the death of Christ in relation to Atonement and Forgiveness rests on the position that death in the world is the consequence and penalty of sin, a judicial infliction by God. But, it may be objected, was not death in the world before sin? Is it not simply a law of physical nature, destitute of moral significance? Christianity is not committed to the position that sin first introduced death into the world. Great Christian teachers (*e.g.* Augustine, Athanasius, Theodore of Mopsuestia) have held that, as being animal, man is by nature mortal. But the higher spiritual nature in man, we may conjecture, would, had his powers been developed in a normal way, have prevented the actual inroad of death. By withdrawing the higher nature from communion with God, sin deprived the physical of those spiritual forces that would have rendered it immortal, so that death followed; and, following in consequence of this withdrawal, it may justly be regarded as the penalty of

And Paul has carried with him the convictions of believers in all ages. Men have felt that there must be Holiness as well as Grace in the Divine Provision by which a new relation was to be established between God and sinners; and they have based their confidence in forgiveness on the death of Christ because they believed that it made this provision, and revealed His condemnation of sin as well as His love for sinners and His desire to reconcile them to Himself. Theology, formulating the convictions of faith on this subject, has adopted now one mould of doctrine now another. Since the revival of Pauline doctrine at the Reformation, it has been customary to speak of the death of Christ as a vicarious punishment inflicted upon Him, instead of upon us, by the Father, in order to satisfy His justice in remitting our sins. Theologians have magnified the significance of His death as a Divine infliction by representing it as designed to take the place of the death that would otherwise have been visited by God on sinners themselves. But the difficulty about this explanation, in its only intelligible form, is that the intended effect has not followed; for men, believers and non-believers alike, do in point of fact die still, and Christ's death has not exhausted God's judgment upon sin, has not relieved any from death as the punishment of it in their own persons.[1] Others, with what appears to me to be a truer insight into the necessities of the case, have emphasised the spirit in which Christ submitted to death as containing in it

sin. In this light it is viewed by the moral consciousness of humanity. If all this is disputed, and death is held to be a natural event and nothing more, it is of importance to observe that the value of the death of Christ to faith remains. It was due, indeed, not to nature but to the violence of men, submitted to in patient love, and its significance will then lie in its being the supreme revelation both of human sin and of Divine love. But the specific Pauline interpretation must then be given up.

[1] On the alternative, whether Christ suffered spiritual death, see Note E.

elements of moral value in which we are to find its real efficacy to expiate sin.[1] For if God is glorified not by a simple endurance of the punishment of sin, but by a submission to it that recognises the righteousness of its infliction, then Christ has truly met our case if He has borne our death in the spirit in which we ought to bear it, if He has, by His holy sorrow for the sins of His brethren, His confession of it and willing submission to its penalty, by His meek acceptance of all its consequences, rendered to God in our name that obedience to His will which we had no power in ourselves to render. Later writers dwell especially on such elements as these in Christ's obedience as what constituted His offering of Himself well pleasing to God and fitted in the nature of things to expiate or atone for sin. And doubtless much light has been shed on the mystery of the Cross by theologians of this class, who, by placing the emphasis on Christ's dealing with sin in His Passion and Death as our Representative, have emphasised the Mind and Spirit in which He bore the burden of our sins—a Mind and Spirit such as only a sinless Being, one with us in His subjection to all evil consequent on our sin, one also with God in His holy love for man, could manifest.[2]

---

[1] Among older theologians who have brought out this aspect of the death of Christ may be mentioned the Puritan, John Owen. I have given extracts from his work on the Holy Spirit to this effect in Note F.

[2] Of writers to whom we are specially indebted in this connection may be mentioned J. M'Leod Campbell, in his well-known work on the "Nature of Atonement"; Gess (*Christi Person u. Werk*, iii. pp. 64-145); and T. Häring, in his *Das Bleibende im Glauben an Christus*, and his recent *Zur Versöhnungslehre*, 1893. Häring insists that forgiveness cannot be received unless in us there be present the consciousness of guilt, and that a Divine provision to communicate forgiveness will be of a sort to awaken at the same time the sense of demerit. In this way he works round to what is very much the position of Mr. Campbell. "We may regard Christ's deed" (in dying for men), he says, "in so far as it is the one sufficient foundation of our consciousness of guilt, as the sorrowful recognition of the guilt of humanity, its great

There is, indeed, in all this no proper answer to the question as to the precise connection between the death of Christ and our forgiveness. We can understand that it was such moral elements as have been mentioned entering into the act of Christ in dying for us that gave that act infinite worth in the sight of God; we can understand that it was because Christ's love and holiness in submitting to death so faithfully reflected the very mind of God towards sinners and sin that His death was so well-pleasing to Him, was, to use the language of theology, "a satisfaction" to the Divine Nature. But the real question is, how, having this worth for God, does Christ's death avail to our forgiveness? What is there in the fact that it possessed this moral glory to bring it about, that because of it and of what Christ is, God restores us to fellowship with Himself, and treats us, although guilty, as if we deserved His love? That the death of Christ had this Godward aspect, that it did something to effect a change, not indeed of the heart or mind of God, but of His relation to men, that it was operative, in some real sense, in reconciling God to us as well as in reconciling us to God, we believe.[1] The language of Scripture seems to point to this. The sense of guilt craves a forgiveness that is based on this

confession of sin by the Head of our Race, the Lord of the Church, who thereby furnishes the condition of Divine forgiveness" (*Zur Versöhnungslehre*, p. 88), See Note G.

[1] We must beware of pressing this thought of God's needing to be reconciled to us, otherwise we will fall into the error of regarding Him as a vindictive God whose wrath has to be appeased before He can look with favour on the human race. We mean by such language that sin separates God from man as well as man from God, that the active manifestation of God's goodwill is withheld till the conditions necessary to its full expression are furnished. Caution must be observed in regard to all the figures of speech in which the effect of Christ's work is described. Pressing the metaphors and extracting from them dogmatic conclusions is a fruitful source of error. Religious language describing what Christ is in the experience of the believer must be used very guardedly when we try to deduce from it truth that lies outside experience.

objective reference of the work of Christ. It is another matter whether we can explain how Christ's work operates in this way. We seem here to have come to an ultimate fact beyond which we cannot get, which we may be able to illustrate by reference to human analogies, but the full rationale of which we cannot fathom. If, then, one or two remarks are added, their purpose is not to attempt an explanation, but to set this fact in a light that may commend it to our acceptance.

It is to be observed, then, that Christ's accomplishment in placing sinners in a new and gracious relation to God by His death is in analogy with facts of life and God's moral government that strikingly illustrate the reign of grace in the world. It is a familiar fact that one who has deserved well of a friend, may, through this circumstance, be the medium of blessing to those who have by their personal conduct deserved punishment at the hands of that friend. We naturally give a portion of the affection that we feel for one who is very dear to us to those who have in themselves nothing to draw forth our love if they are dear to him. We take them into our favour because of what they are to him; we do them good for his sake. This is the basis of intercession, which we know is a real power with God. He is moved (to speak humanly) by the prayers of His saints to bless with His best gifts those who have themselves done nothing to deserve His favour. Their being loved by those who stand high in His esteem is the ground on which they are dealt with apart from regard to their own personal acts. And the gracious relation into which mankind has been brought by Christ's act in dying for us is, as far as we can judge, the supreme instance of this principle. We can see no reason why God should deal with us so differently from what our sin deserves beyond this, that Christ, our Head, is the perfect revelation of God's love and holiness in humanity, and infinitely dear to Him, and that being so He brings blessing to the race to which He belongs, resulting in its being placed in a new relation of acceptance with God. We are restored to fellowship with Him for Christ's sake. This formula, "for Christ's sake," is what our theologisings come to. It expresses in the simplest and most accurate form the thought that is present in all our theories without being open to the objections which can so easily be brought against one and all of them.

Two questions naturally suggest themselves when we follow this line of thought a step further. First, how are we to think of God as influenced in our favour by what Christ has done? What is the precise effect Godward of His work as our Representative? And here, I repeat, we must dismiss all notions of Christ's work having wrought any change on the mind or disposition of God toward us, or having moved God to love us. Rather are we to think of Him as having furnished, by what He did, the conditions that had in the nature of things to be present before the eternal love of God could be seen to be what it is, or could be believed in aright by us. If Christ, by the revelation He has given in His death of God's holy love, brings us into that relation to God in which He can have fellowship with us, then He has on that account abiding worth with God. And God loves and forgives us for His sake because, dying in obedience to the Divine Will, Christ has perfectly revealed the love and holiness of the Father and supplied the conditions, self-imposed by the very nature of Divine love, to its being seen to be what it is, and to its operating, according to its nature, on human hearts.

The other question is, how are we to think of benefit coming to us because of what our Representative has done on our behalf? How can God extend to us, who are unworthy, the favour that rests on His Son, who is all-worthy? Evidently there must be presupposed on our part a connection with Christ that consists in faith and penitence. There can be no mechanical transference of merit here. God can bless us for Christ's sake only because, Christ being seen by us to be the revelation of God's holy love, there is awakened trust in God and penetential sorrow for sin. The condition of our sharing in the Divine favour, of which Christ is the supreme object, is our incorporation with Christ, our attachment to Him by a living faith that reconciles us to God.

While, therefore, the personal obedience of Christ is the objective ground of the reconciliation of the human race to God, and men are dealt with for Christ's sake as if they had themselves rendered that obedience, this is so far only an ideal reconciliation; and in order that it may issue in the actual reconciliation of sinners they must receive the revelation of God's Holy love conveyed in the death of Christ and so share in that vicarious act of His. "One died for all," says the apostle, "therefore all died" (2 Cor. v. 15); but this death of "all" was in idea or intention merely. It is to be realised by each in a faith that enters into the spirit in which the One died, before we can pass into the personal enjoyment of the reconciliation. Faith has, in the teaching of the apostle, this profound significance. It is a religious moral act in which, moved by the love of God, the man consents to the Divine judgment against his sin as expressed in the death of Christ, affirms its righteousness, and accepts what has been done for him by his Representative; and on the ground of this identification of himself with Christ, and penitent trust in the love of God manifested on the Cross, the sinner is forgiven and restored to fellowship with the Father. The work of Christ, then, can take effect in us only when its revelation of Divine love and holiness evokes our trust and the sorrowful sense of our demerit before God. And for the completion of what Christ has done there is needed the Gospel proclamation of what God's will in Christ is, and our consent of mind and heart to its requirement. *God was in Christ reconciling the world to*

Himself not imputing to men their trespasses, that is, not treating them as guilty, *for* (and now the apostle states the Divine arrangement which is the ground of this gracious treatment of the guilty) *He has made the sinless One to be sin for us in order that we might be made the righteousness of God in Him.* And then follows the entreaty of the Gospel, by compliance with which the intended result will take place, *now, therefore, we beseech you in Christ's name be ye reconciled to God.*[1]

The teaching of Paul has been charged with destroying the simplicity of the Gospel idea of faith, and substituting belief in a series of doctrines regarding the way of salvation for the simple acceptance of the message of forgiveness and personal trust in the Saviour. But while undoubtedly the Gospel is presented to us by Paul as a Divine arrangement, whereby, through the death of our Second Adam, forgiveness is conveyed to us in a way illustrative of the wisdom and love and holiness of God,—while there is a doctrine of the Cross that appeals to the intelligence, yet the object of the faith that saves is the Risen Christ, apprehended as the human embodiment of the free grace of God to sinners, as the Divine gift conveying life and righteousness to all who accept Him.[2]

There is one objection, however, that may be taken to this entire scheme of thought by which the apostle inter-

[1] 2 Cor. v. 19–21.
[2] It is when the question arises as to the reception by individuals of the benefit secured by the Death of Christ for the race as a whole, that the importance of the Resurrection in its bearing on the completeness of His work appears. It is as Risen and Living, and appealing to men on the ground of His love, that Christ makes efficacious to individuals that work of reconciliation that has respect to all. The bearing of Christ's resurrection on our justification is referred to in Rom. iv. 25, x. 9. That the faith that justifies has for its object the Risen Saviour, the Personal revelation of God's gracious love, has been illustrated with great fulness by Schäder in his *Die Bedeutung des lebendigen Christus für die Rechtfertigung nach Paulus*, 1893.

prets the saving significance of the death of Christ. It may be said that the analogy on which he proceeds is a mistaken one, that the existence and perpetuation of sin and death through our connection with Adam is a theory borrowed by him from the Rabbinical theology of his time; and, further, that it is disproved by science, which requires us to view the narrative of Gen. iii. not as history but as symbolic truth, as describing the way in which man first realised the consciousness of sin. But if sin, as the evolutionist says, is not strictly an innovation, but the survival of animal appetites that ruled without check during an earlier stage in the history of humanity, and that became sin when the new faculty of conscience had been developed, by which we recognise what is "right" as distinct from what is pleasant —what then becomes of the analogy between the first Adam and the Second? and what becomes of the apostolic interpretation of the obedience of the Second Adam, who is said to bring life and righteousness to the human race, after the same manner in which the disobedience of the first Adam inflicted sin and death upon them? In reference to all this, it is admitted that possibly Paul did proceed on ideas that can be traced to Jewish schools of theology. In Jewish literature ascribed to that age we find the theory of the Fall stated as he states it.[1] And the question may be raised, supposing that he derived it thence, is it a valid reason for our accepting it as true that Paul takes its truth for granted, and uses it to illustrate the Gospel method of salvation? a question that runs up into the further one, whether all the arguments Paul makes use of to illustrate the truth of revelation are to be accepted as equally authoritative with the truth itself.[2] To attempt to answer these

[1] See Note H on the Doctrine of the Fall in Jewish Literature.
[2] "In order to do justice to Paul's theology, we must avoid confusing his principles (which are permanent and universal) with his arguments and illustrations (which in many cases are peculiar to his time or to himself)" (Abbott, *The Spirit on the Waters*, p. 310). It does not

questions satisfactorily would lead us too far afield; assuming, however, the uncertainty or baselessness on scientific grounds of the analogy which the apostle employs, I ask, would this invalidate the interpretation put by him on the work of Christ? Must we regard as simply a bit of religious speculation this whole idea of Christ as a Second Adam, who has by His death lifted mankind into a new relation to God, calling now for our personal concurrence in it in order that life and righteousness may come to us? The conclusion does not, in my opinion, follow at all. For the solidarity of mankind is a fact, whether or not it is rightly accounted for by the theory of our connection with an individual head of the race whose fall involved that of all the rest. Sin is common to the race. Death is the common doom of the race. This is fact, whatever account of it we may give. As a believer, Paul was conscious of facts that meant that this law of solidarity held also in redemption. The righteousness that was the ground of his confidence before God was not his own; it was common to all men; it was the free gift of One who had obtained it for all. It was the result of Christ's dying, for it was in the appropriation and spiritual apprehension of Christ's death that Paul and his fellow-Christians realised their forgiveness and fellowship with God. Connecting his religious life thus directly with Christ and His death, he could well think of Him as a Second Adam, divinely appointed to be the author of a new race of men who should owe to Him their gracious standing before God and eternal life. He is that, He is a Second Adam, although it were proved that the progenitors of the natural humanity were not one but many.

follow that the conclusion is false because the apostle's premises are irrelevant. His quotations may not always bear the weight he puts upon them. What he regards as history may be better understood as parable. But the facts to which he appeals, the conclusions to which he comes, are true all the same, and are borne witness to by the universal consciousness of men.

To Him and to His work for them men have ever delighted to ascribe their forgiveness by God, and all those blessings that flow from forgiveness. The truth of Paul's representation turns on the question whether Christ's death has really that all-determining influence on the religious state of man which faith attributes to it; for if this be so, the idea of the solidarity of men with Christ,—the idea, that is, that an action of His has had so supreme an influence on the human race as to carry with it the actual salvation of all who trust in Him,—is an eminently reasonable conception, and agreeable to what we otherwise know of the moral government of God.[1]

III

But the death of Christ is represented not only as the basis of the forgiveness of sin, as the ground of our religious confidence, but also as the cause of our moral renewal and our deliverance from the power and dominion of sin. He not only died *for* sin, and in order to expiate it, but He died *to* sin, thereby bringing to an end its rule in human nature. This aspect of the death of Christ, its bearing on the destruction of sin, has a larger place assigned to it in the writings of the apostle than the aspect which we have considered; and it is still more characteristic of his interpretation of the saving significance of the event on the Cross. Weizäcker and others maintain that it is in what he says on this subject that we are to recognise the distinctiveness of the teaching of Paul on the death of Christ, and that he is alone and original among the teachers of apostolic Christianity in the emphasis he lays on that event as a death to sin, containing in it the potentiality of our death to it, and our entire deliverance in this way from its power.[2] As a

---

[1] See Dale's *Christian Doctrine*, pp. 325–356; also T. C. Edwards, *The God-Man*, p. 76.

[2] *Das Apostolische Zeitalter*, p. 142. R. Schmidt, in his *Paulinsche*

believer, Paul was conscious of an emancipation from the passions and lusts of the flesh of so complete a character that he could truly speak of himself as "dead" to that old self-life that had been ruled by the flesh. And this he describes as a universal effect of believing in Christ, "they that are Christ's have crucified the flesh with the affections thereof."[1] Union with Christ meant a union with Him in the death He died on the Cross, in virtue of which they had died or had been crucified with Him to the old nature. This is the teaching in particular of Rom. vi., where the very idea of a man continuing in sin who had been saved by the grace of God is repudiated as inconsistent with the fact of his position as a believer, for "baptized unto Christ he is baptized unto a fellowship with Christ in His death," and in that death the "old man was crucified that the body of sin might be destroyed,"[2] that is, that it might for us be brought to an end. But how is this to be understood? The death of Christ was physical, while the death in us that follows as its effect is a moral process, is an inward separation from sin. In what way can a death that is of the body bring about in us a death that is ethical in its character, a dying to sin? This is one of the debatable questions in the theology of Paul. The portions of his Epistle to the Romans that refer to it are among the most difficult in his writings. It has been thought by some that we are not to seek for any intelligible connection between the two things, that while Paul relates them closely together, he probably had no idea in his mind of there being any ethical element in the act of Christ's dying analogous to the moral act of dying to sin to which it gives rise in us.[3] I am reluctant to accept this conclusion. The language of

---

Christologie, makes this the ruling thought in Paul's doctrine of the Death of Christ to the exclusion of every other.

[1] Gal. v. 24.   [2] Rom. vi. 3, 6.
[3] Bruce's *Conception of Christianity*, p. 180.

the apostle seems to imply that there was something in the mind of Christ in dying for us that was the moral equivalent to that death to sin which takes place in us when we believe in Him, something in its very nature fitted to produce that change in us. "In that He died," we read, "He died unto sin once."[1] Not as if sin had had in Him a life that was brought thereby to an end; but He came "in the likeness of the flesh of sin."[2] He partook of our flesh, in which sin has certainly its seat; and His dying in that flesh, in so far as there was an element of will, of personal activity in the act, was the supreme instance of holy obedience. It was in its very nature a death inflicted on the principle of sin that characterises the flesh of ordinary human nature, a slaying of it in its very principle of self-will, a bringing to an end its ascendency over the flesh of man. The power of His death to mortify sin in the flesh of all who identify themselves with Him is derived from the fact that it was in some true sense a dying unto sin in the flesh. He is the Second Adam, in whose flesh that of all mankind received a mortal blow that deprived it once for all of its ascendency over human nature. As the Representative of the whole human race He submitted to the law that conditions our entering on our true life, He was the first to surrender willingly the life of the flesh that He might become the Firstborn of the Resurrection, and was thereby the Ideal and Example of all who were to follow Him hereafter. Heir in His own Person to the weakness of the flesh and its temptations, Christ found this dying to it an essential element of holiness, and in so far as His death on the Cross was the final triumph of His holiness over all those desires of the flesh that furnish to man unregenerate the motive power of his life, it possesses a moral efficacy that constitutes Him the leader of all His brethren in their entering on the inheritance of their true life. And so Paul could speak

[1] Rom. vi. 10 [2] Rom. viii. 3.

of himself and his fellow Christians, "as always bearing about in the body the dying of the Lord Jesus, that the life also of Jesus might be made manifest in our body."[1]

But in accounting for the stress laid by the apostle on the death of Christ as the cause of our death to sin and of our moral renewal, we must take along with us the place he assigns to the Resurrection of Christ in this connection, for in his doctrinal system the Resurrection is inseparably connected with the Death, and is a factor of prime importance in his conception of salvation. As the dying of Christ includes in it our death to sin, so His rising again includes in it our moral resurrection, our reviving to a life of holiness, and is the Power by which that mighty change is effected in human experience. And if the same question that met us before in reference to the moral change attributed to the death of Christ recurs here, in what way can a change so spiritual in its character as the awakening of the soul to a life of holiness be attributed to an event apparently so physical in its nature as Christ's rising from the dead?—the answer is to be found in the higher significance which attached to the latter event in Paul's view; for Christ's emerging from the grave, according to the apostle, was coincident with His entrance on a grander form of being, that gave Him access to the souls of men as Spirit; and it is in virtue of their being subjects of the energy of His Holy Spirit that His people undergo that moral resurrection which is a fact of their consciousness. United to the Risen One by His Spirit, they are said to be "planted in the likeness of the Resurrection," and to rise with Him, partakers of the life that He now lives, and that is eternal as

[1] 2 Cor. iv. 10. Paul's teaching here is the development of Christ's, who represented the inward change necessary to salvation as analogous to death, to the experience of the Cross, Matt. xvi. 25, "Whosoever will save his life shall lose it: and whosoever shall lose his life for My sake shall find it."

He is, "for in that He died, He died unto sin once: but in that He liveth, He liveth unto God."[1] The efficacy inherent in the Resurrection of Christ to effect our moral renewal flows in reality from the Holy Spirit who comes forth from the Risen One, and to this Agent also is to be referred that participation in the death of Christ in which we are said to die with Him unto sin. In the sixth chapter, doubtless, the "new life" of which the Spirit is the author is regarded as preceded by our death to sin, as if the Spirit's work were limited to what follows death, to our being quickened to newness of life. The logical order, doubtless, is so; first, death to the old, and then birth into the life that is new. But the real order is the opposite. Death to the lower life can be accomplished only by the powers of the higher life already working on the soul, and the death to sin is as certainly the effect of the Spirit of life in Christ Jesus as is our moral quickening. Through the energy of His Spirit the Death and Resurrection of Christ are, in accordance with the law of solidarity, repeated in the experience of His people.

At the same time, Paul is careful to show that this work of moral renewal does not take place as a necessary inference. Still less does he give any encouragement to the idea that the virtue of the Death and Resurrection of Christ is dependent on sacramental acts.[2] It is a moral process, conformed to the laws of mind. If in a sense we are already "dead" in Christ, we are nevertheless to "reckon ourselves" to be dead, to cultivate insensibility to

[1] Rom. vi. 10.

[2] Those who take high views of the Sacrament of Baptism make much of Romans vi., where this rite is brought into relation to the Death of Christ, and spiritual results are spoken of as accompanying it. It must be remembered, however, that the Holy Spirit, the essence of the Christian Good, is nowhere said by Paul to be given at baptism, but to faith and the "hearing of faith." This is brought out by Ritschl (*Die Altkatholische Kirche*, second ed. p. 93), who shows that Titus iii. 5 is no exception to this rule. In all cases where spiritual effects seem to

the desires and ambitions of the old life. We are to crucify the desire of the flesh, to live to God, to walk in the spirit of the new life. The imperative mood is used as well as the indicative. We are personally to become what in Christ we already are. We must make our own personal possession that freedom from sin and the flesh which was made good for all humanity when Christ died to sin, and that spirituality of Divine Life which was secured for all when Christ rose from the dead. And here we are to observe Paul's method as a moralist, as one who has found in Christ the secret of a victorious moral life, the key to the attainment of the moral Ideal. He does not say, Act as Christ acted in this and that detail of His earthly life. He does not dwell on separate features of the character of the historic Jesus, or bid us imitate Him in these. He sets the Risen Christ before us as our Model, and bids us follow Him who is as the embodiment of our true life, and contains in Himself the potentiality of all grace and holiness of character. Only die with Christ to the flesh and rise with Him to live the life of the Spirit, and all goodness will grow out of that root; concern yourselves with the principle, details will follow. It has been said, " Take care of the little things of life and the great ones will take care of themselves," is the maxim of the trader which is sometimes, and with a certain degree of truth, applied to the service of God. But much more true is it that in religion we should take care of the great things, and the trifles of life will take care of themselves. Christianity is not acquired as an art by long practice; it does not carve and polish human

---

be attributed to baptism, faith, if not mentioned (as it is in Gal. iii. 26, 27) must be presupposed. Baptism is introduced in Romans vi. merely as an illustration. The parallelism between the rite and the Death of Christ has no dogmatic significance. Karl (*Beiträge*, etc., p. 108) speaks of the thought of Paul in this passage as "nichts als eine Art Augenblicksgedanke." If the apostle had shared the Sacramentarian view he could not have spoken of this rite as he does in 1 Cor. i. 13–17.

nature with a graving tool; it makes the whole man; first pouring out his soul before God, and 'then casting him in a mould.'"[1] It was thus that Paul apprehended and applied Christianity as an ethic. Setting the once Crucified but now Risen Christ before his readers as the embodiment of the principle of the true life, he bids them die with Him, and the Spirit of His life will do the rest. This is his doctrine of the *Imitatio Christi*.[2] And if the question is asked, how may this be? how can we so identify ourselves with Christ as to die with Him to the law of the flesh and live with Him to the law of the mind and spirit? Granted that it is all the doing of His Spirit in us, how does that Spirit become ours? how does it operate? The answer is to be found in Paul's doctrine of faith. With Paul faith is the act of the heart; it is the flower of sympathy and love, it draws us out of ourselves, and makes us one with Him who has now our trust and devotion. The man who loves Christ is a man who "enters into His feelings and lives with His life; he is a new creature; he can do, and he does, what Christ did."[3] As Christ died to self and the impulse of selfishness, the man who believes in Him and loves Him, can out of his sympathy and love die to them too, and can live in the spirit in which Christ lived. This, of course, is the language of affection, that delights in being, and that can be, all that its object is; and, as the language of affection, it is intelligible only to those who love Christ and have experienced the moral changes that are brought about by the power of His love. But that language describes a fact, the most momentous of the Christian life, in which its victorious power is disclosed. It is in the fire of love to Christ that the soul of man is separated from sin as thoroughly as though it were dead to it, and made alive

---

[1] Jowett, *Epistles of St. Paul*, vol. Dissertations (ed. 1894), p. 117.
[2] See Note I on Paul and the *Imitatio Christi*.
[3] M. Arnold's *Paul and Protestantism*, p. 52.

to God and righteousness in the power of a supernatural life, of which the Risen Christ is the Source and Pattern.

It may, indeed, be said, all this is ideal and too much in the clouds. Paul speaks as if our death to sin and life to righteousness and God through our union with the Second Adam were results as natural and necessary as is our inheritance of sin and death through our connection with the first Adam. But how different is the fact! Sin is not, as a matter of experience thus dead in believers; neither is their new life such a glorious reality as it is represented to be when it is spoken of as a participation of Christ's Risen life. Is Paul not utterly regardless of the facts of life in his whole estimate of the matter? Now it is plain the apostle's eyes were open to the facts that militated against his idealism. His letters are directed to the correction of the sins of Christians in the Churches which he founded. But these facts did not breed in his mind any suspicion of the failure of Christ to accomplish in the actual experience of men, so mighty a work of moral regeneration as is implied in their dying to sin and living to holiness. He held by the omnipotence of the Ideal in spite of facts; he could not contemplate the possibility of sin having any lasting significance for those who had entered on the new life in Christ. He transferred to all believers his own experience of the transforming effects of the love of Christ, and insisted that men have only to realise what Christ is to them, and what they are in Christ, in order to exemplify by their character and conduct that God has indeed made Christ to be a Power of real death to sin and of actual holy living.

According to his great conception, then, the death and resurrection of Christ mark a new epoch, a fresh point of departure in the evolution of the spiritual history of man; for they bring to an end the former relation of God to men and of men to God, with the reign of death and sin which characterised it, and inaugurate a fresh period in which man collectively, in the Person of his Representative, has attained to a new standing before God, and started with fresh powers for the realisation of his high destiny to manifest under material conditions the moral image of his Maker. In His Death, sin, both in itself and in its physical consequences, has been destroyed; and in His Resurrection a new order of beings, spiritual and immortal, has been founded. In Him, as its Second Adam, mankind is at once reconciled to God and regenerated in all its powers. Thus is He become the Founder and Head of a new humanity with which He remains united as the permanent source of its life and the pledge of its perfection in glory.

And all this in the view of the apostle was an arrangement for the salvation of man, originating in, and revealing throughout, the wonderful grace of God, as well as communicating that grace in a way that constitutes it a power to which no limit can be set, either in respect of its intensity or the range of its operation. Words seem to fail the apostle in the effort to express his profound conviction of the all-sufficient provision for human need there is in the gracious love of God that reaches mankind through its Second Head, and of the far-reaching effects destined to be wrought out by it for the human race. None knew better than he who lived in that ancient world, and was a witness to its wickedness, what a power sin is in human nature and society, how disastrous the effects of its reign are in the world. But he saw, in the grace of God which had begun to work on the world through the Person of the Risen Christ, a mightier power far than that of sin, and one destined to make its sovereignty recognised in the universal reign of righteousness and life. "Where sin abounded grace has superabounded."[1] Paul's Christianity was characterised by this triumphant faith in the invincible and inexhaustible efficacy of Christ, and of the Divine powers emanating from Him on the nature of man,—by this boundless confidence in the might of the Second Adam to reverse all the effects of the first, and to subdue under Him every form of evil that springs from our fallen human nature. It may be alleged, indeed, that Paul was over sanguine, that the event has shown that he was mistaken in the belief he entertained that the old world was so soon to be replaced by a new in which righteousness and life were to be supreme. We may well believe that it would have been incredible to him had he been told that after so many centuries the world would still be ruled, to so large an extent as we see it to be, by the forces of evil. But were he present with us to-day, a witness to all the crime and wrong that retard the progress of the Kingdom of God and that dishearten those who labour for the well-being of the race, he would not, we may be confident, attribute the failure of Christianity to regenerate the world to any insufficiency in Christ, or to any defect in the moral and spiritual powers that emanate from Him, but to the fault of those who will not receive it, and the pusillanimity of those who receive it in appearance but who will not apply it as it asks to be applied. The world's deepest need now, as in Paul's age, is the need of religion; and the religion of redemption, which Christ administers, is the only one that has proved equal to the necessities of the case. And as for the long-delayed hour of His triumph, who will deny that the Church would have had a brighter story to tell of the prowess of its Master over human souls, had it possessed a little more of the idealism of this Christ-intoxicated man, a little more of his unconquerable faith in its Second Head as the power of God unto salvation?

[1] Rom v. 20.

IV

CHRIST THE LIFE AND THE LORD OF THE NEW HUMANITY

LECTURE IV

Christ the Life and the Lord of the New Humanity

We have been occupied in unfolding the contents of the conception under which Christ presented Himself to the faith of the apostle as the Second Adam. I have dwelt in the preceding lectures on two of the leading truths that enter into that conception: the first being, that, as Risen and Exalted, Christ is personally the Ideal or Archetypal Man, the Type of human perfection; the second, that, in His historic life on earth, He acted as the Representative of man, having by His obedience unto death redeemed the human race from sin and its consequences, and become the Founder of a new humanity. We pass on now to consider the Activity on which He entered when He rose from the dead, by which He communicates to and perpetuates in His people the virtue of His Person and work, and so completes His function as the Second Adam of mankind.[1] This continued Activity is exercised, on the one hand, by His Spirit, and on the other hand by His

---

[1] There would be no proper parallelism between the first and Second Adam if Christ were no more than an example, for Adam is a power of evil in us, and Christ must be in us a power of good in order to be the counterpart of the other. As William Law puts it, in a striking passage in *The Spirit of Prayer* : " If Adam was only an outward person, if his whole nature was not our nature, born in us, and derived from him into us, it would be nonsense to say that his fall is our fall. So in like manner, if Christ, our Second Adam, was only an outward Person, if He entered not as deeply into our nature as the first Adam does, if we have not as really from Him a new inward spiritual man as we have outward flesh and blood from Adam, what ground could there be to say that our righteousness is from Him, as our sin is from Adam ?"

authority as Lord. As Spirit, or in the power of His Spirit, which is the Spirit of God, He has incorporated Himself, as it were, into the very life of the race, in order to distribute in the members of it His own perfected life; while as Lord, He is related to them as their Supreme Authority, representing God to us and receiving from us the obedience we owe to God. Christ as the INDWELLING SPIRIT and LIFE of His people, and Christ their LORD,—this is the distinctive glory of the Exalted One. The change from death to resurrection, we are taught to believe, brought to Him an accession of personal endowment that qualified Him to exert His influence as a principle of new life in men, and it meant also His investiture with supreme power as the Lord of human life and destiny. Accordingly, in the record of Paul's experience in the Epistles, He is recognised both as an energy of Divine life in believers, working towards their renewal and moral transformation, and also as Lord and Sovereign ruling them by the authority of His truth and goodness. In other words, Christ is at once IMMANENT as the Spirit of God in men, and TRANSCENDENT over them as their Divinely constituted Lord. Both aspects of His Person enter into the apprehension of His unique greatness as the Second Adam. Fully to understand His work in this capacity, we must view Him not only as the embodied type of all that a spiritual man should be, not only as having acted on God's behalf and man's, and by His work in relation to sin restored us to fellowship with God,—we must view Him also as living to reproduce and perpetuate in us by His Spirit His own perfection, and as exercising over us the authority of God Himself. It is, as we shall see in this connection, because He works in us with an energy of love and holiness that is identified with the Spirit of God, and commands our obedience with an absoluteness that is identical with the authority of God, that we are to recognise. Christ as truly Divine, and to acknowledge the presence in Him of powers of Godhead that constitute Him the object of our faith and worship.

I

First, then, Christ is IMMANENT in men. According to the teaching of Paul, the Exalted Christ is the medium by whom the Holy Spirit of God is given, He is the source of an energy on human nature that is recognised as the energy of God. The man Christ Jesus, in other words, is the organ of the activity of God's Holy Spirit in the hearts and lives of men, and dwells in them as the Power of a new Humanity that embodies the same principle as that which was realised in Him, and that lives by the same life.

Paul's doctrine of the Spirit is a subject eminently worthy of special investigation. This cannot be undertaken now; but two or three of the more distinctive features of his teaching must be noticed; for if it be true, as a thoughtful writer[1] has remarked, "that the apostle's entire thinking stands under the influence of his estimate of the Spirit," we may expect that his conception of the Person of Christ will be modified by this estimate. While, therefore, it may be convenient for the dogmatic theologian to keep the Pauline Pneumatology and Christology apart, we cannot follow this course except at the risk of mutilating the living thought of the apostle; for in his religious experience, as we shall see, he recognised no hard and fast line between what he owed to Christ and what he owed to the Spirit of God; and to do justice to his intuition of truth we must look at the experience with which it is indissolubly connected.

The bestowal on men of God's Spirit was, according to

[1] Gloel, in his *Der Heilige Geist in der Heilsverkündigung des Paulus.*

prophecy, to be the accompaniment of the Messianic era,—
or rather, it was viewed as an essential part of the salvation
that the Messianic era was to usher in. And the sign to
the apostolic Church that the new age had indeed come,
that Jesus was the Messiah, and that the promised salvation was the actual possession of men, was the fact to
which observation and experience bore witness, wherever the
Gospel was preached, that the Spirit was given. It is an
indisputable fact that certain extraordinary effects followed
wherever men believed the glad tidings. A new energy,
producing remarkable phenomena, took possession of them,
an energy that was spoken of by them as that of the
Spirit of God, thereby intimating their belief that these
phenomena proceeded from a cause that was Supernatural
and Divine. The phenomena themselves were of the most
varied character, being physical, intellectual, moral and
religious. They were all different manifestations of one
and the same Divine power that had taken up its abode in
human nature, and that testified by these extraordinary
effects to the truth of the Gospel and to the advent of a
new age in the history of religion. Paul shared to the full
the belief of the primitive Church on this subject. He
himself enjoyed a measure of the common gift of the
Spirit that was greater, it would seem, than that which fell
to any other, uniting in himself in a singular degree the
various endowments that were conferred on believers by
this new power.[1] He was in the most entire agreement
with his fellow Christians as to the superhuman origin of
the gift and as to its paramount value for the religious
life. His own experience of the Divine life, so full and so
vivid, gave him the most exalted impression of the might
of this supernatural energy and its manifold working within
the sphere of the Church. So far, Paul stood on ground
common to the whole primitive Church. But now it is to

[1] See 1 Cor. iii. 5 ; Gal. i. 1 ; 2 Cor. xiii. 3 ; Rom. xv. 18-29.

be noticed that there were several directions in which he, through the depth of his experience, struck out lines of teaching for himself, that not only bore witness to the originality of his view, but contained truth of the highest importance for a proper understanding of the religious life.

1. He distinguishes between such phenomena as were called gifts (χαρίσματα) of the Spirit and those that are termed the graces of the Christian life.[1] The tendency of the primitive Church was to exalt the extraordinary gifts (χαρίσματα) that pointed a state of ecstasy, and to regard all who possessed such gifts as spiritual in a pre-eminent sense. Paul, on the other hand, emphasised the surpassing worth of the moral and religious effects of the Spirit's working in the renewal of character. He held up the Christian life itself, in the normal exercise of the graces of love, humility, meekness, etc., as being in a special sense the product of the Spirit. "If," says Gunkel, in his admirable little book on this subject, "his fellow believers regarded the extraordinary elements in the Christian life as spiritual, Paul regarded the usual and ordinary ones as being such. They had respect to what was peculiar to the individual, he to what was common to all; they to what stept forth suddenly, he to what was regular. They singled out separate things in the Christian life; the value they attributed to wonderful gifts he placed on the Christian life itself."[2] This marked a great advance on the thought of his age; and by his teaching on this point, as has been well said, "Paul inaugurated that decisive change of view by which Christianity made the transition from the miraculous world of ecstatic feeling and apocalyptic phantasy into the true spiritual world of religious and moral personal life,

---

[1] 1 Cor. xii. 31, xiii. 1, etc., xiv. 1.
[2] Gunkel, *Die Wirkungen des Heiligen Geistes in der Lehre des Paulus*, p. 82.

and by which it could become the regenerating leaven of the history of mankind."[1] In accentuating the moral and religious elements in the Christian life, Paul does not make less of the Divine energy to which they are due. In saying that moral goodness is the best result of the Spirit's working, he holds as strongly as any that only the Spirit of God can produce that goodness. By referring the entire Christian life to the authorship of the Divine Spirit, he taught, in the most explicit way, that there entered into the very conception of Christianity a passion and energy of ethical life, an enthusiasm for God and for man, a power of holiness which was not in man himself and which the Divine Spirit in man alone could awaken and sustain. The fact that the ordinary graces of Christian character were ascribed by him to the Spirit of God, is of itself a testimony to the superhuman worth and Divine origin that were felt to belong to true and noble character in apostolic times.

2. Paul identified the Spirit of God, bestowed on believers under the Gospel, with the *Spirit of Christ*. Effects that are referred by him in some passages to the Divine Spirit, are in others attributed to Christ's Spirit, the two being evidently in his view one and the same power.[2] There was an historical justification for this; for the Spirit of the historic Jesus, that was stamped on all He said and did, was recognised as the Spirit of God Himself. It was the holiness and graciousness and truth of the living God that were expressed in the acts and words of Jesus on earth. Accordingly, when, as Risen and Glorified, He entered on His perfected fellowship with God, the Spirit proceeding from Him, by which He continues to live and energise in the hearts of men, is in the most real sense the very Spirit of God; and the experiences of the life

---

[1] Pfleiderer, Hibbert Lectures, p. 82.
[2] Rom. viii. 9, 14; Gal. iv. 6.

of faith are referred both to the Spirit of Christ and to the Spirit of God. Here, too, we mark an advance on the primitive doctrine, for while it was the original belief that the Divine Spirit is given to men *through* Christ, it does not seem to have been held, till Paul taught it, that this Divine Gift is itself the Spirit of Christ, the active principle of His Personality. And we can understand the significance and value of the contribution the apostle thereby made to a true understanding of the Gift of the Spirit. As long as the connection in men's minds between the Person of Christ and the Gift of God's Spirit was loose and uncertain, manifestations of mere enthusiasm, originating in unsanctified human nature, might be declared to be the outcome of that Spirit which was the peculiar endowment of the Church. But by drawing close the bond between the Gift and the Person, and identifying the Spirit of God with the energy of the Personal life of Jesus, Paul furnished a test by which phenomena really due to the Divine Spirit might be discriminated from others that did not proceed from that source. For what comes from the Spirit of God must authenticate itself as such by its being in harmony with the Spirit of Christ, the Spirit exhibited in the character and deeds of Jesus of Nazareth.

3. But Paul not only identifies the Spirit of God with that of Christ, he identifies both with the very *Person of Christ*. "The Lord is the Spirit,"[1] we read; and, again, "we are changed into the same image by the Lord, the Spirit."[2] The intention of the apostle in this passage is evidently to bring out the fact, that He whom Christians acknowledged to be the Lord was not such an one as the Jews, with their worldly ideas of the Messiah, believed in,—a Messiah distinguished by outward prerogatives, but one

[1] 2 Cor. iii. 17.
[2] 2 Cor iii. 18. Compare also 1 Cor. xv. 45 with vi. 17.

who was Spirit, ruling men by a Divine power at the centre of their lives. Being "in Christ" and "being in the Spirit" are the same thing; and in the thought of the apostle, "Christ," the "Spirit of Christ," and "the Spirit of God" are practically synonymous. At the Resurrection Christ became a Life-giving Spirit to mankind, and by the heightening of the powers of His Personality that then took place, He was so made one with the very life of God as to be constituted a perfect medium through whom the Spirit of God could act upon us; and His Personal Influence and Working being, to the entire exclusion of every lower element, the influence and working of the Holy Spirit, He, Himself Personally, might be spoken of as the Lord, *the Spirit*.

Theologians of a certain school find, in this language regarding Christ, evidence that here again Paul was influenced by ideas derived from outside sources. They point us to the Apocryphal Book of Wisdom, a work which Paul seems to have been familiar with, where we find a striking passage in which Wisdom is identified with the Spirit of God, and is described as the author of operations which are likewise referred by the apostle to the latter source.[1] His familiarity with such-like passages has led him, it is said, to identify the Exalted Christ (or Wisdom of God) with the All-present and Omnipotent Divine Spirit, and thereby to introduce a metaphysical

[1] The passage referred to occurs in Book of Wisdom vii. 22-25: "There is a Spirit, quick of understanding, holy," etc. A very fair account of the traces in Paul's Epistles of his acquaintance with the Book of Wisdom will be found in E. Grafe's Essay on the subject in the vol. dedicated to Weizäcker, entitled, *Theologische Abhandlungen*. Grafe regards it as highly probable that Paul had read this Apocryphal Book, but holds that his dependence upon it is "formal rather than material." "A man of life, with a keen eye for practical needs, Paul borrowed the good wherever it was to be found; and he borrows from the Book of Wisdom a fulness of words, ideas and images, and applies them to express thoughts and convictions which he got from another source altogether."

element into his idea of the Person of Christ; that element, it is added, is the real germ of the later ecclesiastical dogma that has resulted in so glaring an inconsistency between the Christology of the schools and the original picture of the historic Christ.[1] Now the fallacy of this argument lies in the notion that Paul's doctrine of the Spirit was of the nature of a speculation akin to other teachings then current of a quasi-speculative sort; whereas nothing is more certain than that his whole conception of the Spirit was religious, and had its root in his experience of the fruits of the Spirit in his inner life. His idea of the work of the Spirit of God in man has scarcely anything in common with the speculations contained in the Book of Wisdom;[2] and in speaking of Christ as one with that Divine Spirit that was so operative in his personal life, he is not to be understood as setting up any theory of the Person of Christ. He is simply thinking of Him as the unique fountain of that energy of supernatural holiness and grace that was the deepest fact of his own experience. That intensely spiritual influence upon himself could only come from one who was the Personal Embodiment, as well as instrument, of the Spirit of God, and who, in consequence, might with truth be spoken of not only as *having* but as *being* the Spirit, " the Divine Spirit," as Sabatier puts it, " in the form of human individuality."[3]

The identification of Christ with the Spirit of God does

---

[1] Weiss advocates this view in his *Die Nachfolge Christi*, p. 94.

[2] On the Difference between Paul's Doctrine of the Spirit and that of the Book of Wisdom, see Note A.

[3] "The doctrine of the Spirit in Judaism and in the Jewish Christian primitive Church undergoes a transformation by Paul in his doctrine of the Pneumatic Christ; the thought of the ὁ-κύριος-τὸ-πνεῦμα is the specifically Pauline consciousness of the Pneuma, and goes far beyond the representation of his age," Deissmann, *Die N.T. Formel in Christo Jesu*, p. 90. Compare what P. W. Schmiedel says (*Hand Commentar zum N. T.*, II. i. p. 192).

not then warrant any dogmatic inferences bearing on the Person of our Lord; neither are we to attach any speculative significance to it. We are not to infer from it that Paul held that God's Spirit is restricted to the Person of Christ,—that the sphere of the influence of the former is defined by the limits within which the latter is known. The apostle has nothing to say on that subject, though we can scarcely doubt, I think, that he would have recognised the presence and operation of the Divine Spirit beyond the limits within which the historic Christ is known and believed in. It is a mistake to treat the occasional utterances of Paul on this subject as if they were intended to convey to us an exhaustive doctrine of the Spirit.[1] What we learn from his utterances is, that, to the Christian consciousness, Christ and the Spirit of God are one and the same that the influence of the Personal Christ upon us is equivalent, as regards its moral and religious effects, to the energy of the Divine Spirit, and that it is only through our connection with His Person and our faith in Him that we experience that specific working of God's Spirit that was exemplified supremely in His life.[2] And nothing could give us a deeper impression at once of the Personal pre-eminence of

---

[1] When Paul speaks of the "Spirit of God," it is His operation under the Gospel that he has in view, that "enthusiasm," with its manifold gifts and potencies, that followed faith in Christ.

[2] It is to be recognised, indeed, that Christ's Spirit, if we are to judge from the presence of Christ-like dispositions, is found in some who have no conscious connection with Christ Himself. He works even where He is not acknowledged; but in such cases faith in Him cannot fail to follow as soon as He is seen in His real nature. Although His Spirit may be present where He is as yet unknown and unacknowledged, it is, as a rule, faith in Him, and in the revelation of Divine love conveyed in His Person, that is the channel of His gift to men. The attempt to separate the Spirit of God from Christ, to cultivate the higher life without faith in the historical Christ, results in failure. The Life of the Spirit cannot maintain itself unless it is fed from the fountains of spiritual passion that flow from the Person of Christ.

Christ, and the intimacy of the relation in which He stands to God, as well as of the saving significance of His Person to the human race, than this, that He acts on men's souls with the power of God's Holy Spirit, and that His influence conveys to us what is proper to the very life of God.

This practical identity of Christ and the Spirit of God is the ground or reason of that union between Christ and His people that is so characteristic a feature of the experience of the Christian life described in the Epistles of Paul, and that sets his thought of Christ in so original a light. Inasmuch as His Spirit is in them, and is the source of their life, and His Person is in a true sense one with the Spirit, He Himself is said to be and to live in them, and they in like manner are said to be and to live in Him. Everyone is aware of the frequency with which the phrase "in Christ" is used by the apostle in reference to the inner life of the believer.[1] It points to a union with Him as Spirit or Pneuma, in virtue of which He is the very principle of their lives, so one with all that is most deeply personal in them that He moulds and determines their activities, and reproduces in them what is most deeply personal to Himself. Quickened at the centre of their being by the very Spirit of God that formed the principle of His Personal life, and having Christ thus dwelling in them, believers are enabled to live His life over again; or, rather, they are the agents by and in whom He lives over again His own life, reincar-

---

[1] It is to be observed that where this union of the believer with Christ is referred to, it is the phrase ἐν τῷ Χριστῷ or Κυρίῳ that is invariably used, never ἐν τῷ Ἰησοῦ. The latter term describes the Man Jesus in His historical appearing, and is never employed to describe the spiritual fellowship of believers with the Son of God who sends the Spirit. This has been pointed out by Harless (*Commentar zur Epheser Brief*, p. 411). The term "Christ" when conjoined with "*Jesus*" in the Epistles always points to the religious significance Jesus has for believers. On recent literature on this phrase ἐν Χριστῷ, see Note B.

nating Himself, as it were, ever anew in the flesh of His people. The historic Jesus has, with the apostle, passed into the Spiritual and Mystical Christ, who lives in, and reveals Himself through, believers; and we cease to wonder that the past circumstances of the earthly life of Jesus have comparatively little interest for Paul, now that as Exalted, Christ has entered on a present activity in the hearts of men, in which He re-enacts in their experience what was most vital in His historical career, and repeats in them all that was most distinctive of His own Divine life. The poet represents the apostle as longing that he had lived in the days when Jesus was seen of men—

> " Oh to have watched Thee through the vineyards wander,
> Pluck the ripe ears, and into evening roam!
> Followed, and known that in the twilight yonder
> Legions of angels shone about thy Home!"[1]

There is, however, no trace of this feeling in the apostle's recorded words. Why should he or his fellow-believers go back to the past, or dwell with fondness on the recollections of Jesus' earthly life, on what He did and said in Galilee and Jerusalem? Had they not Christ living and working in them here and now? Was he not himself conscious sometimes of the " shock of His possession thrilling and touching " him? Whence that passion for souls that burned in the apostle's heart? Was it not from the contact of Christ's mighty heart with his own? Did not Christ walk the streets of Corinth and Rome and Ephesus to-day as He had done in the cities and towns of Syria? Was He not found in the homes and workshops of men, audible still in the words of grace and truth that came from the lips of His followers, visible to the eye of men in the gentle, pure, devoted lives of

[1] From " Saint Paul," by F. W. H. Myers.

those who loved Him?[1] Where they are, He is, living Himself out from them, embodying His holy will in the actions of their lives. It is this Christ, dwelling in His people, filling them with new experiences, manifesting Himself in and through them to the world, that was the real Christ to Paul, and made the Christ to him no mere dogma, but a personal presence and an immediate life.

The *locus classicus* for this view is Gal. ii. 10, where we have the record of his deepest experience as a Christian. After the remarkable words, "I am crucified with Christ," that express the completeness of his deliverance from the old life of self, he goes on to say, "It is no more I who live, but Christ who liveth in me." It is difficult to translate this into common language. The words at least point to a new moral and religious consciousness formed by his connection with Christ,—a consciousness of what had entered into the inner life of Christ, of Divine Sonship and power over the flesh, power to love and to do the will of God. In this consciousness, indeed, the apostle realised his own proper life, and exercised the functions of spiritual manhood, but its source was not in himself, but in the Spirit of Christ that occupied the place of self, and by the rush of Divine life that pulsed through his soul annihilated almost the sense of his own selfhood. "Not I, but Christ liveth in me." Christ became the true self of the apostle, and what he lost in individuality by the substitution of Christ, the Living Principle of love, for self limited and particular, he gained in personality, for in passing out of his old self into Christ he found his real self and realised his true life in God. The supremacy of this new Principle in his experience was absolute. To the Christ within

---

[1] It was a quaint saying of the great German Reformer, "Should anyone knock at my breast and say, 'Who lives here?' I should reply, 'Not Martin Luther, but the Lord Jesus'" (*Table Talk*).

he attributed all that he did and experienced as a believing man. It was as one who was "in Christ," and was the subject of the activity of His Spirit that he accomplished his life-work,[1] that he formed judgments and came to conclusions,[2] that he followed the courses and modes of conduct that characterised his Christian profession,[3] that he cherished confidence in others,[4] that he suffered,[5] that he rejoiced.[6] He recognised himself to be but an organ for the activity of Christ, a "vessel of earthenware" containing the "treasure" of His light and truth.[7] Christ dwelt in him, Christ in the fulness of His personal life, so that the very love with which Christ loved men impelled Paul to a similar life of unselfish love;[8] and Christ's longing and pity filled the apostle's heart with the same emotions,[9] and Christ's truth and sincerity spoke in the words of truth and sincerity which the apostle spoke,[10] and the will of Christ empowered his own will to do what it had no strength in itself to do,[11] and Christ's mind was his inmost possession, inspiring in him the thoughts and dispositions of His Lord,[12] and Christ's sufferings were repeated in those that fell to him as His servant.[13] It was as if the very personality of Christ had entered into the apostle and used him as the organ of its expression.

To describe at length the specific experience formed in the apostle by the introduction into his inner life of this sinless principle, the Spirit of Christ, would carry us too far afield. It is evident, however, that the result in his experience was the practical solution of the moral problem of his life. Holiness became an actual attainment. The inward contradiction between the higher and lower

[1] Phil. iv. 13.
[2] Rom. xiv. 14.
[3] 1 Cor. iv. 17 ; 2 Cor. ii. 12–14.
[4] Gal. v. 10.
[5] 2 Cor. xiii. 4.
[6] Phil. iv. 10.
[7] 2 Cor. iv. 7.
[8] 2 Cor. v. 14.
[9] Phil. i. 8.
[10] 2 Cor. xi. 10 ; Rom. ix. 1.
[11] Phil. iv. 13.
[12] 1 Cor. ii. 16.
[13] 2 Cor. iv. 10 ; comp. Col. i. 24.

elements of his life which had torn him in twain ceased.¹ We are startled by the language in which he speaks of himself as a Christian—a pneumatic man. He has no hesitation in appealing to his own character and conduct in proof of his moral integrity.² Again and again he describes himself an example in respect of Christian discipleship, and bids others follow him.³ He does not indeed claim to be sinless. He has not yet reached the ideal, but is always pressing on toward it.⁴ The flesh still lusts after what is condemned by the Spirit,⁵ and he has to keep it in subjection.⁶ But his moral state is now one of harmony with the will of God. He is freed from the "law of sin and death."⁷ He is done with the old life, and has entered on a new life characterised in its aim and normal attainment by sinlessness.⁸ The one serious hindrance to the perfection of his state is the sufferings of this present life, the mortality of the body, the vanity and perishableness of existence; but this feature is destined soon to pass away, when, with the second coming of the Lord, the full glory of the new age ($αἰών \; μέλλων$) shall dawn upon the world.⁹

¹ I regard Rom. vii. 21-25 as referring to Paul's state while still unregenerate; his normal state as a Christain man is described in Rom. viii. 1-5. To this, the view held by all the Greek Fathers, first departed from by Augustine in his later writings, most modern commentators have now returned.
² 1 Cor. iv. 2-5, ix. 15; 2 Cor. i. 12, iv. 11, vi. 3, x. 7, etc.
³ 1 Thess. i. 6, ii. 1-12; 2 Thess. iii. 7, 8; 1 Cor. iv. 16, xi. 1.
⁴ Phil. iii. 13.   ⁵ Gal. v. 17.   ⁶ 1 Cor. ix. 27.
⁷ Rom. viii. 2.   ⁸ Rom. vi. 1-14.

⁹ Rom. viii. 18-25. Ritschl has called attention to the consciousness of moral integrity that characterises Paul's Christian experience. After enumerating passages, he goes on to say: "Diese Zusammenstellung beweist, dass neben der Ueberzeugung von der Rechtfertigung durch den Glauben ein Bewusstein persönlicher sittlicher Vollkommenheit, insbesondere vollkommener Treue im Beruf möglich ist, welches durch keine Gewissensrüge getrübt ist, aber auch nicht den Grundsatz verlezt dass man sich Gottes rühmen soll, welches endlich von der Gewissheit eines besonderen göttlichen Lohnes gemäss dem von Gott verliehenen Erfolge der anstrengungen in seinem Dienste begleitet ist" (*Rechtfertigung u. Versöhnung*, ii. p. 370).

Now this indwelling of Christ is asserted as true of all believers. To secure an entrance for Him into the inner life of men was the very object of the apostle's ministry. To the Galatians, hesitating between the flesh and the Spirit as the principle of their lives, he writes, in that strange mother-cry, "my little children with whom I travail in birth till Christ be formed within you."[1] Nothing less would satisfy him than Christ's taking shape and form within them so as to be the all-controlling power of their lives. Believers were certified to be God's children by their willingly allowing themselves to be led by the Spirit within.[2] By the Spirit they have power to crucify the flesh and its affections,[3] to mortify the deeds of the body,[4] to rise superior to the law of sin and death.[5] Being "in the Spirit" constitutes believers πνευματικοί; and apart from the possession of the Spirit, they have no claim to be ranked as Christians at all.[6] As πνευματικοί, they are distinguished from others who are mere "men."[7]

This indwelling of Christ, and participation by His people of His Spirit as the principle of their lives, abolishes all separateness of life or function in them. If individuality can be said to remain, it is only as the sphere in which that One life, of which Christ is the source, is to be embodied in a distinctive form. "He that is joined to the Lord is one Spirit;"[8] he loses that selfhood or separateness of being in which self, as long as it is the principle of life, is intrenched; and his life is henceforth merged in a Higher than his own, in the life of love and goodness that animates all in whom Christ dwells. The place and function of the individual is to be a *member* of Christ, one by whom a portion of the common life is exercised and manifested. And the collective society of believers is constituted the

---

[1] Gal. iv. 19.   [2] Gal. v. 18.   [3] Gal. v. 24.
[4] Rom. viii. 13.   [5] Rom. viii. 2.   [6] Rom. viii. 9.
[7] 1 Cor. iii. 1, 4.   [8] 1 Cor. vi. 17.

Body of Christ, the living organism united to Him as the body is to the soul; and as His natural body in the days of His flesh was the means by which He had intercourse with the world, the medium by which His Personal life expressed itself and accomplished its purposes, as well as the vehicle by which He conveyed His gifts of healing and blessing to men, —so His Church, or the Society of believers, is His Mystical Body in which He reappears on earth. It is the instrument by which now He effects His purposes in the world, reveals Himself and transmits His saving energy.[1] Its function is to interpret and represent Him, to be the "Epistle" of Him, declaratory of His Mind and Will,[2] to be the Mirror "reflecting" the glory of His Face,[3] the "Body" that through its various members does His Will,[4] the "Temple" or "Shrine" that is to be kept holy from all coarseness so as to let His Divine Presence shine through it.[5] The language in which the Indwelling of Christ in His people is described excludes the idea of there being any save One principle of personal life in them. Each, indeed, is but a part of the one supreme Personality of Christ who lives in them all, absorbing into His own their individual lives; and they, on their part, reach their perfection in the measure in which their own separate lives are lost in the common One that flows

---

[1] "The Church," says Gore, "is the extension and perpetuation of the Incarnation in the world." And again, "This visible human society exists to receive, to embody, and to communicate a spiritual life. And this life is none other than the life of the Incarnate. The Church exists to perpetuate in every age the life of Jesus, the union of Godhead with manhood" (Bampton Lecture, p. 219). This exalted conception of the Church is too much lost sight of. We are grateful to the school to which Canon Gore belongs for the prominence it receives in their teaching. But we must differ from them in the use they make of this conception to support the theory of sacramental grace. Surely it is to the influence of the sanctified personalities that make up the Body of Christ we must look for the conveyance of the blessing of the Spirit of God that resides in His Church, and not to the handling of material things.

[2] 2 Cor. iii. 3.   [3] 2 Cor. iii. 18.
[4] 1 Cor. xii. 12.   [5] 1 Cor. vi. 19.

from the all-inclusive personality of Christ,—"ye are all one man in Jesus Christ."[1]

This mystical Body is the New Humanity, which, in accordance with the eternal purpose of God, Christ came into the world to create. And it is in thus entering into the very springs of our being by the energy of the Spirit, in order to make us alive toward God and victorious over sin and death, and to mould us inwardly and outwardly into His own likeness, that He discharges His function as the Second Adam of the human race. The language in which the union between Christ and His people is described is not to be understood in a metaphysical sense, as if the supremacy of His life in us and our union with Him involved the literal absorption of all personalities into His own; it is the language of religious feeling and experience, and is not to be taken as psychological truth.[2] It expresses the feeling that in the relation that subsists between Christ and His people there is no room for self as a principle of moral action, and that the Spirit of Christ, of love and of holiness, is the all-controlling principle of the personal life of each. It indicates, too, that this supernatural element made itself felt in the experience of the believer as an overmastering impulse, operating almost after the manner of a natural force of a lofty order, manifesting itself not so much in works which a man did as in dispositions and affections which he experienced.[3] At the same time, the language that speaks in this wise of the Spirit alternates with language that is of a different sort, and that suggests that in the consciousness of the believer the Spirit was an

---

[1] Gal. iii. 28.

[2] "This possession by the Spirit is a fact for the explanation of which we will seek in vain in the categories of our psychological systems, but it is none the less real on that account. We are led to it by the simple analysis of the Pauline consciousness, and there will come again a time when it will be better understood than it is to-day" (Paret).

[3] Gal. v. 22.

exalted form of the *nous* or inner man himself, a new faculty or exercise of will due to the influence at the roots of our personality of the Personal Christ; for we are enjoined to "walk in the Spirit," and to "sow to the Spirit" and not "to the flesh," as if this new force left us still masters of our own destiny and laid on us the duty of acting in accordance with its movements.[1] It is plain that along with Christ's dwelling in us, and His possession, as it were, of the seat of our life, there may coexist independent action on our part, that proceeds from the old self-life and shows that our own personal being is not wholly one with the Higher Principle. Paul recognised this; he was not blind to the sins into which Christians fell. We can see that it was a perplexity to him how they who had Christ dwelling in them could sin; but he does not allow himself to deny, on that account, that they had Christ dwelling in them. "He bates no jot of his ideal Gospel."[2] He rather impresses upon them more strongly than ever the fact with which their conduct was in such flagrant contradiction. "Know ye not," he exclaims (recalling to them what they were as members of Christ), "that the Holy Spirit is in you, that ye are the temple of God?"[3] It was the remembrance of what they were "in Christ" and of His indwelling in them that alone could give the impulse to conduct that was in keeping with it. Whatever difficulty this great idealist might have in reconciling the actual facts of the Christian life with the operative presence of Christ living out His own Divine life in Christians, whatever account he might give to himself of the discrepancy in believers

---

[1] Gal. v. 16, vi. 8.
[2] "It was beyond all doubt a wonderful faith that, in spite of appearances to the contrary, held fast to the reality of these gifts of God, and that could in patience wait till it manifested itself also to the senses, a faith that was supported by the near approach of the Parousia" (Wernle, *Der Christ u. die Sünde bei Paulus*, p. 60).
[3] 1 Cor. vi. 19.

between the Ideal and the Real, he saw that the true remedy and the secret of the approximation of the latter to the former lay in their realising more constantly this Divine Presence. Thus only would they be enabled to act in a manner worthy of their real selves, and true to their deepest life.

This doctrine of the mystical Christ is an essential part of the Pauline conception. The power of Christ to dwell in His people and to communicate His own spiritual life to them was an aspect of His Glory that the apostle could not make enough of; it was everything to him. The presence of Christ within was the *summum bonum* of man, it was the very essence of the Christian Good; if he rejoiced in being a child of God, it was because he was one with the Exalted Christ who is the Son. It was the fountain of moral inspiration and strength, for he was one with the mighty Spirit of God. It was, moreover, the ground of his hope of immortality. We can see from the Epistles that Paul deeply desiderated for himself a well-grounded assurance that death would not be the end.[1] And it was a welcome thought to him that, through fellowship with the Spiritual Christ, he was partaker of a principle of life that had in the Person of the Risen One already proved its imperishableness, and that could not fail to impart immortality to all who had it from that source. "If Christ be in you, the body is dead because of sin, but the Spirit is life because of righteousness; if the Spirit of Him that raised up Jesus from the dead dwell in you, he that raised up Christ Jesus from the dead shall also quicken your mortal bodies through the Spirit that dwelleth in you."[2]

---

[1] A recent writer (Teichmann, *Die Paul. Vorstellungen von Auferstehung*, p. 1) says, "The Pauline faith in Christ is at bottom a faith in the Power of the Christ to rescue man from the perishableness of time and to confer upon him the imperishableness of life eternal." This is perhaps an exaggeration. But there can be no doubt about Paul's deep personal interest in a Christ who had overcome death and could fulfil the destiny of man as created for immortality.

[2] Rom. viii. 10, 11.

This truth of Christ's immanence has always been a most influential one in the life of the Church. It is true, indeed, as T. H. Green reminds us, "that in a generation or two the intuition of the present Christ, which Paul even seems to have been unable to convey to others as it was to himself, had faded away, and that in its stead came the belief in past events or in present mysteries, transactions external to the man which had to be stated in a creed."[1] But it is also true that the intuition has been recovered again and again in the course of the Church's history;[2] and that in times especially when the religious life has been crushed under the weight of tradition and ecclesiastical observance, this truth of the Spiritual Presence of Christ has come home with wonderful power to devout souls who sought God in secret, restoring to their hearts that Gracious Figure that had become a tradition of the past or a mere formula of theology. Wearied with the arid notions and verbal definitions of scholastic theology, men have turned to the revelation of the Indwelling Christ as the traveller turns to a well of water in the desert, finding themselves brought thereby into direct communion with the living God for whom their souls thirsted, and made glad by the contact of their hearts with the realities of the spiritual world.[3] It is a truth very congenial, especially to all forms of Mystical Piety; and some of the most precious works on heart religion that have come from the school of the

---

[1] *The Witness of God*, p. 27.

[2] In speaking of this doctrine of the inward Christ, Gore says, "Mystical as it is, and transcending, as it does, our faculties of intellectual analysis, it has been ridiculed as fit only for enthusiasts in a rationalistic age such as the last century; but every revival of vital Christianity brings it to the front again, and roots it anew in the consciousness of serious and devout Christians, though they be 'plain men' and unimpassioned" (Bampton Lecture, p. 221).

[3] The intensity that characterised the religious life and experience of the late General Gordon was due to his vivid realisation of the Indwelling Christ. He often refers to it in his *Letters to his Sister*. He speaks

Mystics owe their power to move us as they do to the experiences they contain of communion with the Christ within. There are certain dangers indeed that accompany the one-sided cultivation of a religious life in which this truth is all in all. And these may be mentioned if only to point out how Paul, the first evangelical Mystic and the greatest of them all, escaped the dangers of mysticism, and what further view of Christ's Exalted Activity it was that saved him from the exaggeration and error into which many of his successors have fallen.

It is doubtless true that with those who make much of the Mystical Christ and of communion with Him, the picture of the historic Jesus is apt to fall into the background. Their impressions of Him come to be determined by what they are too ready to accept as private communications made to their souls by the Exalted Christ, more than by the truth that is conveyed through the facts of the historic life; and the abiding value of Christ's historic work suffers in other ways when the Indwelling of the Spirit of God is emphasised. The mediatorial office of Christ comes to be dispensed with, and the individual is tempted to feel that being in a sense an incarnation of the Spirit of Christ he is also a Christ to himself, and to say, with a certain Quaker of old, "I too am Christ." It is inevitable, also, that the habit of dwelling exclusively on the Spirit's presence should tend to dissolve the connection that ought to subsist in our minds between the Spirit and the historic Christ. Dependence on a vague impersonal Spirit or principle of life, in minds predisposed to pantheistic exaggeration of the Divine side of our nature, comes to take the place of trust in the living Personal Saviour. There is nothing of all

of our "realising our identity with and absorption in Christ," of "the Holy Spirit being incarnated in us," of "the power and peace that flows from the truth that God dwells in us." It is to be remembered, too, that this type of religious experience was associated in his case with extraordinary efficiency in the practical affairs of life and in the management of men.

this, however, it must be noticed, in the thought of the apostle. His conscious possession of the Spirit of God never broke down in his mind the sense of his absolute dependence on the historic Christ for that Divine Gift; nor does he ever use language that betrays the faintest consciousness that he stood on a level with his Master because possessing a measure of the same Spirit of God. He could indeed say to his converts, "Be ye followers of me,"[1] because he was conscious that his own life, being an interpretation of Christ's and inspired by His Spirit, was an example to them; but he hastened to add the words, "as I am of Christ," recognising the supremacy of his Master and of His example for all alike. Now, what saved the apostle from any exaggeration to which the view of Christ as the Immanent principle of life in His people might have led, was his equally vivid apprehension of His Transcendent relation to His people as their Lord. It belongs to Paul's greatness as an interpreter of Christ that he set forth His relation to men as being not only of the nature of a mystical union, but also as a practical fellowship based on a community of aim and purpose that calls into exercise their independent energy as moral beings,—a fellowship in which He is Lord or Master and they are servants. This truth of Christ's Lordship has a large place in the thought of Paul. He was a mystic indeed; he was conscious of a oneness with the Exalted Christ that finds expression in words that are startling to us who lag so far behind him in religious feeling and intuition. But he was also a practical teacher; he never forgot for a moment that he was a servant or a "slave" of Christ, as he delighted to call himself, recognising thereby the separateness of Christ from His people, their mystic union with Him notwithstanding, and His Lordship over them giving Him a supreme claim on their obedience and service.

[1] 1 Cor. xi. 1.

II

We pass on then to consider the teaching of Paul on the Transcendence or Lordship ($Κυριότης$) of Christ. The term "Lord" occurs hundreds of times in the Epistles, and expresses the conviction of the Supremacy of Christ which the apostle shared with the entire primitive Church. From the moment they received the evidence which was furnished by the gift of the Spirit that Jesus was Risen and Exalted, He was to them *Lord*. Supremacy, universal dominion, entered into the very conception of the Christ or Messiah; and to believe in the Lordship of Jesus was to confess Him to be the Christ. "This Jesus whom ye crucified," was Peter's solemn declaration to the people, enforcing the message of the resurrection, "God hath made Lord and Christ."[1] The terms were synonymous, and the wider currency which "Lord" obtained was due to the influence of Paul, who made large use of it, not only because it was more acceptable to Gentile believers, for whom the term "Christ" had a Jewish-national significance, but because it so well expressed the authority of Christ and the relation of believers to Him as His servants ($δοῦλοι$). Paul's conception of the Lordship of Christ did not differ from that of his fellow-believers, but it was a larger and fuller one, as was to be expected from his richer experience of Christian truth; and at a later stage it was characterised by a breadth and comprehensiveness that went far beyond the content of the original faith. His conjunction of God and Christ in his stated greetings to the Churches indicated his belief that a co-partnership of Divine power and honour was included in the exaltation of Christ to be Lord. And that there was nothing accidental in this conjunction we infer from the express

[1] Acts ii. 36.

statement in which he contrasts the polytheism and idolatry of the heathen world with the pure religious faith of the Christian: "Though there be that are called gods, whether in heaven or on earth; as there are gods many and lords many; yet to us there is one God, the Father, of whom are all things, and we unto Him; and one Lord Jesus Christ, through whom are all things, and we through Him."[1] In the Christian religion there is one Father = God, to whom the term Θεός in its integrity is applied, and One who possesses the nature and measure of Divinity that Κύριος describes.[2] In the nomenclature of the apostle the Father is ὁ Θεός, Christ is Κύριος.[3]

This name, as well as the dignity and authority denoted by it, belong to Christ as Exalted. He is not spoken of as Lord absolutely, or on the ground of the authority of His teaching as the historic Christ. At the same time, His Lordship is the appropriate result of the entire life-work of Jesus on earth, and is the Divine recognition of its Worth. It was the intended issue of all that He underwent in the flesh. "He died and rose again that He might be Lord both of the living and the dead."[4] The confession that He is Lord is regarded as inspired by faith in the almighty power of God who raised Him up from the dead;[5]

[1] I Cor. viii. 5, 6. Weizäcker's translation brings out the sense better than our R.V. Gibt es für uns nur Einen Gott, den Väter, den Schöpfer aller Dinge, der unser Ziel ist, und Einen Herrn Jesus Christus, den Mittler aller Dinge, der auch unser Mittler ist.

[2] The Christian conception of God as related to us contains, as this passage shows, two elements—Fatherhood and Lordship. They constitute one God (ver. 4), but ὁ Θεός is applied to the Person of the Father; ὁ Κύριος to the Person of the Exalted Christ.

[3] The term "Lord," except where he quotes from the O. T. (in which case Κύριος is used of God, being the Septuagint translation), uniformly denotes Christ in Paul's Epistles. That he regards it as Christ's proper designation we see from the above passage, also from Eph. iv. 5; I Cor. xii. 5. Wherever "Lord" occurs we are to understand him as referring to Christ. I Cor. iv. 19, iii. 5, vii. 17; Rom. xiv. 4, which Weiss adduces as exceptions, are so only in appearance.

[4] Rom. xiv. 9.   [5] Rom. x. 9.

and in Phil. ii. 7–10 we are told that He received the Name of "Lord," conferring the right to universal worship, as the reward of His voluntary self-abasement in the assumption of our nature. The dignity and power to which He was thus raised are declared to continue to belong to Him till He has accomplished the work of our salvation and all His enemies have been subdued. The "Lordship" shall then be laid aside, and the delegated Supremacy over all that has respect to the salvation of man shall be surrendered to the Father again.[1]

The Lordship of Christ, which belongs to Him as Exalted, stands, therefore, in the closest connection with His earthly life-work, and is its natural consummation. It meant an enlargement of power and endowment such as was needed to make His supremacy operative and influential in the world of humanity, but all this as the outgrowth of His historic life, as carrying to its final issue, as well as setting in its true light the glory that existed in Him in a concealed form before, and was discoverable in the days of His flesh by all who had eyes to see. Paul never forgets that He who is now Lord, and is so much more and greater than He was when on earth, is essentially the same with Him who had suffered and died, and that His present exaltation is, in its deepest meaning, simply the recognition of the Divine Worth that belonged to Him even in the days of His flesh. Witness the beautiful combination that occurs in the epistles, "the Lord Jesus," as if he clung to the thought that He who is now Supreme is one and the same with Him who had made Himself known and loved by His pure, unselfish life. Jesus was Lord; that meant that He, whose goodness had

---

[1] 1 Cor. xv. 24–28. In reference to this passage Mr. Gladstone in his paper, "Proem to Genesis," makes the suggestive remark: "It may be we shall find that Christianity itself is in some sort a scaffolding, and that the final building is a pure and perfect theism; when the kingdom shall be delivered up to God, that God may be all in all."

so little impressed the world at large, had now been acknowledged as the Supreme and Final manifestation of God; that the gracious love to sinners and the lowly spirit of service that had shone forth from the life and death of Jesus were declared and authenticated to be the strongest and Divinest things in the universe, and to have represented the very mind and heart of God; that He was victorious over the powers of sin and death that appeared at the Cross to have triumphed over Him, and that He was now the Pledge of His people's supremacy over these forces and of their final deliverance from present subjection to them. We do not wonder at the importance assigned by the apostle to the confession that Jesus is Lord, or that he should have referred it to the enlightenment of the Divine Spirit.[1] "The acknowledgment of the Christ without is evidence of inspiration from the Christ within." The world worships the supremacy of power;[2] but the Lordship of Jesus means the Supremacy of Love and Holiness, and the confession of it signifies the bowing down in heart before the Greatness of the God whom Jesus has made known, and before the personal Ideal that His life embodied, an act of homage of which only he is capable who has been taught of God.

The Lordship of Christ is in Paul's teaching no empty title, no inoperative prerogative; it is exercised actively on His people's behalf, and is, for one thing, their security against all evil that may threaten their well-being. Under the inspiring influence of the thought that Jesus lives and reigns, the apostle bursts into the splendid song of confidence at the close of Rom. viii. that concludes with the words, "I am

---

[1] 1 Cor. xii. 3.

[2] The Antichrist that Paul has in his eye in 2 Thessalonians is power used for merely selfish and sensual ends. Paul saw this power impersonated in the frivolous sensuality of the Emperor Nero. But Antichrist is incarnate in all who use power for selfish and degrading ends in contrast with Him whose supremacy is that of love and self-sacrifice.

persuaded that nothing shall separate us from the love of God which is in Jesus Christ our Lord," the Exaltation of Christ binding believers to His love and care with a bond that is indissoluble.[1]

But more is secured than their protection from evil by Christ's Lordship over His people. As Lord He has proprietary rights over them purchased by what He has done on their behalf, and He has that interest in them, and in their becoming all that He desires them to be, which one cannot help taking in those who are one's own. They are the objects of His gracious regard, and He is engaged in the business of their sanctification and is actively carrying on the work of grace in their souls. He causes them "to increase and abound in love."[2] He strengthens them in good works, and establishes them.[3] Judicial functions are also ascribed to Him, and the exercise of these will fitly close His activity as the Exalted Lord. On the "Day of the Lord" He will descend from heaven and appear as Judge on earth;[4] and before His judgment-seat all shall stand,[5] "bond and free,"[6] the living and the dead, that "each may receive the things done in the body according to what he hath done, whether it be good or bad."[7]

This truth of Christ's Lordship imparts to the Christian life its distinctive character, makes it at once a life that is devoted to Him and to the advancement of His Glory, and that issues in our conformity to His Image. The believing response to it is expressed in such utter-

---

[1] It is said of Luther that in times of depression he wrote for himself the words, *Dominus Vivit, Vivit*, on the table, door, and walls of his room to serve for the encouragement of his faith.

[2] 1 Thess. iii. 12. [3] 2 Thess. iii. 3. [4] 1 Cor. iv. 5.
[5] 2 Cor. v. 10. [6] Eph. vi. 8.

[7] 2 Cor. v. 10; 1 Thess. iv. 16; 2 Thess. i. 9. The apostolic picture of Christ coming in judgment (1 Thess. iv. 16; 2 Thess. i. 7, etc.) has not a little in common with the descriptions of the Messiah found in the apocalyptic literature of that age. On this, see Teichmann's *Die Paul. Vorstel. in Auferstehung u. Gesicht.*, 1896, p. 24, etc.

ances as these,—"to me to live is Christ";¹ "whether we live we live unto the Lord, whether we die we die unto the Lord."² To "please the Lord" is represented as the supreme aim of the disciple;³ to "glory" in the Lord his one legitimate boast;⁴ "to do the will" of the Lord his chief business, for the Lord's will is the highest standard of conduct, even as the Lord Himself is the Supreme Example.⁵ The perfection that is to crown His people's effort consists in the "glory of the Lord,"⁶ that is, in perfect likeness to Him who is victorious over sin and death, who is "Lord." The process of transformation is being carried on now by the Risen Christ who reproduces Himself in the inner life of believers; "reflecting the glory of the Lord, we are changed into His image from glory to glory."⁷ The power that belongs to Christ as Lord is, we learn from all this, a power that is exercised on His people's behalf; the effect of His working is their complete salvation, the gradual lessening of the distance that still separates them from Him, and the communication to them by successive stages of His own distinguishing "glory." He is the "Firstborn" of many brethren, and is constituted Lord over them, in order that, by what He is able to do for and in them, He may impart His own superiority to all evil.⁸ This is the end or purpose of His Exaltation to be Lord. Its object is the carrying on of His mediatorial work, and when it is accomplished in their complete redemption from evil, and in their participation of that mastery over all hostile forces that is as yet His exclusive possession, His Lordship will cease, and the Son shall also be subjected to Him that did subject all things unto Him, that God may be all in all.⁹

¹ Phil. i. 21.   ² Rom. xiv. 8.   ³ Col. i. 10.
⁴ 1 Cor. i. 31.   ⁵ 1 Cor. xi. 1.   ⁶ 2 Thess. ii. 14.
⁷ 2 Cor. iii. 18.   ⁸ Rom. viii. 29–30.
⁹ 1 Cor. xv. 28. While the immediate sphere, according to the above, of the active exercise of Christ's Lordship is the community of believers, His Sovereignty itself embraces all men, and extends to every

But the further question remains, how does He who is related to us as Κύριος, or Supreme, stand to God? He to whom we are subject, answers the apostle, is Himself subject to God, as the Son is to the Father; this subjection is at the same time consistent with an equality with God, inasmuch as in mind and heart and will the Son is absolutely one with the Father. The subordination is expressly stated. In all the Epistles God is spoken of as the "God and Father of our Lord Jesus Christ."[1] "The head of every man," we read, "is Christ, and the head of Christ is God";[2] while "all things are ours, and we are Christ's, Christ is God's";[3] and as the passage already quoted states, He who now rules by God's authority will by and by return His trust, that all may be subject to the Father as Supreme.

On the other hand, inasmuch as the very basis of His "Lordship" is His perfection as the Son of God, His full participation of the very life of God qualifying Him to

human interest. To suppose that His Dominion is not coextensive with that of the Father, that His Spirit is not to rule over the entire life of man, would be to introduce a dualism into our thought of the world that is intolerable to the mind. But His Lordship over the world at large is made effectual through the instrumentality of His people and through the universal application of the principles of His kingdom, which it is their business to make. He is Lord over them that they may in turn subject all to the authority of His Love and righteousness, and so illustrate the supremacy of His Rule and the world-subduing Power of His Spirit. They who speak of the failure of Christianity point to the feeble influence Christ has exerted upon national and social life; and what truth there is in this assertion is due to the fact that Christians have not testified as they ought to have done to the universal validity of those principles of love and self-sacrifice by which Christ reigns. That Christ's Lordship over all, with the corresponding duty of believers to assert His supremacy in every sphere of life, does not hold so large a place in Paul's teaching as we might have expected, is no doubt to be accounted for by his belief in the near approach of the end of the world, and the setting up of an Ideal order of things by the exercise of Omnipotence.

[1] *E.g.* Rom. xv. 6; 2 Cor. i. 3; Col. i. 3; Eph. i. 3.
[2] 1 Cor. xi. 3.   [3] 1 Cor. iii. 23.

represent the Father and to be the instrument of the Father's saving will, He is one with God. And while the Father and the Lord Christ are spoken of as two, they are also spoken of as to the religious consciousness one. What the One does, the Other is said also to do.[1] Sometimes it is the "Lord" who is represented as bestowing upon us the blessings of redemption, "calling us into His Kingdom," "establishing us in grace";[2] in other passages, it is the Father who does for us these same things.[3] Now, it is the "grace of the Lord Jesus," that Paul prays his converts may receive;[4] again, it is "the grace of God," the Father.[5] The identity is also implied when the action of the historic Christ is viewed as the equivalent of the action of God, as in Romans v. 8, "God commendeth His love to us, in that, while we were yet sinners, Christ died for us"; also, where Christ's present activity is spoken of as the instrument by which God is carrying out His Saving Purpose. It is the Lord *through* whom we now receive from God "grace and apostleship."[6] "Being justified by faith, we have peace with God *through* our Lord Jesus Christ."[7] "Who shall deliver us from this body of death? I thank God *through* Jesus Christ our Lord;"[8] "thanks be unto God who giveth us the victory *through* our Lord Jesus Christ;"[9] "obtaining salvation *through* our Lord Jesus Christ."[10] Sometimes the preposition "in" instead of "through" is used,—"the gift of God is eternal life *in* our Lord Jesus Christ";[11] the only difference being that in these passages, instead of the instrument *through* whom God

---

[1] *E.g. God* is declared to be our Judge (Rom. ii. 16); and in another place we are told we must all appear before the Judgment-seat of *Christ* (2 Cor. v. 10). [2] 1 Cor. vii. 17; 1 Thess. iii. 13.
[3] 1 Thess. ii. 12; 1 Cor. i. 9. [4] Rom. xvi. 20.
[5] 1 Cor. i. 4. As a rule, "the grace of God and of the Lord Jesus Christ" are conjoined (1 Cor. i. 3; 2 Cor. i. 2; Gal. i. 3).
[6] Rom. i. 5. [7] Rom v. 1. [8] Rom. vii. 25.
[9] 1 Cor. xv. 57. [10] 1 Thess. v. 9. [11] Rom. vi. 23.

blesses us, Christ is viewed as the Man *in* fellowship with whom the Divine blessing is received.

The idea we gather from these passages is that, as Lord, Christ discharges a mediatorial function. It is through Him " that all things are,"[1] that communications between God and men take place. In relation to us, He is God's Vicegerent, who is at the same time subject to God, as one who represents another and dispenses the favour of that other, is subject to him whom he represents and whose kindness he dispenses. But as God's Vicegerent and Representative He is to us as God. He is not separate in our minds from God, but one with Him. In what He does for and in us, God is active. It is always in and through the exercise of the Will of Christ that God accomplishes His Will. Christ and God seem to form in Paul's mind one image, and he passes naturally from the one to the other when the same form of activity is referred to.[2] The authority of Christ is indistinguishable from that of God, for it is the authority of righteousness and love. His power working in our hearts and lives is the power of God accomplishing for us what only the Divine energy can accomplish. If our highest thought of God is that of the *summum bonum*, then Christ answers to that thought, for in Him, Exalted and Lord, all moral and religious good is found, the forgiveness of sins, the participation of life everlasting, power to live as children, a supreme moral ideal and authority; all this, answering to our highest conception of the Divine, makes Him one with God in our thoughts and regards.[3]

We have found in the first part of this lecture that as Immanent in His people, Christ is spoken of by the

---

[1] 1 Cor. viii. 6.

[2] *E.g.* 1 Thess. iii. 11, 12, where a prayer is directed to God and the " Lord," and continuing it, the apostle contents himself with naming the " Lord " only, although God is as truly concerned in the answering of the second part of the prayer as in the first. Although he understands by the " Lord " Christ, it is evident he does not think of Him as separate or distinct from God (comp. 2 Tim. i. 18).

[3] The doctrine of Christ's intercession (so prominent in the Ep. to

apostle not only as the Giver of the Spirit of God, but also as Himself that Spirit, so identified in his experience was the influence of the Personal Christ with the energy of the Spirit of God. And we are prepared to find, similarly, that in speaking of Him in His transcendent relation as Lord, Paul should call Him expressly God, for, as we have seen, the same activities are spoken of indifferently as the activities of God and of the "Lord." But it is very doubtful whether Paul so designates Christ. There is only one passage that can be adduced in this connection,[1] and that one is not conclusive, since it depends on the punctuation, whether the words "who is over all, God blessed for ever" are to be taken as a doxology to the Father, or as an integral part of the preceding statement about Christ; and there is apparently little prospect of unanimity among scholars on this point. Paul does not elsewhere use the word Θεός of Christ, and although there is nothing in his thought that could prevent him doing so, it seems hazardous on the strength of this one passage, that is of doubtful interpretation, to conclude that he has actually called Christ God.[2] But the fact that he habitually applies to Christ the term Lord (Κύριος), a term that in the Septuagint is practically equivalent to God (Θεός), and is the rendering Hebrews), suggesting the idea, not of God accomplishing His Will through Christ's activity, but of Christ's activity as moving that of God in accordance therewith, is foreign to the theology of Paul. The intercession of Christ in heaven is only once referred to in his writings (Rom. viii. 34), and there the word describes the activity of His Love generally, at the Right Hand of God, in befriending and taking the part of His people against everything that threatens their well-being. Their having been justified by God (ver. 34) seems to exclude the idea of God needing to be interceded with on their behalf.

[1] Rom. ix. 5.
[2] In Sanday and Headlam's Commentary on Romans a long and careful note will be found on this text, which, as they say, has been probably discussed at greater length than any other verse of the N. T. Their conclusion is that the "balance of probability is in favour of referring the expressions Θεός and ἐπὶ πάντων to Christ." In Ritschl's view there is no doubt of the truth of this interpretation (*Altkatholische*

of the most solemn name of Jehovah in the Old Testament, shows that in his regard He was entitled to the worship and obedience that are due to God.[1] To such an extent is He the object of religious worship that Christians are spoken of as those who "call on the name of Jesus Christ our Lord," this invocation of Christ being referred to as the common mark by which they are distinguished,[2]—a striking testimony to the supremacy of Christ in the faith of His followers, and of the practical identification of Him with God in their religious feelings.[3] If further proof were *Kirche*, p. 29). It must be admitted, however, that it is against his usage for Paul to call Christ Θεός, a term reserved by him for the Father alone; and the additional epithet ἐπὶ πάντων, equivalent to the idea of Κύριος, would, if viewed as descriptive of Christ, make the apostle speak of the latter as the "Lord God," a combination that goes beyond the thought of the apostle regarding his Master as expressed in his writings.

[1] See Note C on the use of the term Κύριος in the Septuagint.

[2] 1 Cor. i. 2 ; Rom. x. 13.

[3] We find, accordingly, that prayer is directed to Christ. Paul specifies an occasion when he prayed to the "Lord" (2 Cor. xii. 8), and "the calling on the name of the Lord Jesus Christ," which he attributes to believers, includes prayer besides other exercises of worship. Some who pray in Christ's *name*, recognising the revelation of God that Christ has given as the ground of their expectation of being heard, shrink from direct prayer *to* Christ. Their minds cling to the image of the earthly Jesus, who was Himself a Man of prayer, and they think it is derogatory to God, the Source of all Blessing, to ask Christ to give what He must Himself first receive from the Father. But by His exaltation Christ has become so one with the Father and with the Spirit that it is natural for us to think of Him as not only the Medium of blessing to His people, but the Dispenser of it ; and since it is God in Christ we appeal to, we feel it to be in no wise inconsistent with what is due to God to direct our prayer to Christ. At the same time it is to be noticed that, as a rule, in his Epistles God the Father is spoken of as the *Source* of all good, to whom we are to look for what we need and to whom we are to pray, while Christ is the *instrument* by whom it is given. And nothing could be more contrary to Paul's thought than the notion that lurks in the minds of some whose habit it is to pray to Christ, that He is more accessible to men than the Father is. The ease and naturalness with which Paul passes from the thought of God to that of Christ shows that he knew of no other God save the God who was one with Christ and Christ with Him, that in turning in faith and prayer to Christ he was conscious he was drawing near to God in the truest way, and that in calling on God he was calling on Christ in whom alone God is accessible to men.

wanted of the Divinity claimed by Paul for his Master, it is found in the words of the benediction, " The Grace of the Lord Jesus Christ, and the love of God, and the communion of the Holy Ghost be with you all."[1] Our ears are so accustomed to the words of the formula that we are apt to miss the force of the testimony they furnish to the extraordinary impression of Divine glory made by the Risen Saviour on the hearts of His followers. The fact that He is mentioned in the same breath with the Eternal God and the Life-giving Spirit—in a way, too, that betrays no consciousness whatever that the juxtaposition of Christ with God and the Spirit will be thought by any to savour of extravagance or an exaggerated sense of what is due to Him—is surely a remarkable proof of the exalted place He held in their regards.

The confession of Christ's Lordship is the confession of His Divinity. There is no doubt that to Paul and the mass of believers the Man Christ Jesus, Risen and Exalted, stood in the place of God, and was the object of worship. In Him thay saw God manifested in a human form. In His influence upon them they perceived the influence of the Spirit of God. Of His Divine power they had the most convincing evidence in the consciousness of the new life, with the moral strength it imparted, which He had quickened within them. In contact with Him, and in the experience of His gracious love forgiving their sins, they were in communion with God in the riches of His love, and were conscious of changes of thought and feeling and purpose which could only be ascribed to the Will of God. They were not withheld from the worship of Christ because He was Divinity in a human form. The only knowledge of God that can inspire religious worship is that which comes to us through a human manifestation of Him. Religious worship is impossible without reverence and love; and in

[1] 2 Cor. xiii. 14.

order to command these feelings God must reveal Himself through human qualities that express our highest conceptions of worth in character, and through the medium of acts that satisfy our highest expectations of what may be experienced from the energy of the Divine Will. And Christ is the proper object of worship, because in Him God comes to us, appeals to us, works upon us in these ways. How Paul's monotheism is to be reconciled with this practical acknowledgment of Christ as Divine,—for monotheist he remained, as we see from the distinction he observed in speaking of the Father as God and Christ as Lord,—is a matter on which we expect some light to be thrown by those passages in his Epistles that suggest a transcendent relation of Christ to God over and above that in which He stood to Him as the Man exalted to be, in the faith of His people, One with the Father and with the Spirit. The passages referred to will fall to be considered as we proceed in our inquiry. Meanwhile, it is to be repeated that the Divinity in Christ on which Paul based his faith in Him as Lord was a truth to which his own conscious experience of Christ, and of the effects of His working on his inner life, bore witness. And we learn from this that in order to know Him to be the Son of God, and to justify our faith in Him as truly Divine, we do not need more than the evidence of experience which flows from the practical acknowledgment of Him as Supreme. I conclude with the words of the late Dr. Dale, which seem to me fairly to represent the Pauline view: "It may be that some of you who have constructed for yourselves imposing conceptions of God as the Creator of all things, the Infinite, the Absolute, the Almighty, the Unchangeable, the Omnipresent, the Omniscient, a God of your own making, an hypothesis to render the universe intelligible, may be perplexed and confounded when you attempt to find this God in Christ. But if you have found in Christ the supreme and ultimate authority over your moral and religious life, you have found God in Him. If you have found in Christ the Infinite Mercy through which your sins are forgiven, you have found God in Him. If you have found in Christ the Giver and Source and perpetual support and defence of that Divine life which renders righteousness and saintliness possible in this world, and is the beginning of immortal power, you have found God in Him. Even if your lips falter when you are asked to confess that He is God, He is of a truth God to you. These realms of moral and spiritual truth, in which for you Christ is supreme, lie far above the realm of material things. He who is supreme in the spiritual order cannot hold any secondary place in the physical; you have already confessed, even if you meant it not, that Christ is eternally one with the Highest."[1]

[1] *Christian Doctrine*, pp. 120, 121. It is well known with what emphasis Luther insisted on the truth that the Man Jesus is the proper revelation of God, and that all speculations are unprofitable that relate to the Divine nature outside of Him. "See to it," he says in his *Table Talk*, "that thou know of no God and pay homage to no God except the Man Jesus Christ, but lay hold of Him alone, and continue hanging with thy whole heart on Him, and let all thoughts and speculations about the Majesty go their own way! In this business look straight at the Man alone, who presents Himself to us as Mediator, and says, 'Come to Me all ye that are weary and heavy laden.'"

V

LATER DEVELOPMENTS: CHRIST THE FULNESS OF GOD, THE HEAD OF THE CHURCH AND OF ALL PRINCIPALITIES AND POWERS

LECTURE V

LATER DEVELOPMENTS: CHRIST THE FULNESS OF GOD, THE HEAD OF THE CHURCH AND OF ALL PRINCIPALITIES AND POWERS

THE subject of the present lecture is the development in the later Epistles of Paul, the so-called Epistles of the Imprisonment, of that doctrine of Christ which in its main features we have now considered. And I shall confine myself at this time to the Epistles to the Ephesians and Colossians, reserving the teaching of Philippians for the lecture to follow, where its special contribution to our subject will find its proper place. No one can fail to be struck by the contrast these two Epistles present to those from which we have hitherto drawn our material for this study. They evidently belong to a much later period in the history of the planting of the Church. That to the Ephesians marks the close of the epoch with which the earlier Epistles deal. We hear only the echoes of the controversy that rages so loudly in the letters that were penned by the apostle under the strain of the conflict which he had carried on with the Jewish section of the Church. The battle had been won when the letter to the Ephesians was written. The ideal of a new society, of which believing Jews and Gentiles were members on equal terms,—that ideal of which Paul had been so powerful an advocate,—is now an accomplished fact. This splendid achievement of the Christian faith gives him occasion to expatiate on God's eternal purpose to reconcile to one another in Christ all sections of the human race.[1] And if this Epistle is manifestly an *eirenikon*, marking the peaceful settlement of the controversy which the announcement of the free grace of the Gospel had provoked and encountered in the first days of the Church's history, that to the Colossians as plainly marks the beginning of a new era; for it places us in the thick of a second controversy,—this time not with national but with intellectual exclusiveness,—a controversy that grew in intensity as time went on, and that was destined to reach dimensions and to involve in it issues that made it one of the most memorable in which the Church was ever engaged.

And the point of interest for us is that both Epistles are remarkable for the fresh points of view from which the Person and Work of Christ are regarded in them, and for the impressiveness both of the ideas and of the language in which these are couched, in reference to the Supremacy of Christ. New terms are applied to His Person; significant hints crop up as to the bearing of His Work and Influence on superhuman intelligences. Such is the wealth of language called forth by the contemplation of the Exalted Son of God, that we seem to lose sight of the historic Jesus in the blaze of glory that surrounds the throne. This advance of thought in reference to the Divine Pre-eminence of Christ, has been represented as so pronounced as to amount to a change of view that is inconsistent not only with the Pauline authorship of these

[1] Eph. i. 10–11, ii. 13–18. "The Christian doctrine," says Principal Rainy, "rests upon and rises out of the Christian facts,—the persons, the transactions, the events." And again, "Christian doctrine is the light that illuminates for us the transactions of a divine history" (*Development and Delivery of Christian Doctrine*, pp. 100–101). The doctrine of the Epistle to the Ephesians is a case in point. The reconciliation of Jew and Gentile had been wrought out and had become a fact of history. The theology of the Epistle is the Divine interpretation of that fact, and of the work of Christ in its bearing upon it.

Epistles, but with their having been written in the apostolic age. With regard to the Epistle to the Colossians in particular, with which we have chiefly to do in this connection, it is alleged that the use in it of terms that were current in later speculative discussions points to its having been written in the middle of the second century, and suggests the propriety of regarding it as a monument of the great conflict with heathen systems of thought through which the Church then passed. It has, however, as it seems to me, been conclusively shown, both by Lightfoot and Klöpper in their splendid contributions to the elucidation of this Epistle, that there is nothing in it that requires us to refer its composition to sub-apostolic times, and that the entire course of thought becomes luminous when we regard it as directed against a system of error that was Jewish in its origin, and was certainly influential in apostolic times in circles liable to be affected by it. We know comparatively little of the Jewish sect of the Essenes, but we are sure that the mediation and worship of angels were prominent features of their religious system, and that the Ideal of life which they practised was modelled on the spirituality of angelic intelligences. And once assume that a leaven of that sort had invaded the Churches on the Lycus through their Jewish adherents, we shall then have a sufficient background of historic fact for the understanding of the Epistle, and a sufficient explanation of the emphasis placed on the higher aspects of Christ's Person and Work.[1]

It is another and distinct question whether it came from Paul's pen, and whether we are warranted in drawing from it material for our reconstruction of his thought. The

---

[1] Ritschl infers from the mention of those who abstained from flesh and wine in Rom. xiv. 21, that there was in the Church of Rome also a leaven of the doctrine of the Essenes. He accounts for the presence of Jews in Rome and Colosse by the dispersion through the cities of the empire of the Jews whom Pompey had carried off from their native land as prisoners of war (*Altkath. Kirche*, 233).

answer will depend on the estimate we form of its teaching, and whether we regard the ideas it contains as a development of truth found in germ in the undisputed writings of the apostle, or whether we must view them as a fresh departure pointing to another mind. The more we consider the matter, the more does the former view commend itself. A mind like Paul's, ever in living contact with the truth, might well be stimulated to make an advance in the apprehension of his Master's Greatness by the crisis that arose when men attempted to engraft the ideas of that Jewish sect on the Christian faith.

The inevitable tendency of these outside ideas was to lower Christ in the esteem of believers, to exalt other beings to a share of the worship that belonged exclusively to Him, and to encourage the ascetic treatment of the body rather than communion with the Risen Lord. Paul must have felt that the truth of the Christian Religion itself was at stake when the question was raised, Where is Christ in the universe of being, what rank does He hold in relation to other intelligences and to God? He knew he could give, out of the consciousness of the New Life in Christ, an answer to these questions that met the wants that had given birth to them, and that overcame the error into which men fell when they tried to answer them by speculations of their own; and he hastened to give the answer. He was not afraid to use the terms that were current in these speculations, because he could fill them with ideas that made them express the very truth of the Christian faith. We need not wonder that in its advocacy of the universal Supremacy of Christ, his teaching bears the impress of the system of thought he opposed. It is the same truth that we find in the Epistles of an earlier period, but unfolded and applied to meet new circumstances, cast into the mould of the theological thought of the time. If we assume Paul to be the writer, his procedure is a fine instance of wisdom in the performance of the task by which the Christian theologian is confronted in ages of intellectual movement and spiritual unrest,—the task of adapting the eternal truths of religion to the wants of the new age by seizing on the thoughts that set forth its aspirations and gropings after certainty, in order to point men to the revelation of God in Christ for the satisfaction of every craving that is rooted in our religious nature.

We find, then, in these Epistles a doctrine of the Exalted Christ that undoubtedly exhibits an enhanced sense of the Greatness of His Person; and the progress of statement in this direction is along the various lines of truth that set forth the thought of the apostle in the earlier letters. And I proceed to indicate as briefly as I can the development of the original elements of the Pauline Christology under each of the three heads of the preceding lectures, the interpretation of the Person of Christ we find here, as well as of His work, and of His present relations to mankind.

I

With regard to the interpretation of the Person of Christ that is characteristic of the Epistles now under review, it is to be observed, on the one hand, that while a new terminology is used, the idea of His Archetypal Significance is still plainly the master-thought, and, on the other, that the terms employed emphasise more strongly the qualitative as well as quantitative distinction between Christ and other men. The new terms applied to Christ are "the Fulness of God,"[1] and "the Image of the Invisible God."[2] These correspond with the designation of Him as the "Spiritual man" and "Son of God," but they give us a grander view of His Pre-eminence over the human race.

[1] Col. ii. 9, i. 19.   [2] Col. i. 15.

1. The term FULNESS OF GOD is evidently a theological one, and is borrowed from a vocabulary familiar to those to whom the Epistle was written. When we ask what precisely it signified on their lips, we are left to a certain extent to conjecture. We know what it meant in the later system of the Gnostics, in which it played an important part. But we are dealing with a period antecedent to that heresy, a period when ideas that afterwards attained to a full-blown activity were as yet in germ only. And while the intellectual forces that were then shaping men's thoughts, whether from Jewish, Greek, or Oriental sources, all tended in one direction, and imparted a certain similarity to the religious speculations of thinking men of all schools, —it is not so much to the influence of Greek thought that we are to look for the explanation of this term that was in use among the churches at Colosse, as to the ideas that had grown up under the later Judaism on the soil of the Hebrew religion. The Essenes shared the view of God that we find in the Old Testament Scriptures, where He is represented as a Being possessed of a fulness of life that is manifested in the innumerable forms of created being that stand around the throne to fulfil the behests of Jehovah. But later Judaism, speculating on the Infinitude of God,— influenced, doubtless, also by the feeling that has its roots in the religious consciousness, of the distance between God and man, and the difficulty of direct access to the Almighty, —had concentrated its regards exclusively on the complex of forces and beings that issued from God, and that constituted His "Fulness." The Divine Being Himself was contemplated as inaccessible except through the beings that filled up the gulf between the Infinite and the Finite, into whom He poured forth the fulness of His life and energy; only in communion with them, and by following the Ideal of the spiritual life, unfettered by the flesh, which they presented, could men have communion with God, or

become partakers of His Life. We can understand what an immense stimulus such views would give to the cultus of angels, which was practised by those whose errors this Epistle was written to combat, and which we know from other sources was a feature of Jewish worship at that time.[1]

We do not know what precisely was the place assigned to Christ by those who had engrafted this speculation on their faith, but He could be only *one* of this multitude of intermediate beings, possessing but a fraction of the "Fulness" of God that was distributed among them all. And very soon He would be lost sight of altogether amid the hierarchy of Celestial Beings. All this was directly subversive of the Christian faith, and was contradicted by the consciousness of the life of God, and of direct fellowship with Him, which the believer owed to Christ. The perfection of our religious state and standing was incompatible with any place other than that of supremacy being assigned to its Author—with any endowment of Him by the Spirit that fell short of the very Fulness of God. Hence Paul proclaims that that "Fulness" of the Divine life, which false teachers had said was distributed among the Many, was concentrated and had its home in One, "in Christ," "in whom it pleased the Father that all fulness should dwell."[2] In a passage further on[3] he repeats the expression, adding the words "in a bodily form," claiming for the perfect

[1] "The worship of angels was assuredly a widely spread Jewish habit of mind at this time: the Epistle to the Hebrews shows how prevalent it was where there is no sign of what we should call a philosophy" (Hort, *Judaistic Christianity*, p. 122). Baldensperger has some striking remarks on this feature of the religious thinking of that age, on the prying curiosity of devout people into the secrets of the spiritual world, which grew as men felt the mystery that surrounded the Divine Existence. "Is it not," he exclaims, "as if, in the measure in which God withdrew behind the thick clouds, the Heavenly world for a moment disclosed itself to the longing heart of man, and made known to them its secrets?" (*Das Selbstbewusstsein Jesu*, p. 51).

[2] Col. i. 19.   [3] Col. ii. 9.

Humanity of Christ a participation in the Divine Fulness, and a fitness to receive from God, and to communicate to us, all of God and of His Life that can be communicated and received.[1] And this in opposition to those who exalted the angelic nature above the human as the proper organ of Divinity.

The term then, in its origin, or as used by the theosophists of Colosse, may be metaphysical or not; in the mouth of the apostle it expresses a religious truth, a truth of reflection based on religious experience, the truth learnt in communion with the Risen Lord, that in Him there is a full endowment of life by the Spirit of God that answers to all the religious needs of human nature. It is as the embodied organ of the Spirit of God that He is called His "Fulness"; and the apostle is here putting into fresh language, language borrowed from speculations then in vogue, the conception of Christ as the "Life-giving Spirit," that from the beginning was so fundamental with him. The most cursory reader of the Epistle to the Colossians must have been struck by the fact that there is scarcely any mention in it of the Spirit of God,[2] a fact that seems unaccountable in a writing which professes to be Paul's. But the explanation is that other terms are employed to express the idea; and this term "Fulness of God" is one of them. The simple word "Spirit" would have failed to set forth what the apostle meant now to teach: that there is in Christ that totality or manifoldness of Divine energies and spiritual qualities which false teachers said had been distributed among a host of created intelli-

---

[1] In Eph. iii. 19 we learn that Christ is the "Fulness" of the Divine life to us, in so far as He is Love, and makes us partakers of the love of God "that ye may know the love of Christ, and might be filled with all the fulness of God." This idea of Christ being the plentitude of the *moral* attributes of God, especially of Love, distinguished Paul's conception of the "Divine Fulness" from that of the false teachers.

[2] It occurs only once, i. 8.

gences. What required to be insisted upon was, not only that Christ was the organ of the Spirit of God, but the organ of the Spirit in the manifoldness of His gifts, powers, operations,—the perfect type of humanity in whom converges every grace and function that is needed for the purpose of His coming, which is the complete redemption of man. In magnifying the endowment of the Servant of the Lord for his office, the prophet Isaiah had said, "the Spirit of the Lord shall rest upon him, the Spirit of wisdom and understanding, the Spirit of counsel and might, the Spirit of knowledge, and the fear of the Lord" (Isa. xi. 2). It is this all-inclusive endowment of spiritual gift and Divine qualities in relation to the wants of men that the apostle ascribes to Christ when he speaks of Him as the "Fulness of God"; and the expression certainly conveys to us a profound impression of His inexhaustible value for the religious life of men.[1]

2. He is also designated in this Epistle, the IMAGE OF THE INVISIBLE GOD (εἰκὼν τοῦ Θεοῦ τοῦ ἀοράτου, i. 15). The phrase is found in Philo's writings, and is applied by him to the Logos,—the principle of self-manifestation and self-communication in the Godhead. But although a philosophical term, it is used by the apostle not to teach anything about the metaphysical nature of Deity, but to set forth a religious truth regarding the Exalted Christ. It is evident from the context that in speaking of Jesus, the Son of God's love, "as the Image of the Invisible God," he is not predicating anything of His Preincarnate Being. He means to differentiate Him from others who may be spoken of in a secondary sense as sons of God, in so far as they exhibit a certain degree of resemblance to God, or separate

---

[1] The vision of Christ in the Apocalypse as having the Seven Spirits of God (Rev. iii. 1), conveys much the same idea as the apprehension of Him as the "Fulness of God," and brings Christ before us as the Giver of the Spirit in the sevenfold perfectness of His operations.

features of likeness to Him. Christ is *the* Son, because He is the Image or perfect embodiment, the complete revelation, of the hidden nature of God. This holds, in the absolute sense, only of Him as Exalted. Only in Christ thus perfected and glorified do we behold the very Image of God, the perfect expression in a form apprehensible by our faculties of the Divine nature, which must otherwise have remained hid from us. This truth is also taught, as we have seen, by Paul in 2 Cor. iv. 4, where Christ's glory is said to consist in His being the Image of God; but occurring in the Epistle to the Colossians, where the characteristic description of Christ is that He is the Fulness of God, it receives additional meaning, and points more unmistakably to a something in Him that raises Him above all others.

There is nothing indeed in these expressions, as applied to Christ, that is inconsistent with His Archetypal relation to mankind, for the peculiarity of His Person which they set forth is declared to be transferable in measure to His people. If He is the Son and Image of the Invisible God, we also are sons, and are called to imitate the perfections of our Heavenly Father; if He is the " Fulness of God," His believing people are also spoken of as the " Fulness of God." In connection, however, with this transference to His people of what is distinctive of Christ, there are two things to be remembered. On the one hand, what they have in common with Him is derived from Him, and is theirs only through their organic connection with Him. It is through their union with Him who is the " Son " and " Image " of God, that they are sons and share in God's image. It is because they are in the first instance so related to Christ as to be in a true sense His " Fulness," that they in their turn are called the " Fulness of God." And on the other hand, this participation by His people of Christ's distinctive Being is only a partial participation of that which He possesses in its integrity. No individual believer is said to be the "Image of God"; that is His prerogative. He alone answers to the idea of perfect resemblance to God. The most that can be said of us is that we partake of His Image: we are fragmentary resemblances. This realisation in Christ of the Divine idea in its completeness, in contrast with its incomplete realisation in His people, is strikingly illustrated in what is said of the "Fulness of God." While believers share this distinction with Him, and are also called the "Fulness of God," it is to the body of believers that this term is applied, never to the individual; the truth conveyed being, that only the Church as a whole can appropriate that fulness of spiritual life which, found in Christ personally, entitles Him to be called the "Fulness of God." It is the body of believers that is destined through the ministry of the various agencies given for this end, to attain "to the Perfect Man, to the measure of the stature of the fulness of Christ."[1] No individual, however closely he may resemble his Master, can reveal all that is in Christ. A body, a society of men, is the only adequate receptacle for His fulness. The truth suggests the inexhaustible energy of the Spirit of Christ and His adaptation to the manifold varieties of type in the human race. While, then, it gives us an idea of the Greatness of His Personality that goes beyond anything that we find in the early Epistles, it is yet altogether in keeping with the position that is there assigned to Him as the Second Adam. For as the successive generations of men are simply the unfolding of the possibilities of natural life contained in the First Man, so that not until the race is exhausted can we form any proper conception of the power and faculty that lay in him at the first in germ, — we are warranted in saying of Christ, the Second Adam, or Spiritual Head of Mankind, that no adequate representation can be furnished of the

[1] Eph. iv. 13.

possibilities of spiritual manhood and likeness to God of which He is the Germinant Principle and the Pledge, till Humanity as a whole has been brought into living union with Him, and every variety of human nature and culture has come under the influence of His Spirit.[1] The "Fulness" of Christ can be contained in and expressed by a Redeemed Humanity only, which will then become the counterpart of Christ in sharing with Him the glory of being the "Fulness of God."

This magnificent conception of the Church or Redeemed Humanity as being the "Fulness of God" is expounded in the Epistle to the Ephesians. The theme of that Epistle is the Grandeur of the Church, that new Brotherhood, in which men of every nationality and of the most diverse religious training were bound together by the one Spirit. To the imposing spectacle of this Body in living fellowship with God and with one another, the apostle directs the attention of his readers, who at the time were being enamoured of that idea which false teachers were holding before them of an invisible host of angels mediating between God and men. Not to that world of angelic intelligences were they to look; not from it would they learn what the "Pleroma" of God was, but from the Church of Christ, the new Brotherhood of men, filled with love and holiness, the true recipient, through the presence and working of its Divine Head, of the Fulness of "Him who filleth all in all."[2]

[1] Canon Gore in his Bampton Lecture (p. 170) insists that only a really Catholic society can be "the fulness of Him that filleth 'all in all.'" He adds these words, which I gladly indorse: "Thus we doubt not that when the day comes which shall see the existence of really national churches in India and China and Japan, the tranquillity and inwardness of the Hindu, the pertinacity and patience of the Chinaman, the brightness and amiability of the Japanese, will each in turn receive their fresh consecration in Christ, and bring out new and unsuspected aspects of the Christian life; finding fresh resources in Him in 'whom is neither Jew nor Greek, neither male nor female, barbarian, Scythian, bond nor free, but Christ all in all'" (Gal. iii. 28; Col. iii. 11).

[2] Eph. i. 23, iii. 19.

II

This leads us to the second point, the account we have in these Epistles of the Work of Christ as compared with that which the earlier Epistles contain. We find, then, that here, as there, supreme importance is attached to the Death of Christ, both in relation to the forgiveness of sin and to deliverance from its power. It is set forth as the means of reconciliation to God, and as the Power of our dying to sin itself, as well as of our being quickened to a new moral life.[1] But besides what they have in common with the teaching of the early Epistles, they contain two new points of view from which the Cross is regarded, that are most instructive as opening up fresh fields of thought.

In the Epistle to the Ephesians the dominant idea is the RECONCILIATION effected by the Gospel BETWEEN MAN AND MAN, the removal of the old antagonism between Jew and Gentile, and the union of both in one brotherhood or family. At the time it was written Christianity was showing itself to be a great social power. The groups of Christians that sprang up in every place to which the Gospel came were communities in which all alienations of race and religion were forgotten in the enthusiasm of a new love. The Church was presenting itself in this light. It was drawing to itself the wonder and admiration of the world because of this striking feature of its life; and in his letter Paul dwells on it, and points out that the reconciliation of man to man, the unification of the different sections of the human race that had been effected, was the result of Christ's Death, and the in-

---

[1] *Reconciliation*—Col. i. 14, 19-20, ii. 13-14; Eph. ii. 13; *Quickening*—Eph. ii. 5; Col. ii. 11, 12, 20, iii. 3. The enlarged conception of the Person of Christ in these Epistles is observed in the fact that He is spoken of as the Agent in certain Divine acts in which the earlier Epistles speak of the Father as the Agent. Compare 2 Cor. v. 18 f. with Eph. ii. 16. The subordination of the Son to the Father is implied in i. 17 ("The God of our Lord Jesus Christ").

tended result of it. "He is our peace, who made both one, and brake down the middle wall of partition, having abolished in His Flesh (*i.e.* His body offered in death) the enmity, even the law of commandments contained in ordinances; that He might create in Himself of the twain one new man, so making peace; and might reconcile both in one body (*i.e.* the mystical body of believers) unto God through the Cross, having slain the enmity thereby."[1] Formerly Paul had dwelt on the efficacy of the death of Christ in removing the dualism between man and God, as well as that in human nature itself, between the higher and lower elements of our being,—a dualism which in both cases he showed had been intensified by the law working on a nature opposed to it. This dualism had been taken away by the Cross, and by the removal of the law that had been effected by the Cross. And now we find it is still this same effect of the death of Christ, the abolition of the law, that is insisted on, only it is followed by a new effect, by the removal not only of the dualism between God and man, but also of that between man and his brother man. For the law had created a breach between the Jew who had it and the Gentile who was without it, fostering a pride in the former that was resented with contempt on the part of the latter. But the Cross "broke down the middle wall of partition between the two," removed the law, liberated men from the obligation of ordinances affecting the flesh, and restored them to a fellowship of love with one another. It is an instructive fact that we have an entire Epistle devoted to the exhibition of Christ as the Reconciler of men to one another, and to emphasise the intention of His death to sweep away all customs and ordinances, however sacred, that divided man from man. Most instructive is it, also, to observe that His Church is held up to our admiration as the Society in which has been realised this ideal of a new Brotherhood, where all differences are

[1] Eph. ii. 14-16.

merged in the consciousness of one faith and one love. Subsequent history shows that the Church has often proved a Divider rather than a Reconciler, falling sadly short of the apostolic ideal. This Epistle is an abiding witness to the Catholicity of the Church; it is a perpetual protest against those who exalt ordinances and dogmas to a place of supremacy, only to produce discord and division thereby. Ritual and sacrament and formularies of belief are matters of secondary importance, and are mischievous when they alienate us from our fellow-men, and hinder the realisation of the New Testament ideal of a Church, in which love and brotherhood, based on equality of religious privilege, is everything. We need to catch anew this vision of Christ as the Breaker of all the bonds of creed, ritual, caste that mar human fellowship, as the "Opener of men's hearts to one another, the well-spring, never to be dry, of a new humanity."[1]

The Epistle to the Colossians goes still further in its account of the consequences of the death of Christ, for it attributes to it an efficacy in removing the DUALISM BETWEEN MAN AND ANGELIC INTELLIGENCES, and, it would seem, between these angelic intelligences and God Himself. In chap. i. 19 we read, "it pleased the Father that in Christ should all the fulness dwell; and through Him to reconcile all things to Himself, having made peace through the blood of His Cross; through Him, I say, whether they be things on the earth or things in heaven." Here the reconciling power of the Cross is extended so as to embrace the intelligences of the unseen world who were hostile to man, and who, till the effects of the Cross reached them, had stood outside the harmony that was to prevail among God's creatures. A further light is shed on the matter in chap. ii. 13–15, where we read that God has forgiven all our trespasses, "having blotted out the bond written in ordinances that was against us which was contrary to us; and He hath taken it out of the way, nailing

[1] Dean Church.

it to the Cross; having put off from Himself (*i.e.* as one divests himself of a garment) the principalities and the powers, He made a show of them openly, triumphing over them in it." Two errors characterised the religion of these Colossians: they worshipped angelic powers,[1] and they practised a ritual designed to liberate them from the flesh and to conform them to an angelic spirituality.[2] Their angelic worship and their law-observance were very closely connected. Underlying both was the belief that they were subject to the angels, and that the authority of the angels over them was declared in those legal enactments about meats and drinks that they observed so scrupulously. The belief of Judaism in regard to angels, which has left its stamp especially in the later Epistles of Paul, is a subject requiring more thorough investigation than has been given to it, before this passage and its significance for the first readers of it can be fully appreciated.[3] But evidently the aim of the writer is to show that Christ has freed men from their real or fancied subjection to the angels, inasmuch as in His death He has abolished the law. By releasing men from the law and its obligations, Christ had broken the authority of the angels over men, for its unfulfilled obligations had been the hold that these angelic powers had upon them,—a hold which the Colossians acknowledged by the law-observance that entered into their religious life. The apostle would point out to them, that the abolition of the law accomplished by Christ in His death was in its effects equivalent to the subjection of the angels to a power greater than their own, and involved the freedom of men who had formerly been in bondage to them. A view of Christ's death in its relation to law that is strange to us whose minds are so little exercised with questions about angels, but a view that had a profound significance for those to whom angels were a power to be reckoned

---

[1] Col. ii. 18. [2] Col. ii. 16, 20–23.
[3] See note A on The Angelology of St. Paul.

with in their religious life, as much so as sin and guilt are to us. It is a view also very closely connected with the Headship of Christ over the angels which is emphasised here as a distinctive Feature in the Picture of the Mediatorial Glory of the Risen Lord. This Doctrine of the Headship we now proceed to consider, as the third point in the marked development of the Doctrine of Christ that characterises these Epistles.

III

When we inquire, then, as to the account they give us of the activity of the Exalted Christ, we are struck by one feature of difference between it and the account in the earlier Epistles; and that is, the frequency with which the term HEAD occurs in describing the relation of the Risen Christ to men, and the insistence on the ideas which it suggests. The Headship of Christ over man is indeed implied in the idea of the function of the Second Adam as that idea is worked out in Romans v. 12–19. But of this Headship in relation to man, which certainly seems to follow from His place and Function as the Progenitor of a spiritual Race, we do not hear much in the Epistles under consideration. It is His relation, first, to the Church or New Humanity, and, second, to the world of supernatural intelligences, that is emphasised in them. Of both He is said to be the Head.

1. He is HEAD OF THE CHURCH, the ecclesia, "which is His Body."[1] Now, we do not find Him so designated till we come to these Epistles. In the earlier, the apostle spoke of Him as "Lord" and "Spirit," but not as "Head." The idea of Christ as the Indwelling Spirit, which, as we saw, is so supreme in the apostolic thought, is certainly present in Ephesians and Colossians; it underlies the whole structure of the thought, and occasionally finds very definite

[1] Col. i. 18; Eph. iv. 15.

expression.[1] But his language in describing the Indwelling of Christ is new. It is not as Spirit that He is now conceived of as related to us. Indeed, as I have already pointed out, the Spirit is only once mentioned in the Epistle to the Colossians; and the absence would be inexplicable but for the fact that the term "Head," which is used so often, includes in it the idea of Spirit, and has the advantage of combining the two notions of Immanence and Transcendence which, as we saw in last lecture, set forth the relations to men of the Exalted Saviour as Spirit and as Lord.

Headship is a larger conception than Lordship: it implies not only authority over us, as the latter does, but union with us. As Head, Christ is organically related to His people, and one with them. They partake of His life. As Head He is the noblest member of the organism. His office is not only to direct the activities of the Body, but to send fresh life into its members, so as to secure the health and growth of them all. He also represents the body, and takes the initiative in its movements, having first undergone the experiences which His members now share with Him. The term brings out, better than any other, both the distinctiveness of Christ and His community of Life and Spirit with His people; for the Head and the members have the same Life in them, the one originating and directing its outflow, the others receiving and appropriating it, that they may grow up in all things unto Him.

The germ of this fruitful idea is found both in Romans and 1 Corinthians, where Christ is declared to be the Bond or uniting element of the whole Body of believing men: "We, who are many, are one body in Christ, and severally members one of another"[2]; and again, "As the body is one and hath many members, and all the members are one body, so also is Christ."[3] The truth in these passages is

[1] Eph. iii. 17; Col. iii. 4. [2] Rom. xii. 4–5. [3] 1 Cor. xii. 12.

that Christ is the animating Soul or Spirit who dwells in believers and makes them one Body; while in the later Epistles it is not as the Soul, but as the Head of the Body of believers, that He is referred to. But evidently Head and Spirit or Soul are congruous conceptions; and the same author might freely use the one term or the other, according as he had in view the truth of the controlling Authority to which Christians are subject, or the Life they share in common with their Lord. In the early Epistles it is the latter truth that is prominent; hence we hear much there of the Indwelling Spirit. But circumstances had emerged by the time the later Epistles were written that made it necessary for the apostle to shift the emphasis to the other truth which Headship taught. Everywhere scattered communities were appearing, each with its gifts, its beginnings of organisation, its recognised and variously endowed members contributing blessings on which the Church's life and growth depended; and it became necessary to enunciate the truth of the subjection of all to a supreme Authority, in following whose inspiration and direction the various communities would work together towards the attainment of a common end. It is not surprising that we should hear much now of the Headship of Christ and the recognition by the Churches of One all-controlling Authority. The term, as we have seen, combines both ideas of supreme Direction and a common Life, which are the two aspects of the relation of the Exalted Christ to His people. While the former idea, I think, is the more prominent, we would certainly err were we to exclude the latter idea of Life from Paul's use of the term in these Epistles. The basis of Christ's Headship over the *ecclesia* is declared by him to be His vital relation to it. He is the Head of the Body, " who is the beginning, the First Born from the Dead."[1] He is the First who has entered on a

[1] Col. i. 18.

Life that is in its own nature victorious over death; and being so, He is the "Beginning" or the living Principle of a new creation,—a passage in which the notion of Head is brought into very close connection with that of the Second Adam, and where Headship is thought of, not only as the Source of authority over, and of direction to, His Church, but also and chiefly as the Source of its Divine and Supernatural Life.

2. But the most striking evidence that these Epistles contain of progress in the estimate of the Greatness of the Exalted Christ is furnished by the doctrine taught in them (especially in the Epistle to the Colossians) of the HEADSHIP OF CHRIST OVER ALL PRINCIPALITIES AND POWERS.[1] Now, it would be an entire mistake to suppose that in asserting Christ's Sovereignty over the world of Celestial Beings, Paul is teaching truth that had a merely speculative interest for himself or for his readers. Nothing could be further from the fact. The belief in angels—in their existence and functions in the government of the world, and in the ordering of everyday events—was an influential article of religious faith at this period. The idea prevailed that God could have no direct communication with the world, characterised as it is by so much that is undivine. The interval between the Infinite and the Finite was, in the vulgar imagination, peopled with beings of various orders and gradations, all concerned in the work of mediating between the Most High and His creatures on earth. The Judaism of Paul's day was dominated by this idea. The Gospel, by its revelation of a way of direct access to God in Christ, had emancipated Paul from all notions of the power and influence of angels in the religious life; but no doubt, before he was converted, he shared the common belief of his countrymen on the subject, and there are indications in the Epistles that his mind sometimes went back to those early days

[1] Col. ii. 10.

when he was under bondage to it. Witness the splendid passage in which he exults in the confidence he can cherish as a Christian man, and spurns the idea of inferior beings having power to endanger his eternal security: " I am persuaded that neither angels, nor principalities, nor powers, nor any other creature, shall be able to separate me from the love of God, which is in Jesus Christ our Lord."[1]

The Colossian Christians, however, had not attained to this confidence. They were entangled in a heresy that accentuated in the strongest way the belief in principalities and powers, and the subjection of men to them. Holding that angelic beings were permitted to exercise influence over the lives and destinies of men, they were withdrawing from Christ the worship and service of which He was the sole legitimate object, in order to bestow them on these intermediary intelligences. The belief in the mediation of angels had resulted, as it must ever result, in the degradation of Christ to an inferior place in faith and life, and in the removal of the Father, who had graciously revealed Himself in Christ, to a distance that made Him practically inaccessible. Against all this Paul lifted up his voice. He will brook no rival to his Master in the affections of men. Christ is the sole Mediator between God and the human race. Angels and principalities have no power either to hinder or to promote our fellowship with the Father in Him. All such beings are under Christ. He is Lord and Head, not only of the Church, but of all " principalities and powers," Supreme in the Universe of Being. In Him Christians are complete:[2] in need of nothing that He cannot give them either for the perfection of their religious state, or for the realisation in them of the Divine Ideal of life.

This pre-eminence of Christ over created intelligences is traced back by the apostle to His Priority to them in origin, in a passage where He is called the " First Born of

[1] Rom. viii. 38-39.   [1] Col. ii. 10.

all creation."[1] But this reference to the Cosmical Significance of Christ is not meant to explain His Supremacy over the angels, but simply to make it more credible. The death of Christ is the true explanation. One effect of the Cross, as we have seen, was to liberate man from enslavement to supernatural powers. To use the expressive language of chap. ii. 15, "God had on the Cross stript Himself" of that vesture of created intelligences under which He had formerly appeared to men; and in token thereof Christ had been exalted over all created beings. "Let no man," exclaims the apostle, "by bringing you into subjection to angels and the ascetic practices that follow, rob you of your prize (the prize won for you when God triumphed in the Cross), by a voluntary humility and worshipping of angels, vainly puffed up in his fleshly mind and not holding the Head."[2]

It will be apparent, I trust, from what has been said, that in all this teaching about the Headship of Christ over unseen powers, Paul was setting forth an aspect of Christ's Exalted Activity that had a profound religious significance for those to whom he wrote. Christ could not be a Second Adam to men unless He were Supreme over the angelic world, to which they, as fallen under sin, had become subject, and unless He were in this way the fulfilment of Man's Destiny to be Sovereign over all things. This idea is more fully worked out in the Epistle to the Hebrews, and constitutes one interesting point of connection between that Epistle and the Pauline writings.[3]

But it may be asked, What is the worth or value of this doctrine for us, who have no lively belief in angels, and are not troubled by the thought of intermediate beings coming between us and God? Has not this truth of Christ's supremacy over angelic intelligences lost significance for

[1] Col. i. 15.   [2] Col. ii. 15-18.   [3] Heb. ii. 5-9.

us, since we have lost all practical belief in that to which it appeals? The religious consciousness does not indeed now conceive of the world as ancient thought conceived of it,—a sphere in which unseen agents are continually at work, producing the phenomena that make up what we call the course of nature.[1] Where the ancient mind saw spiritual beings or angelic powers engaged in carrying out the will of God, viewed as friendly or hostile according as the events they were the instruments of bringing to pass affected the weal or the woe of men, we see natural forces acting according to sequences that we term laws. Besides, the thinking of the world at that time was ruled by the notion of the intrinsic evil of matter: the belief in intermediate beings rested on the supposition that matter could not have been created by God Himself, but was the work of beings that emanated from Him in an endless series, becoming less and less perfect as they receded from the original source of all. The scientific view of the world by which we are all influenced nowadays makes it difficult for us to throw ourselves back into this ancient habit of mind. And yet although we speak of the laws of nature where they spoke of angels, the same problem faces us that faced them, and we are not brought any nearer to a solution of it than they were, by our altered conceptions. The existence of evil and suffering in the world is a problem that baffles us, as it baffled them. We encounter the same difficulty in rising from the facts of nature to faith in God. The scientific knowledge of the world does not help us; it has rather increased the difficulty, for it reveals to us the working in nature, as the very law of its progress, of the principle of evolution, which, through a selfish and ruthless struggle, sanctions and perpetuates cruelty and wrong. We seem to be removed farther from God than before by that

[1] See Illingworth's interesting chapter on the "Development of the Conception of Divine Personality" in his Bampton Lectures.

knowledge of the processes of nature, so relentless in their operation, that we call science. The same fears are suggested to our minds by the aspect of a world that has so much to perplex and terrify us. A dread creeps over us, as if we might find that God and nature were hopelessly apart. And this feeling comes to affect our religious experience, and tempts us to say, Christ may be indeed the Lord of the inner life, the Saviour of the soul, the Head of His believing people, but His rule reaches not beyond. Nature rolls on in its course, governed by forces that science can give account of, but whose action cannot be related in any way to faith, or to the God of love and righteousness whom faith embraces. Thus we slip back into the error of the Colossians, who, while they gave Christ a certain place in their thoughts, acknowledged the angels to be the real influences on human affairs, and were in bondage to them; only in the place of angels we put, what is their equivalent to us, the laws of nature and the forces of the universe, that work out their results in reckless disregard of human happiness.

Now, when Paul held up the Exalted Christ as the " Head of all principalities and powers," he meant that the love of God in Christ is Supreme over all the forces that govern the world and bear on human happiness. These forces were viewed by him, in accordance with the thought of his age, as angelic agencies. But were he present with us to-day, and to speak to us in the language appropriate to our conceptions of things, would his message not be substantially the same? The Dominion of the Christ (would he not say?) is over all things visible and invisible. There are no powers, however destructive they appear to be, or however opposed to the moral life of man, that are not under Him, that cannot be made to work out the perfection of man by faith in His love. Misfortune, unfavourable environment, maladjustment of circumstances, heredity, perverse habit, and other forces hostile to our highest good, that arise out of the physical system of things, are subject to the spiritual power embodied in Jesus Christ. They who have fellowship with Him in faith and love are victorious over the evil that assails them from this lower plane of existence, and can attain, in spite of them, to the Perfect Life. And do not human experience and history bear witness to the truth of Christ's Sovereignty over nature in this sense? Do they not bear witness to a power at work in those who believe in Him, that is stronger to lift them up and make them holy, than are the forces of evil to drag them down? Are we not taught thereby that Christ's dominion is coextensive with the world of nature and humanity, that He opposes a Divine Power and All-Triumphant Love to all influences, from whatever quarter they come, which retard or threaten to make impossible the true progress of man? The "Head of all principalities and powers," He is clothed with ability to subdue all things for those who believe in Him and are ruled by His Spirit.

I can only in a sentence point out the bearing of this view on the practical Ideals that are now to regulate human life and conduct. As long as the Colossian Christians thought that the authority of Christ was contested or restricted by other powers in the world that shared authority with Him, they cultivated a false spirituality. Looking with fear and suspicion on the material world, that was supposed to be under the government of spirits, they practised asceticism, and strove to reach what seemed to them the higher perfection that belonged to beings that are immaterial. A dualistic way of thinking ever leads to a false ideal of life, and, viewing the world as evil, aims at a spirituality that is unreal, and leaves the nature we have unsanctified. In insisting on the universal Headship of Christ, Paul warns us against the ascetic ideal under every form. He teaches that Perfection is reached not by avoiding intercourse with the world, but by claiming the world and all the interests of human life for Christ, and in giving effect to the universal supremacy of His Love and Righteousness. With our changed way of looking at the world, indeed, the ascetic ideal has little charm for us. Nor are we in danger of setting Christ aside from an anxiety to attain to the spirituality of angelic beings. Our danger is that we may become enslaved under that false ideal of conduct that results from the exclusive study of natural law, an ideal that has nothing moral in it, that exalts mere strength and selfishness. As against this tendency we are to hold up Christ, in Whom the supremacy of Love and Goodness is manifested, in Whom we see the true idea of Personality realised, and made triumphant over all hostile powers.

IV

What has been said of the Supremacy of Christ over all will help us to understand the meaning of the apostle in the claim he makes for Him in his Epistle to the Colossians as the END or goal of creation itself,[1] where a still higher view of the Greatness of Christ is presented. In Ephesians the God of redemption is said to have for His aim in the work of Christ, "to sum up all things in Him,"[2] that is, to bring all things under Christ as their Head; where the truth darkly hinted at seems to be, that He is the intended Bond or principle of universal harmony in the universe, representing the law of life for all moral beings, and revealing the one ground of health and stability in the moral world, in subjection to Whom all are united to God and one another. In Colossians a different phrase is used to express much the same thought: "it pleased God by Him to reconcile all things in

[1] Col. i. 16.   [2] Eph. i. 10.

heaven and earth."[1] Instead of "recapitulation," the idea of "reconciliation" is chosen here in order to describe the effect of Christ's work on the "all" of created existence, because the Colossians imagined that the angels had a part to play in reconciling them to God, which made the cultus of them obligatory on believers; and the apostle would point out that so far was this from being the case, that the angels owed to Christ their own standing in full harmony with God, and that it lay in the Divine Plan that He should be the instrument of a universal reconciliation, that all might realise their perfect harmony with God in their common subjection to His Son.

This, the apostle says, was a result of the work of Christ that was intended from the first. "All things were created unto Him,"[2] that is, with a view to Him, to the universal acknowledgment of His Supremacy and His claim on the worship and obedience of created intelligences. This doctrine, that Christ is the End or Final Cause of creation itself, is criticised by some as extravagant, and as un-Pauline in going beyond what the apostle has elsewhere said. But, as it seems to me, the mind welcomes this conception as in keeping with the whole idea of Christ in the Pauline writings, and as introducing a unity into our thoughts of God's government. It means that redemption is not an after-thought of the Divine mind consequent on the Fall, but that the thought of it was present in the very act of creation. It means that the natural order does not stand alone, does not exist for its own sake, but that from the very beginning it was intended to be followed by that spiritual order which explains it, and which has Christ for its Head. As the first Adam, according to Paul's earlier teaching, looked to the Second, and was the Type of "Him that was to come," so now we find him advancing to the position that the creation of

[1] Col. i. 20   [2] Col. i. 16.

the Kosmos itself looked to Him who was to be supreme, and under whom all created intelligences were to rank themselves. This grand view is in full harmony with the trend of modern thought. Man, science tells us, must be regarded as the object or end of creation—the culminating point in the ascending series of forms of life, in whom is explained all that went before. What is it but an enlargement of this idea to regard Man in Christ, the Risen and Exalted Man, as the end of the human development that began with the appearance of the first Adam on the scene? The Supremacy of Christ then becomes the goal of the previous history of mankind, and at the same time the instrument or agency by which is reached the final end, which is the glory of God.

Thus are we to reconcile the apparent divergence of view in this passage, which declares that Christ is the " End " to whom creation and redemption had regard, from the statement of Paul in an earlier Epistle,[1] that the universal sovereignty of God is the end, and that Christ's mediatorial glory is but the means to its realisation. From one point of view, and looking at the matter from the close of the present dispensation of Grace, the Glory of God is indeed the true end of Redemption, and Christ's Supremacy is the means by which it is advanced. While, from the point of view of the present order, and remembering that Christ is God's Vicegerent, and that all things are intended to advance the interests committed to Him, we may say with equal truth that His Supremacy is the object or end of all. In the passage in 1 Cor. the apostle is speaking of the close or consummation of all things. The issue is the Glory of God. In Colossians he has before him the dispensation that is running its course, whose object is to illustrate and extend

[1] 1 Cor. xv. 24–29.

the present Sovereignty of Christ. The point of view is different, but there is no discrepancy of thought.

From this account of the Christological doctrine which these Epistles contain, it must be evident there is ascribed to Christ by their author a greatness in the scale of Being, a Dignity and Pre-eminence of position in the universe of God, that surpasses all we find in the early ones; but it must also, I think, be evident that the loftier views are but the full expression and development of truths present to the apostle in the early stage of his spiritual history, and that they, too, have their root in his experience as a Christian man. It is often said, regarding the exalted conceptions of Christ contained in these later writings of Paul, that they are testimonies to the feelings of love and admiration that he and his fellow-believers had for their Master, and to the profound impression made upon their minds by His Personality, but that they cannot be regarded as objectively true. "They are but sallies of love and admiration," says Emerson, "which in our ecclesiastical theology have been petrified into official titles that kill all generous sympathy and liking."[1] It may be true that we do often empty the expressions that bear on the superhuman Greatness of Christ, of the power they possess to stir our affections, by our theological treatment of them. But, on the other hand, it is doing them less than justice to view them simply as the language of ardent love dwelling with a natural exaggeration on the worth of its object. It is nearer the truth to say that in such language we have the utterance of convictions regarding Christ's Divine Power and all-sufficiency that are inseparably connected with the experience of the new life He quickens in the soul. They have more than a

[1] In his address delivered before the senior class in Divinity College, Cambridge, 1883.

subjective value. They state what is true of Christ in His relation to us; and however lofty such statements may be, and however inappropriate to any but Himself, they come with the force and authority of truth to those who believe in Him as Living and Supreme. Experience of what Christ is to us decides what we believe to be true regarding Him. Our conceptions of Him will be exalted in the measure in which He is realised by us as a Power in our life of thought and action. The thoughts of others regarding Him may seem to us strange, and may be difficult to make our own, but the reason of that may be explained by the meagreness and poverty of our experience.[1] It is not too much to say that the representation of the Christ contained in these Epistles has found an echo in the minds of most who have attained to the largest discoveries of His Redeeming Power, and who have been led by the strength and light He has brought into their lives to rest in Him as both the Wisdom and the Power of God, the solution of the problem of the world as well as of the contradictions of the human soul.

[1] My revered teacher, Professor J. T. Beck of Tübingen, used to insist on patience with ourselves in the study of Scripture, inasmuch as the understanding of spiritual truth depends not on processes of logic, but on processes of life; and with the deepening of the higher life our horizon of truth widens and things become plain that before we doubted the reality of. I have given in the Appendix an extract from one of his opening lectures to his students in which he enforces this lesson. See Note B on Beck on Truth and Life.

VI

THE ETERNAL NATURE OF CHRIST

LECTURE VI

THE ETERNAL NATURE OF CHRIST

THE course of our inquiry into Paul's conception of Christ has, up to this point, led us to dwell exclusively on those elements of the conception that are derived from the experience of the Christian life, and are verifiable by the Christian consciousness. In Paul's view, the only Christology that is of value is that which is Soteriological in its character—is that, in other words, which is gathered from the impressions of Christ's personal saving grace received in the life of faith. We rise to the understanding of what He is through the experience of what He proves Himself to be, where the inner life is under the influence of His Personality. There is, however, one aspect of his Christology which is of a different character, and to that our attention is now to be directed. There are in the Epistles statements in which Christ is spoken of as existing in a Preincarnate state. Affirmations are made regarding a Life prior to that which He lived on earth, that belong to an entirely different category from the affirmations that constitute the great bulk of the apostle's teaching. The latter concern Christ in His relation to us, and as the Author of religious benefits that fall within our conscious experience. The former concern Him as He is in Himself, antecedent to that connection with the world into which He entered when He became Incarnate. They are metaphysical in nature and unverifiable by human experience. A peculiar difficulty must, of course, attach to the understanding of statements of this sort; and had a sense of this been more present to the minds of theologians, it might have had a salutary effect in restraining the confidence with which these statements have been made use of by them to explain the Person of Christ on its metaphysical side, and to form theories that have served only to perplex, and to endanger one part or another of the faith regarding Him. This difficulty has been more vividly realised in modern times; and, pressed by it, later theology, in an influential section of its representatives, has rejected the authority of these statements over the faith of the Church, viewing them as belonging to the category of opinion in theological matters, in contrast to what is to be regarded in the light of essential truth. This attitude of mind is, no doubt, a recoil from the excessive tendency of the theologians of the early Church to deal with those passages that bear on the pre-existence of Christ as if they furnished material for a dogmatic understanding of the Person of the Lord of Glory. We are required, therefore, to consider in this lecture not only the question of the objective value of the statements that relate to the Premundane life of Christ, but also the further question how far these statements admit of being employed to construct theories that aim at explaining the mystery lying at the root of His Person. But before entering on these difficult and delicate inquiries, let us see what Paul's teaching on the pre-existence of Christ really is, and in what connection the references to it occur.

I

Paul is not alone among the writers of the New Testament in asserting a PRE-INCARNATE life of Christ. John and the author of the Epistle to the Hebrews give this doctrine a greater prominence than Paul gives it. They set it forth in forms that are even more explicit. From the almost incidental way in which it is mentioned we are justified in concluding that it was a familiar representation among the apostolic churches, a self-evident truth. Whatever account may be given by us of the origin of this belief, it seemed to them in harmony with the profound impression made upon them by the Personality of Jesus, and by the contrast between the lowliness of His earthly life and the Divine glory which He had reached, to believe that He who was the subject of so wonderful a history, and had proved Himself in their experience to be so great a Saviour, had existed in heaven before He appeared on earth, had come from a higher sphere into this world. The belief was certainly prevalent, and the Epistles bear evidence of having been written to those who did not need any proof of it.[1]

This is the character of most of the allusions in Paul's Epistles,—at least in the earlier and undisputed ones, to which we turn our attention in the first instance. The references, then, to the Pre-existence of Christ in the four leading Epistles are exceedingly scanty, and so incidental as to suggest the inference that, while intimately related to his own deepest convictions about Christ, this doctrine formed no part of his formal teaching, until, at least, the necessity for it arose in the special circumstances of the Church at Colosse. We have the two great announcements of the change effected on the religious destinies of men by the mission of Christ: "God sent forth His Son, made of a woman, made under the law, to redeem us,"[2] and "God, sending His Son in the likeness of sinful flesh, condemned sin in the flesh."[3] The "sending forth" of the Son implies that He existed before He was "made of a woman," and came "under the law," before He appeared in the "like-

---

[1] "What strikes us in these statements about pre-existence is, that the apostle nowhere really establishes or teaches the pre-existence of Christ, but, especially in his earlier Epistles, presupposes it as familiar to his readers and disputed by no one" (Beyschlag, *N. T. Theology*, vol. ii. p. 78, Eng. Trans.).

[2] Gal. iv. 4. [3] Rom. viii. 3.

ness of sinful flesh," and that He existed in a form that was contrasted with that of His historic life, in its being one of Sonship and Spirit, while that which followed was one of subjection to law and participation of flesh. In 2 Cor. viii. 9 we learn positively that, in coming into the world, Christ exchanged a state of riches for one of poverty: "He who was rich for our sakes became poor." His coming is here described as His own act, and not, as in the previous case, the result of the decree of God—as an act that revealed the generosity and self-sacrificing spirit of the pre-incarnate One. It is instructive, as suggesting the slight importance the apostle attached to the details of Christ's early life, that, in order to exhibit the Lord as the Pattern of Generosity, and to draw from His life and Person motives for our practice of a similar spirit, he passes over the many incidents of the Divine Life that could so well have served his purpose, and appeals to the sublimest exemplification of it that was furnished by the prehistoric act of Christ in consenting to be born. "He who was rich for our sakes became poor, that we through his poverty might be rich." In 1 Cor. xv. 47, where we read of "the Second Man," who "is from heaven," the Exalted Christ is referred to, for, as we have found, it is only as Exalted that He is called the Second Man; but it is implied that He belonged to heaven as His home, and that He existed before as a Heavenly Being. In 1 Cor. x. 4 the Prehistoric Christ is spoken of as accompanying Israel of old in their wilderness journey and, ministering by His communications to their religious wants. "They drank of that spiritual Rock that followed them, and that Rock was Christ."[1] And in chap. viii. 6 we have a significant hint

[1] It may be that the apostle had in his mind the Rabbinical tradition that the rock smitten by Moses followed Israel through their wanderings. Not that we can suppose that he believed this grotesque idea. "The Rock that followed them" was Jehovah (Isa. xxx. 29), a "spiritual" Rock, because the supernatural source of blessing to Israel.

of the part He played in creation itself. Contrasting the faith of Christians with that of the heathen who have "gods many and lords many," Paul says, "to us there is one God the Father, of whom are all things, and we in Him, and one Lord Jesus Christ, by whom are all things, and we by Him"; or, as Weizäcker in his translation has it, bringing out the sense more fully, "our Lord Jesus Christ the Mediator of all things, who is also our Mediator." The range of meaning to be given to "all things" is indeed doubtful. Many of the best exegetes restrict it to the "all things" of the Christian economy, and understand Paul as here claiming for the Lord that mediatorial Function in virtue of which He carries on, in the name of the Father, the government of all things. On the other hand, the words "we by Him," in which Christ is declared to be our Mediator, by whom we reach the end of our being, seem to point to a wider activity, and to base Christ's present Mediatorship in regard to men on a prior Mediatorship in regard to creation itself. There seems at least to be a hint of a prior relation on His part to "all things" corresponding to, or a shadow of, the relation of Grace in which He now stands to the human race as its Lord and Mediator.[1]

When he adds "this rock was Christ," we are not "to disgrace Paul," to quote Hofmann's words (*Der Schriftbeweis*, i. 171), "by making him say that Christ, not yet Incarnate, followed the march of Israel in the form of a rock." The reason why he says "Christ," and not "Jehovah," is that his readers may make the application to themselves. "All activity bearing on the history of salvation on the part of the God of whom the O. T. testifies was an activity of God coming into the world, and an activity, so far, of the Christ whom the N. T. Church acknowledges as its Lord. For, since He has been revealed, believers know to distinguish between Him who came into the world, who is God, and the God who sent Him into the world, while formerly the distinction lay concealed in the one name of Jehovah" (Hofmann, *Der Heilige Schrift*, ii. 2, p. 209).

[1] Mr. Hutton has criticised Paul's Doctrine of the Pre-existent Life of Christ as less full than that of John. "He held, doubtless, that the Son of God had been the centre of Jewish unity and nationality throughout the history of the Jewish nation (1 Cor. x. 4). He held, too,

When we turn now to the expressions on this subject that occur in the Epistles of the captivity, we find that they are equally rare, and that they are either to the same effect, or expansions of the thought, in keeping with the undoubted growth of the apostolic conception of the glory of the Exalted Christ which characterises these Epistles. The most noteworthy passage of all is the familiar one in Phil. iii. 3-10, in trying to understand which one cannot take a single step without being challenged by the voice of controversy. I can only state in the briefest way what appears to me, after the fullest consideration I have been able to give to them, to be the natural meaning of the words. The Supreme Pattern of Christian conduct is the Exalted Christ, to whom God has given a name "above every name in heaven and on earth"; and it is evidently the intention of the apostle, in commending the grace of humility and the duty of each looking to the things of others as well as to his own, to exhibit the Exaltation of Christ as the grandest instance of the recognition by God of the infinite worth of a spirit of self-effacement for the good of others. He is not content to dwell on the successive stages of the earthly career of Christ as marking the steps of a course that was marvellous for the spirit of self-denial it disclosed: "He humbled Himself, and became obedient to death, even to the death on the cross" (Phil. ii. 8). He goes back to what antedated Christ's earthly experiences, to show that the humble self-denying spirit that characterised the life of

that Christ was equally the centre and root of the social unity of the Christian Church, that His life was in all its members, and the real bond of its organisation, but I can see no trace that he had learnt to extend the same truth to the whole world of heathen humanity,—that he had grasped the fulness of St. John's teaching,—that He is the light which lighteth every man that cometh into the world" (*Essays*, vol. *t*. pp. 250 ff.). In the passage quoted in the text, however, as well as in those to follow (*e.g.* Col. ii. 15-18), our apostle does seem to assert a relation, antecedent to the manifestation in time, in which the Son of God stands to every human being.

Jesus was the reproduction of the mind of the Eternal Pre-existent One, and exhibited in detail the spirit that was manifested in the very act of coming into the world in the "form of a servant." He existed before in the "Form of God." The phrase points to a state of being that is to be regarded as implying at least the absence of the limitations, weakness, corruption, that belong to creaturely existence. What more we are to understand by it will depend on which of the two alternative meanings of the word, translated "form" ($\mu o \rho \phi \eta$), we adopt. The great majority of modern commentators take it in the sense of "outward appearance,"—that which expressed the nature of Christ, but was at the same time separable from that nature. And this "form" or "appearance" of God they regard Him as having laid aside, or "emptied Himself of," that He might assume the "form of a servant." On this understanding, the "being Equal with God," which "He did not cling to as a prey," will explain more fully what is meant by the "Form of God," will describe it as consisting in an Equality with God in respect of rank and dominion. The chief difficulties in the way of accepting this interpretation are these: first, "the being Equal with God" is with more appropriateness, I think, referred to that "Lordship over all" which, as we read in vv. 9, 10, was conferred upon Christ at His resurrection, and was not therefore His actual possession in His pre-incarnate state; and second, the word "Form" is a philosophical term, and has a definite sense, meaning that "appearance" of a thing or person that is inseparable from the person or thing itself. It is equivalent to "nature"; and we cannot conceive of Him who "was in the Form of God," understood in this sense, divesting Himself of it without His ceasing thereby to be Divine. This is the view of the Greek Fathers; it is also the view, in modern times, of Canon Lightfoot, and it has been advocated lately with great force by Gifford in his masterly examination of this passage.[1] On this understanding, then, the "Form" of God implies a relation to the life of God which signifies perfect resemblance to Him; and the term means much the same thing as "Image of God" (εἰκων), which is elsewhere used of Christ (Col. i. 15).

We are further to recognise in this relation of the Pre-incarnate Christ to God that which constituted His Fitness to be raised to the "Equality with God" which, in actual fact, became His only after He had finished His earthly career, when God "highly exalted Him." The word is "*highly* exalted" (ὑπερύψωσε). The idea conveyed is that the Exaltation glory marked a certain advance on that which belonged to His Eternal state when He was " in the Form of God." We are to picture to ourselves a situation in which the Pre-incarnate One had presented to Him the career by which He was to realise the possibilities that lay wrapt up in His being "in the Form of God." The course by which the "Equality with God," or the Divine lordship of His exaltation-state was to be reached, was conceivably one that would have outwardly illustrated His superiority to all others and His Personal Claims to Divine honour. But such an assertion of His right to be worshipped as God would have been the act of one who looked at "his own things," and not at "the things of others." And Christ did not choose the way of self-exaltation to reach His present position. He did not regard the "Being Equal with God" as a thing to be grasped or clutched at in this way, as one would a prey or booty; He looked rather to the good of men, and renounced His own things to enter on a course of self-denying service of others, and of humble obedience to the will of God. He "emptied Himself," and took upon Him the "form of a servant." He preferred to receive from the Father the sovereignty over all as the Divine recogni-

[1] *The Incarnation, a Study of Philippians* ii. 5-11, by G. H. Gifford, 1897.

tion of His self-effacement for others (ἐχαρίσατο), rather than obtain it by the assertion of His own right. The temptation of Christ in the desert, where we see Him choosing the path of self-humiliation in preference to that of self-glorification, in order to reach the Messianic supremacy, is perhaps the best commentary we can have on these words.[1] We cannot fathom the depth of them. We cannot understand that act of "self-emptying"; we can only say that it was the analogue, the eternal counterpart, of the spirit of self-annihilation for the interests of His brethren, by which the earthly life of Christ was distinguished, and which had its reward in His exaltation to be supreme in the affections and worship of men. And it seems to be the design of the apostle to enhance our admiration of that spirit, by representing it as the continued manifestation of an eternal act in which the Pre-existent One of His own free will relinquished a glory personal to Himself, in order to enter our state and win the higher glory of being loved and honoured and adored by all on the ground of service rendered to them.

A further insight into the pre-existent life of Christ is afforded in the opening of the Epistle to the Colossians (i. 15–18), where He is designated the First-born of Crea-

[1] Luther, it is well known, viewed the passage in Phil. ii. as referring to the historical Christ, and many others besides have so understood it. Amongst later writers of this class may be mentioned Schenkel (*Christus-Bild der Apostel*, p. 296), who thinks there is an intended contrast in the words between Christ and the first Adam. The latter, made in the image or "form" of God, abused his original gift by seeking to reach equality with God ("ye shall be as gods"), through eating the fruit of the tree of knowledge, and fell into bondage to sin. The Second Adam did not yield to the temptation to pride and self-assertion which His possession of the "form" of God brought with it, but accomplished His Messianic task by His humble obedience. Beyschlag, in his *New Testament Christology*, also advocated Luther's view, but in his later work has abandoned it, accepting the interpretation which finds most favour with exegetes, according to which the Pre-incarnate Christ is the subject. But it remains true that it is in the study of the Historical Christ and of His earthly life that we learn what that spirit was that was exemplified in the eternal act of self-emptying.

tion, " in whom all things were made, things in heaven and things in earth, visible and invisible; whether thrones or principalities or powers, all things were made by Him, and for Him and in Him all things consist." This passage may be regarded as an expansion of 1 Cor. viii. 6, to which allusion has been made, and which states that as Christ in His present relation to us is the instrument by whom we reach the end of our being, so He was related to creation itself in a prior state of existence as the instrument by whom it came into being. The object of Paul in amplifying this thought in the striking terms of the passage in the Colossians, is to assist us to understand that supremacy over all powers and intelligences which he claims for Christ in this great Epistle. That supremacy, as we have seen, belongs to Him as Risen and Glorified, and is based on His historic work; but it goes back, he tells us here, to a relation of superiority to, and primacy over all angelic powers that was prior to His incarnation, and was the eternal counterpart of the Supremacy which He now exercises. He is the "First Born of every creature," and owes His Being to a mode of the Divine Activity that places Him in a higher category of existence than that to which others belong. They derived their being from His agency, the Divine Power that called them into existence travelling to its goal through Him. And this constitutes Him at once the Ground of their Being and the Ideal in whom they reach the completeness of their powers. Words could not more emphatically proclaim the truth, that while the relations in which Christ now stands both to men and angels are of grace, flowing from His deed of love on the Cross and conveying blessings that are entirely gracious in their character, they at the same time go back to relations that are of nature, and that are grounded in the original constitution of Christ, making Him the Natural Head of all, so that to believe in Him, to accept Him as our Ideal, and find our life's end in doing His will, is to be true to a relation that lies in creation itself, and that expresses the eternal law of our Being.[1]

II

We have thus hurriedly passed under review the passages in which the Pre-incarnate life of Christ is spoken of in the Epistles. And the first inquiry which is suggested, and to which we must now address ourselves, is this, What value is to be attached to these statements? Do they express truth that is literal, or that is symbolic merely? Are we really to believe on their authority that Christ existed before He appeared on earth? and are we to take as literal truth the things that are said of Him in that prior life? Or may we regard this language as simply expressing, in the forms of theological thought natural to that age, the profound sense Paul, in common with the other writers of the New Testament, entertained of the Greatness of their Master and His superiority to all others? Can this doctrine of His Pre-existence be adequately explained by viewing it as the intellectual clothing of their faith in the moral and spiritual supremacy of Christ? If this account of the matter be accepted, then the belief in His Pre-existence must be viewed as an excrescence on the doctrine of Christ, and as forming no part of the Christology which the Church of all time recognises as the expression of its

[1] I have not thought it necessary to discuss the question whether the pre-existence asserted in Paul's Epistles is ideal (in the mind of God) or personal, for most are now agreed that it is doing violence to the language of the apostle to understand it in anything else than a personal sense. Beyschlag, who in his former work (*Die Christologie des N. T.*, 1866), which gave such an impulse to the study of this subject, maintained that the pre-existence predicated of Christ is ideal simply, has in his recently published work on N. T. Theology abandoned that opinion, and now explains the apostle's statements about the personal being of Christ in a pre-incarnate condition as an imperfect mode of setting forth the truth that the " temporal appearance of Christ must be traced back to an Eternal Basis."

faith regarding Him. This is the position of a certain school of theologians of the present day; and it is necessary to consider the grounds on which it is defended, and the intellectual tendencies which, in their judgment, account for this belief.

Two sources of influence are mentioned in this connection. The one is the influence of Palestinian theology, with which presumably Paul was familiar, and which ascribed pre-existence in heaven to all objects and persons connected with religion, by way of accounting for their existence and the worth that belonged to them. Moses, the temple, the Sabbath, the law itself, are all spoken of as pre-existent in heaven. It would not surprise us to find that the Messiah, while still an object of hope, is referred to in the literature of the period as existent in heaven, and waiting to be revealed. It is alleged that this is actually the case, and that the notion of the Pre-existent Messiah was a part of the ancient teaching of the synagogue. The evidence of this is indeed not quite conclusive. Modern research into the opinions prevalent among the Jews before the Christian era has done something to clear up this subject; but more has to be done before we can form a confident judgment; we cannot be sure that the passages in the apocalyptic writings that contain this dogma are not Christian interpolations.[1] At the same time, it must be admitted that the conditions were present for the springing up of this idea. Daniel's vision of the Son of Man coming in the clouds of glory suggested His pre-existence to those

---

[1] The Christology of the Jewish *Book of Enoch*, which belongs in its older portions to the century before Christ, is very striking. The Messiah is spoken of as the Son of Man, who "is waiting in heaven" to be revealed. The section, however, in which this occurs (called the Similitudes) is by many scholars referred to Christian times. See Stanton, *The Jewish and the Christian Messiah*, page 153; *The Jewish Messiah*, by Drummond, i. 4. Mr. Charles believes it to be pre-Christian (*Book of Enoch*, pp. 29, 30, 107, 108).

who understood it of a personal Messiah. The habit, to which I have alluded, of attributing an existence in heaven to objects and persons to which the religious hopes clung, which arose, as Baldensberger says, "from the desire, in an age that threatened general dissolution, to place the cherished ideals of the soul beyond the crumbling hand of time, and the changes incident to all things earthly":[1] this predisposed the Christian consciousness to believe that He who was the fulfilment of the Messianic Hope had existed in heaven before He came into this world. Thus, it is said, we may fairly regard the belief as the product of the human mind, borrowing from ideas then in vogue the conception in which it expressed its conviction of the greatness of the Master, translating its faith into language that was supplied by the theological thought of the age.

A second intellectual influence, it is alleged, combined with that just mentioned to bring about the same result, and that was the prevalence even in Jewish circles of religious ideas that were more congenial to Greek philosophy than to the original spirit of the Hebrew religion. The Greek notion of a transcendent Deity, separated from the world of matter, necessitated the conception of an intermediate power, called reason or logos, by which the Creator and the creature were brought together, a conception which played a large part in the system of the Alexandrine Philo. The later Judaism felt the influence of the Greek notion of the absoluteness and transcendence of God, and its theology betrayed the same tendency to rest in some intermediate Being, corresponding to the logos of Greek speculation, as a Bond of intercourse between God and man. This it found in the Old Testament ideas of the creative "Word" of God, and the "Wisdom" of God, and the "Spirit," or Breath, of the Almighty. In the books of that time we find a religious philosophy that employs these terms no longer as express-

[1] *Das Selbstbewusstsein Jesu*, i. 3.

ing different modes of the Divine activity and self-manifestation, but as names for a separate hypostasis of the Divine nature, with Divine attributes and functions towards creation similar to those assigned to the logos in the cognate system of Philo. This idea of an intermediate Being, who makes possible the transition from the uncreated to the created, furnished the mould into which the Christian consciousness of the Superlative Greatness of Christ would pour itself. To Him became transferred those conceptions that had been associated hitherto with an object of religious speculation. Thus there attached itself to the faith of Jesus Christ the belief in His Pre-existence, and in His possession in a pre-incarnate state of such Divine attributes as are ascribed to Him specially in the later Epistles of Paul. In this way the conclusion is reached that the belief, originating in the speculative thought of the age, and rendering a religious idea into language borrowed from that thought, has no objective validity, and does not enter into the doctrine that expresses what is true regarding Christ for all time and for every age.

This view possesses great plausibility, and is attractive to those who are wearied with the metaphysical subtilities that surround the doctrine of the Person of Christ, and long for a return to a simpler faith, to a faith that is confined to what is historically true, and that can enforce its authoritativeness before the bar of reason and conscience. The facts mentioned prove, indeed, how prepared the soil was for the reception of a doctrine of the superhuman origin and pre-existent life of Christ, and may well account for the infrequency with which it is alluded to; for it was not necessary for the writers of the New Testament to dilate on an aspect of truth which was not called in question by their readers, and which it was so easy for them to believe. But the more we consider the matter, the more difficult is it for us to accept as exhaustive an explanation of the doctrine that refers it to what was peculiar in the religious thought of the age. The Christian consciousness has acquiesced in this doctrine as not only consonant to its convictions of the Divine Greatness of its Master, but as required by those convictions to justify them to itself. When we reflect on what the exaltation of Christ means, on the essential grandeur that must belong to a Being who receives such recognition, and the power to rule human destiny that is thereby conferred upon Him, we feel that it is reasonable to believe that He had an origin different from that of all others; and that, when Scripture refers to Him as preexistent and possessed of a nature and prerogatives that are eternal, identifying Him in a peculiar way with the eternal life of God, it presents Him under an aspect which, however difficult to make plain to our minds, is one that has in favour of its truth the antecedent probabilities of the case. One who is so High in the universe of Being, who has been and is so powerful an Agent in the moral and religious renewal of the race, could not at His human birth have begun to be—must have a history antecedent to that which was wrought out on the platform of time. It is a religious datum, or an implicate of our religious consciousness. It seems to originate in the very faith itself, or to be necessitated by it.[1]

Those speculative systems that repudiate the claim of this doctrine to a place in the creed of the Church acknowledge the necessity of recognising, in one form or another, in the true doctrine of Christ, His connection with a superhuman order of events in the kingdom of God, in order that

[1] Kähler puts the matter thus: "Christ has, with His Glorification, entered on a state of Activity that embraces the world and penetrates into the hearts of men. That fact points to an Independence of Being in contrast with the ordinary life of Humanity such as cannot by any magic belong to any mere child of man. Such a position can be held only by the Eternal in His Majestic Independence in contrast with creaturehood. His exaltation, therefore, finds its only explanation in uncreated Being" (*Die Wiss. der Christ. Lehre*, p. 324).

justice may be done to the consciousness of His supreme religious significance. Proceeding to translate this consciousness into language more appropriate to modern modes of thought, they say: This ascription of pre-existence to the person of Christ comes of mixing up two things that must be kept separate, a religious idea or principle—the relation of sonship to God—and the Historic Person in whom that idea or principle is embodied, Jesus Christ. The pre-existence is to be ascribed to the principle or idea; the Person in whom it is embodied is a Man like any other man, born under similar conditions, pre-incarnate only in thought. He is but the temporal manifestion of the Eternal idea of the sonship of man to God. This is the construction of the Person that is offered by the speculative theology of the school of Lipsius, Biederman, Pfleiderer, and others. It is not pretended that it accords with the representations of Scripture, which assert a real and personal pre-existence; but it is claimed for it that it does equal justice to the idea of Christ's supernatural worth in which these representations of Scripture originated, and that it conserves the religious interest in a form more consonant to the modern consciousness. The difficulty, however, appears to me insuperable of conceiving how one who is no more, by original constitution, than a human individual, can possess so exclusive an authority over the religious life of men, and an authority which rests not simply on what He said, but on what He personally was; or how such an one could become the recipient or embodiment of the idea in so absolute a sense as to constitute Him the Creative power by whom it is reproduced in others. The mind seems to me to demand that One who is to stand in such a relation to others should be in his own Person distinctive, should be more and greater than they who are to benefit by their connection with Him; and the Scripture representation of Him as eternally pre-existent, descending into a connection with us from a higher life, best meets that postulate, and is most in keeping with the religious conviction of His superhuman greatness and supreme significance for the religious Life of Man.[1]

III

But the further question remains, whether the language of the apostle supplies us with the means of formulating a doctrine of the Person of Christ on its metaphysical side; whether, in addition to the moral and spiritual understanding of the contents of His Person, we can form any definite idea of its original constitution, of His place and rank in the system of Being; whether, in short, we can know Him as He is in Himself, apart from His relations to us which are the proper matter of revelation. We are here called to consider the theories which theologians, on the authority of statements in Paul's Epistles, have formed of the Person of Christ, and by which they have attempted to solve the problem of who and what He is in Himself. And, in approaching these theories, two things are to be kept before us as canons of judgment by which we may test their claim to be based on the teaching of the apostle and to represent his thought. On the one hand, it is to be noticed that it is always of one and the same subject that Paul speaks in his references to the different stages of the Being of Christ. However contrasted these states may be with one another,

[1] Besides, it makes a difference in our conception of the grace of God in the Incarnation whether we regard that grace as manifested in the Son of God leaving heaven that He might enter on the humiliation of our earthly life, or as manifested simply in His Passion and Death for us. There is an added element of condescension in the former case that is absent in the latter. It is not often that Paul speaks of the act of the incarnation itself as a revelation of the love of God, but he does so represent it in two passages at least (Phil. ii. 3-10, and 2 Cor. viii. 9). And it would deprive those of meaning were we to regard him as mistaken in believing in the personal pre-existence of the Son of God. See Rainy on Philippians, p. 127.

it is one and the same Christ who is the subject of them; the continuity of His life and consciousness unites them as parts of one history extending over the Eternity that is past, the brief episode of His earthly career, and the Eternity that followed. And, on the other hand, there is the no less indisputable truth that, as Paul represents the matter, Christ's experience of these successive states marks the progress of His Personality from what is (in one point of view) a less perfect form of Being to one that is perfect and complete. While His life in the flesh was a state of Humiliation compared with His life as pre-incarnate, His state as Exalted involved an increase of personal glory (or personal qualification for the work of our redemption) compared not only with the earthly state, but also with that which was prior to it. The exaltation was not simply His return to a glory He was in possession of before, but an accession of personal greatness for which His earthly career furnished the needed preparation and discipline.[1] What Christ became as Risen and Glorified at once revealed what was distinctive in His eternal and unchanging nature, and crowned it with the perfection for which He was destined from the first. These two points must receive recognition in any theory professing to set forth the more speculative aspect of Christ's Person that would commend itself as Pauline.

There are but three possible views to be taken of this subject, and each of them has received support.

1. The first is that Christ, in Paul's teaching, is in His essential nature a Man, and no more. Starting from the undoubted fact that He who lives in heaven, our Lord and Saviour, is genuinely human, the advocates of this view refuse to claim for Him more, and in predicating pre-existence of Christ they hold that the New Testament

---

[1] As Haupt (*Philip. Brf.*, p. 96) puts it, "Σύνθρονος Gottes ist er erst kraft seiner Erhöhung geworden, denn der Platz zur Rechten Gottes bezeichnet die Teilnahme an der göttlichen Herrschaft."

contemplates Him as Man in that prior state. This opinion is based on their interpretation of 1 Cor. xv. 47, " the Second Adam is from heaven," according to which Paul is supposed to teach that Christ existed before as the heavenly Pneumatic Man, clothed in a celestial body, to be revealed in due time as the Pattern Man in order to communicate to His people that spiritual body that is the appropriate organ of the higher manhood. The passage is confessedly one of the most difficult in Paul's writings. Holtzmann, who himself accepts the view taken by so many modern scholars, that Paul taught the doctrine of a Pre-existent Heavenly Man, and that it formed part of the inheritance he had brought with him from his Rabbinical training to the understanding of Christian truth, includes this in his list of several passages noted by him in Paul's writings, in regard to which he says we can never be sure that we understand him in the sense which the apostle intended. With commendable fairness that writer allows that it is to Christ as Exalted that Paul applies the term "the Second Adam," since it is only as Exalted that Christ can be spoken of as the New Spiritual Head whose glorified body is the pledge of a similar resurrection-life to His people. While this is so, Holtzmann still maintains that indirectly there is a reference to the Heavenly Pre-existent Man in the phrase "from Heaven," indicating the apostle's belief that Christ had a prior existence as the Primal Man. The difficulty in the way of our acceptance of this interpretation, and it is one that seems to me insuperable, is that in other passages quoted above His pre-existent life is described in terms that are incompatible with His being no more than human, or the created Model of other human intelligences. He is declared to be the instrument by whom creation itself was effected;[1] and when He is said to have existed in the " Form of God," the " Form " whether held to be something essential to His Being

[1] Col. i. 15.

and inseparable from it, or something He could divest Himself of, points in either case to a relationship with the very life of God that seems inconsistent at least with creaturehood.[1] And therefore, although it is going in the face of what, up to recently at least, was almost an accepted result among modern students of Paul, I am unable to agree with the opinion that the apostle conceived of Christ as the Heavenly Man of Jewish Theology.[2] The truth in this view, and it is one that must find a place in any theory that is to reflect his thought, is that Christ is a True Man; and that inasmuch as He is the same through all the stages of His history, the reality of the human element must be recognised in Him as belonging to His essential nature, however difficult it may be for us to conceive the fact.

2. The second view by which Paul's statements have been interpreted, is that Christ pre-existed as a Divine Person, the second Person of the Godhead, who in His birth assumed human nature into personal union with His Divine nature, each maintaining its own distinctive attributes unchanged by the union. The co-existence of two natures essentially different from each other is regarded as having been effected by the Divine Omnipotence, and as constituting the mystery of the incarnation. The strength of this interpretation lies in the fact that it does full justice

---

[1] It may, besides, be urged that if He was Pre-existent as Man, it could not be said that it was not till He appeared on earth that He was made in the "likeness of man," and was found in "fashion as a man." Ritschl, indeed, thinks (*Altkath. Kirche.* p. 80) that if it had been the apostle's view that Christ was Man only in His earthly appearance, he must then have written μορφή ἀνθρώπου instead of δούλου as the proper contrast to μορφή Θεοῦ (Phil. ii. 6). But we cannot isolate μορφή δούλου in this way from what follows, where it is explained as meaning His Humanity.

[2] Later commentators are opposed to this idea. Haupt, in his commentary on Philippians (1897), says he cannot "discover the Pre-existent Man Christ in Paul's writings" (p. 71). Klöpper has a long note in refutation of it in his *Brief an die Philip.* (1893), pp. 134–140. R. Schmidt also is opposed to it. See his *Paulinische Christologie.*

to the Divine Factor in the Person of our Lord, and to those passages that assign cosmological functions to the Pre-incarnate One; and further, that it finds a reason in the original constitution of His Person for His present supremacy over all as Lord. Its weakness is that it sacrifices the humanity of the historic Christ, and with that, His moral and religious significance for the life of man to what is conceived to be the interest of His essential or metaphysical Divinity. There is no question as to the basis of His Personality being truly Divine. The only question is whether His Original Godhead is to be conceived of under those attributes of Infinity that are incommunicable to human nature, or as having affinities with and relations to what is human that explain the Divinity of Man as "made in the image of God." The idea of His essential or Metaphysical Divinity is, to say the least, not actively present in our conception of Christ. For our belief in Him is not that God "in all His absoluteness, omniscience, omnipresence, took on the form of a Man and walked among men in Galilee," so that Jesus was everywhere present at the same time and knew all the occurrences on earth and all the secrets of science and philosophy; but it is the belief that God was in Christ in so far as He can be present in a human personality, revealing Himself under those features of moral character which we can understand and appreciate in virtue of our moral affinity with God. But if, as a certain class of theologians allege,[1] there is all

[1] I refer to those theologians who, in conceiving of the union between the Divine and Human in Christ, start, not from the affinity of the one with the other, but from their essential unlikeness and disparity. The Divine is with them the Infinite, the Omniscient, the Omnipresent One, incapable of union in the real sense with the human or finite, inasmuch as a human consciousness possessed of omniscience and omnipresence would be no longer human. As a modern instance of this metaphysical treatment of the subject, I would refer to the elaborate work of Powell on the *Principle of the Incarnation*, 1896. Approaching the problem from this point of view, the author regards Jesus as the subject of a

the difference between what Christ in His transcendent nature is and what we are, that there is between One who is possessed of the Infinite attributes of Divinity and those who are finite and exist under the limitations of creaturehood, then it is hard to see how there can be any real union between the Divine and the human in His Historical Personality, or how He could be in any true sense a Man, with a human consciousness and the subject of human experiences. Inevitably the entire worth of His Person for the life of faith is impaired by a doctrine that denies all affinity between the original constitution of the Person of Christ and our personal life, or that forces us to conceive of Him in His original pre-existent being as contrasted with and essentially separate from us; and were the latter supposition true, Paul's language would have no meaning in which he speaks of Him who had pre-existent relations with God and creation as essentially one and the same with Him whom he knew as a "man."

This difficulty has of course always been felt, and the long controversy of the ancient Church that preceded the fixing of the dogma exhibits the wavering of theologians in their endeavour now to maintain the unity of His Person, involving the practical surrender of the Human factor, and now the duality of the Natures, with its consequent surrender of the unity of the Person. The decision of the Council of Chal-

---

double consciousness, a Divine and a human, in virtue of which He was, in one and the same moment, in the one sphere of consciousness, omniscient and in full possession and exercise of His Divine nature, and in the other, ignorant and subject to the limitation of His creatures. The union of the Divine and human in the Person of Christ is, on this view, however, a purely formal one. The human remains really dissociated and separate from the Divine. To speak of Christ as at once omniscient in the Divine sphere and ignorant in the human, as filling all space on earth while at the same time locally confined to one place, the subject of attributes that are disparate and naturally exclusive of one another, is to use language to which no real meaning can be attached, and which certainly does not describe the Christ of the Gospels. But we are landed in this when we attempt to construe to our thought the fact of the Incarnation starting with metaphysical postulates, cedon was no solution of the problem, but it brought the controversy to an end for the time; and the Church acquiesced in a judgment which, in exalting the Divine at the expense of the Human, gradually widened the breach between the dogmatic and the historic Christ, lessening very seriously the influence of His Humanity on the life of the Church, and obscuring it from the view of men, except in so far as it was brought home to their minds by His suffering and death. "The God-Man of the Catholic Church," says a German historian, "is too prevailingly only God to be at the same time also Man. He is Man only to undergo the Passion. It is the holy Virgin that represents normal Humanity in its Spiritual Perfection."[1]

The Reformers accepted the Christology of the ancient Church. But with the revival of the evangelic faith there came a fresh realisation of the truth of our Lord's humanity and its supreme worth in the salvation He has procured for men; and new attempts were made on the old lines to formulate the doctrine of the Person of our Lord in a way that would rescue the human element from the Doketism that resulted from the old view. The two branches of the Protestant Church had each its own type of doctrine on this subject. Lutheranism, holding that the natural effect of the union of the Son of God with our nature was the communication to the latter of the Divine attributes of the former, saved itself from the charge of reducing the humanity to a mere semblance by maintaining that the exercise of these Divine attributes was in abeyance during the earthly life of Jesus, that they existed in Him only in a concealed or hidden form. Abandoning this unsatisfactory position, the later representatives of the Lutheran

[1] Schneckenburger, *Vergleichende Darstellung des Luth. u. Reform. Lehrbegriffs*, vol. ii. p. 229. His words are: "Der Katholische Gott-Mensch ist zu præponderirend nur Gott um zugleich wahrer Mensch zu sein. Er ist Mensch nur um die Passion zu dulden. Die normal geistig vollendete Menschheit repræsentirt die Heilige Jungfrau."

type of thought have maintained that the eternal Son of God laid aside the Divine attributes in becoming Man, so as to leave room for a genuine human consciousness and development. Hence we have the dogma of the Kenosis of the Son of God, which, propounded in the most extreme and most consistent form by Gess, asserts that in becoming Incarnate the Eternal Son of God denuded Himself of the essential qualities of His own nature and all that prevented Him becoming the subject of true human experiences. The criticism of this dogma has been accomplished in a way that has brought out its irreconcilableness with right reason by my predecessor, Dr. Bruce; and I think it has been amply shown by him, that however attractive the theory may be as the basis, in the hands of Gess, of a faithful representation of the Christ of the Gospels, the supposition of an act of "self emptying" on the part of the Second Person of the Trinity, that means the divesting Himself of those qualities that constitute His Divine Nature, is one that just views of God do not allow us to entertain.

The theology of the Reformed Church deals with the difficulty in another way. It accentuates more strongly than the Lutheran the disparity between the Divine and the Human, and holds in opposition to it that the Human cannot partake of the qualities of the Divine. The union that is implied in the Incarnation would thus seem to be an impossibility. But here it brings in its doctrine of a Double Life and dual consciousness of the Son of God. As the Second Person of the Trinity, the Son of God remains in the exercise of His Divine prerogatives, knowing and upholding all things. But He has another life, as the principle of the Person of the God-Man. In the Man Christ Jesus He limits Himself so as to make possible a genuine human life, and is truly united to the human nature by the Holy Spirit. He is wholly in the Humanity of Jesus according to its nature and at each stage of its development, but also wholly outside of it in the sphere in which He lives and acts as the Second Person of the Trinity.[1] This view has been lately revived and advocated by Canon Gore. "There is reason to believe," he says, "that the apostolic writers contemplate the continuance of the Divine and Kosmic functions of the Son of God through the Incarnation; that the state of humiliation within the sphere of His humanity must have been compatible with their exercise in another sphere, by the same Divine Person, of the fulness of the Divine Power. In other words, that the Son of God, even when He walked the earth, was actively engaged in ruling this world from a different centre, so to speak, that, while in the sphere of His humanity He was ignorant of many things, in another sphere He knew all things."[2] I do not, however, see that on this view we

---

[1] The Logos, as the Reformed theology has it, is *totus extra Christum et totus in Christo*: He is in heaven while a man. The truth expressed in this language is that the Redeeming Love of God is not lessened in God by its being the life of Christ, any more than a man's virtue is lessened by being communicated to another man. The Lutheran Christology maintains that the Logos is *totus in Christo*, and denies that it is *extra Christum* at all. Gess goes so far as to say that "the Logos became man only if He ceases to feel, to perceive, to act, except in the human nature which He animates" (*P. u. W.* iii. 315). This means, of course, the temporary extinction of His Divine self-consciousness. The truth that finds so imperfect an intellectual expression in the Lutheran system is that God is *wholly* revealed in Christ, that in Him we have very God, and not a God reduced to the measure of our capacities, or different from God as He is.

[2] Gore's *Dissertations*, the "Consciousness of our Lord in His mortal Life." Mr. Hutton, in his essay on "The Incarnation and Principles of Evidence," seems to suggest a similar view in the following words,—words which indicate also a thorough-going doctrine of Kenosis: "It seems to me the most presumptuous of all presumptuous assumptions to deny that the Son of God might have really become what He seemed to be, a finite being, a Jew of Jewish thoughts and prepossessions, and liable to all the intellectual errors which distinguished the world in which He lived. If there is an indestructible moral individuality which

can believe in a Divine Personality as the principle of the Personal life of Jesus Christ, since it is only outside of the latter and as extramundane, that this Divine Person is conceived as existing as He really is; or that we can affirm more of Christ, if this theory is true, than that He possessed in an extraordinary measure that Spirit of God that is the principle of every true human personality. And in that case the union of the Divine and the Human in His person is no more than the supreme instance of the union that is normal of every true Christian. And to this the Christology of the Reformed Church, it seems to me, inevitably comes.[1]

constitutes self, which is the same when wielding the largest powers and when it sits alone at the dark centre,—which, for anything I know, may even live under a double set of conditions at the same time,—I can see no metaphysical contradiction in an Incarnation" (*Essays*, vol. i. p. 242).

[1] Dorner has attempted the solution of the Christological problem in a way of his own. He regards the union of the natures as the result of a moral process. The incarnation is to be understood properly in an ethical sense, as the result of the Divine (the Personal Logos) gradually communicating Himself to the Human in the Person of Christ, as the man grew in moral receptivity. This theory implies a dual personality in Jesus till the union of the two natures was completed, and the logos entirely communicated Himself to the man. Conscious that, in this form, his doctrine was a revival of the error of Nestorius, Dorner in his latest work (*System of Christian Doctrine*) no longer maintains the separate personality of the logos, but, with Rothe, views the logos as a "principle" or factor of the Godhead. The real contribution of this theologian to Christology is the emphasis he places on the truth (which receives such prominence also in Rothe's construction of the doctrine of the Second Adam) that the union of the Divine and Human in the Person of Christ was a gradual process and proceeded from the Indwelling of God in the Man Christ Jesus, the fulness of the manifestation of God in Him keeping pace with His growth in personal holiness and love. The study of Christology, ancient and modern, is valuable for the fresh points of view for the understanding of the *religious* contents of the Person of Christ which it furnishes. The failure of theologians one and all to interpret *intellectually* the Person of Christ in the light of the special religious truth that in each case gives interest to their speculations, illustrates the inability of the human mind to deal with the metaphysics of the subject. It is plain that only such deter-

3. Whether, then, we think of the Pre-existent Christ as the Heavenly Man merely, or as the Second Person of the Trinity, bare Divinity and no more, we fail to account for the Christ of whom Paul speaks, in whom the Divine and the Human both co-exist and are brought home to our hearts in a way that defies explanation on any theory that views them as originally and antecedent to the Incarnation, distinct and opposite in nature in the way they are regarded in both the explanations that have been criticised. But a third view remains to be considered, that which represents Paul as teaching that Christ pre-existed, not as Man nor as God, but as God and Man in essential union. Denying that there is any such original antithesis between the two natures as ecclesiastical theology presupposes,—maintaining, on the contrary, the original and essential identity of the two,—certain Christian thinkers have held that Christ was from all eternity God-Man, at once Son of God and Son of Man, the Image of God and Revelation of Him to His creatures, and the Ideal or Archetypal Man in whose image the human race was made. The Incarnation was not then properly the assumption of human nature, for before creation itself Christ was Man and our Brother; it was the assumption of our flesh, and involved a change of state or condition merely, the laying aside of the Divine Form of His Humanity that He might partake of it in its flesh-and-blood form, so that under its conditions He might do and suffer what He could not while in the Form of God. The Incarnation, then, simply revealed the essential oneness of the Divine and the Human, and the relation that already existed between the Son of God and Mankind.

minations of Christological opinion as reflect the light that comes from the historic life and work of Christ can be regarded as expressions of Christian truth; and that all views must be set aside that fail to do this, or that reflect a light borrowed from outside speculation.

This understanding of the Eternal Nature of Christ has commended itself to speculative minds in all ages, and is widely held at the present day.[1] It is maintained not only by continental theologians of note, but by many in recent years in our own country. Readers of F. D. Maurice's works will remember the vitality of this belief in his theological thinking; and the late Dr. Dale advocated it not less strenuously, and insisted on the appreciation of the truth of Christ's Eternal Humanity and pre-existent relation to the Human race, as necessary to the understanding of the relation between God and man as set forth in the Scriptures.[2] This doctrine, indeed, belongs to the best days of Greek Theology, and was held by those who were most eager in doing justice to the unity of the Person of Christ. For if He was throughout all states the Son of God, one and unchanged, then the humanity He took to himself could be no new thing, but must have been already rooted in His Eternal Being. He must have been Man as well as God before He came into the world.

There is much in this view to commend it. It recognises the kinship between God and Man, and the essential correspondence between the Divine and human. It rebukes that false conception of what constitutes the greatness of God that makes some hesitate to see God in One who shares the frailties of human nature, and who is wanting in those Infinite attributes of the Godhead which they identify with His Glory. By emphasising the truth that Jesus Christ in His historic life is the manifestation of God, it exalts the moral and religious qualities by which He is known, the righteousness and love that appeal to our trust and love, and it proclaims the significance for the

---

[1] See Note on The Different Forms of this Theory of the Pre-existent God-Man.

[2] Edwards (*The God-Man*) seems also to hold this view. He speaks of the Logos as "Eternal Man," though he explains this as only "an idea of what the Logos Incarnate will be" (p. 18).

Eternal Life of God of the idea of human nature with the elements that make it up and as it is realised in Jesus of Nazareth.[1] At the same time I doubt whether, as formulated by theology, this doctrine of the Eternal God-Man can be accepted as a solution of the problem of the Person of our Lord. It is involved in the same difficulties as have been referred to in connection with the Lutheran and Reformed types of Christological doctrine. For the limitation of the Divine in the Man Christ Jesus has to be accounted for, as in these cases, and we are driven, in our attempt at explanation, either to the theory of Kenosis or that of the Dual consciousness. The religious truth to which this view seeks to give expression is of priceless moment, but the intellectual form in which it is expressed eludes our grasp, and the truth seems imperilled when we make our faith in it dependent on our apprehension of the form.

A special emphasis was given to this mode of conceiving the Person of Christ in the Christology of Apollinaris; and some reference may be made to his view, since he has been recently regarded as having reproduced more faithfully than any other the original Pauline thought. According to that great thinker, the Logos (word) or the Pneuma (spirit) was the pre-existent factor in the Person of the historic Christ, and took the place of the human pneuma or nous. This teaching was condemned because it followed, his opponents urged, that His Humanity was an imperfect thing, consisting only in His participation of the human body or material side of our nature, wanting in those higher elements of will and freedom that enter into our conception of a true humanity. The charge was well

[1] "All religious philosophy will admit that in God there is the Eternal Prototype of Humanity. All intelligent religious thinking must recognise in the Deity an eternal basis for the nature, the advent, the career, and ideal of mankind" (*The Christ of To-day*, by G. A. Gordon).

founded. He held, indeed, that the pneuma in Christ was in its very nature human as well as Divine; the flesh or natural physical man of the historic Christ was but the organ through which the Divine Spirit, essentially human in its nature, manifested itself. Still, it remained true that the humanity which He brought with Him into the world was, in its ideal character, its immunity from temptation, its natural incapacity for sin, a very different humanity from ours. Nor could He, as long as He was thus human only in His eternal nature, redeem from sin and death the humanity that is ours, or reconcile us to God. The Church saw that it was but a form of Doketism to say that the only thing Christ had in common with ordinary men was the flesh or material part of His humanity, and in rejecting such teaching it was guided by the instinct of truth.

At the same time, the general conception of the Eternal Humanity of the Son of God, and of Christ as predestined, in virtue of being in His pre-existent state human as well as Divine, to realise the union of God and man in the flesh, is a very attractive one; and the *language* at least of Apollinaris, in his advocacy of it, seems to answer strikingly to that of Paul. In his *History of Dogma*, Harnack has remarked on this. These are his words: "One cannot but express his astonishment that in Apollinaris speculation has returned to its first beginning, for this Christ is really the Christ of Paul, the heavenly Spirit-Being who assumed the flesh."[1] This judgment, however, seems to me to go too far in magnifying the resemblance between Apollinaris' doctrine and that of Paul. There are certain features common to both that tempt us to identify the one with the other, and we are not surprised to find in modern biographers of the life of Christ the influence of Apollinarism when they deal with the mystery of His Person.[2] It

---

[1] *Dogmen Geschichte*, vol. ii. p. 217 (note).
[2] The Kenotic Christology of Gess bears a strong resemblance to

accords with Paul's view of the identity of the Pre-existent Christ with the Christ Incarnate, to think of His Person as being, under both conditions, at once Human and Divine. And Apollinaris' theory seems to be echoed in Paul's language in reference to the transition from the Heavenly to the earthly state of being, suggesting, as that language to all appearance does, that it was not so much the assumption of another nature that took place in His Incarnation, as that of a lower form of the same nature, the assumption of the flesh, a distinction being implied between humanity as it existed at the roots of His own Person, and humanity as derived from us, destitute of the Divine pneuma, and simply flesh. The language Paul habitually uses in reference to the Person of Christ is psychological and moral rather than metaphysical. The contrast, according to him, is not so much between the Divine and the human, as between the Spirit, which is at once Divine and Human, and the flesh. And from this circumstance his language lends itself to the support of theories such as that of Apollinaris, which, going behind the historical in order to form a conception of the Pre-existent One, regard Him in that state as the Divine-human Pneuma, and the humanity He assumed as being only flesh that concealed the true inner personality of the Eternal God-Man.

But notwithstanding what has been said, the resemblance is more in appearance than in reality; and I am unable to regard the view of Apollinaris as warranted by the thought of Paul. The terms "Spirit" and "Flesh" are used by the apostle in a psychological sense to describe the Person of Christ from a religious point of view, and not to denote

---

Apollinarism. For according to him it was the Logos nature that took the place of the human soul in the body that was born of Mary; only (and here he differs from Apollinaris) it was the Logos nature depotentiated of all Divine attributes and reduced to a Receptivity for the Divine. See *Person u. Werk*, iii. p. 379, etc.

metaphysical entities. In His being Spirit, clothed in flesh, Christ, according to Paul, simply fulfilled the idea of our humanity, and was what we are all called to be, and what He makes us. And we seem unable to find in that which was the religious basis of His human personality a clue to the understanding of what He was in His own distinctive Being as Pre-existent and Eternal.

I confess I have little confidence in any speculation that has been formed on the subject, or in the power of the human mind to grapple successfully with the difficulties of it. It lies beyond our experience; all forms of speech about Christ as pre-incarnate must necessarily be figurative and imperfect. The references of Paul are incidental and insufficient to form a basis of theory. We are not to look for that exactness of definition in Paul's Christology which the conflict of later theologies developed. The age of definition was not yet. A love so intense, so all-absorbing, as the love of Christ that consumed the heart of the apostle, cares not to inquire about the nature of the Being that is loved.[1] The contemplation of Christ in His Risen Glory was enough for him. With this Glorified Man to love, to live and labour and die for, to follow now and to hope in for hereafter, he was indifferent alike to questions that related to His Human Birth and His Eternal pre-incarnate nature. It does not appear that he ever made the Incarnation the subject of reflection except in the one passage in Philippians that has been considered; and there, the difficulty that is felt by us as to how One, Divine in His pre-existent state, could become a Man and remain the same in His original Personal Life, does not seem to have occurred

---

[1] "As soon as we can give a reason for a feeling we are no longer under the spell of it; we appreciate, we weigh, we are free, at least in principle. . . . Love must always seem to us indivisible, insoluble, superior to all analysis, if it is to preserve that appearance of infinity, of something supernatural and miraculous, which makes its chief beauty" (Amiel, *Journal*, vol. ii. p. 21).

THE ETERNAL NATURE OF CHRIST 215

to him. It is the Resurrection rather than the Incarnation, I must repeat, that in Paul's view gives us the Christ with whom we have to do, and who is the object of a faith that has a definite content, who is known to us as at once the Man who is Spirit, the instrument of the Energy of the Holy God upon our souls, and the Son of God or perfect image of the Father.

It is to be observed, then, that the previous stages of Christ's Personality, His terrestrial and preterrestrial stages, are spoken of by the apostle only incidentally and in their contrast with His Present Life. His earthly state is represented as one of imperfection contrasted with His state as Exalted, for His real glory was concealed and obscured by the flesh; while, in relation to His pre-existent state, His life on earth is declared to have been a state of impoverishment and voluntary self-abasement for our sakes. No doubt what has always given to the Gospel Message its power to touch human hearts is that Christ, in being born into the world, is declared to have come from glory to dishonour for us men and for our salvation, and that He was aware of this humiliation. But wherein that humiliation consisted, and what the differentia was between His historic life on earth and His prior life in heaven, is a question that could only be answered were we able to tell what precisely is meant by the apostle's phrase, "He emptied Himself." It cannot be of "the Form of God," if we are to understand by "Form" not what is accidental but what is characteristic of God, which is essential to Him and inseparable from His nature, for of that the Pre-existent One could not denude Himself without ceasing to be God. Or, turning to the other clause in his remarkable statement, "He thought the being-on-an-equality-with-God was not, like booty, to be grasped at by Him,"—can we find here any clue to what is meant by the phrase "He emptied Himself"? Some answer in the affirmative, regarding the "equality with God" as a condition of glory and majesty that was the manifestation of the Divine nature, and which could be resigned for a time by His taking the form of a servant.[1] But against this there is, as I have pointed out, much to be said in favour of the view that we are not to understand "the being equal with God" as the actual possession of the Pre-incarnate Christ, but as a glory in prospect, that was *destined* to be His; and we can scarcely speak in literal truth of one "emptying" himself of an object that is not yet his own. But if any meaning at all is to be attached to the phrase "He emptied Himself," it is in this clause we are to find it, in connection with what is said in what immediately follows about His taking the "form of a servant." By this term, however, we are to understand, I think, not a surrender of metaphysical attributes or prerogatives, but a moral act of self-abnegation in which He declined to seek that predestined glory to be Lord of all in a way that would be easy to Himself or that would have indicated a spirit impatient to grasp its own, preferring to assume the form of a servant that He might win it by humble obedience to the Will of God and loving service of His brethren. On this view there is no hint of the metaphysical change involved in passing from the one state to the other. We have the simple statement that there lay at the root of it a sublime act of self-renunciation that involved all the issues of an earthly history, such as He passed through.[2]

[1] Whether the τὸ εἶναι ἴσα Θεῷ can be understood in this sense as a something separable from Deity is of course open to dispute. Gess explains it as something belonging to the inner nature of Christ, without which He would cease to be Divine. He, with the majority of commentators, regards the "Form of God" as that of which He "emptied Himself" (*Per. u. Werk*, vol. ii. p. 313).

[2] This passage (Phil. ii. 6-8) has no real bearing on the metaphysical questions that have been raised regarding the Kenosis of the Son of God. There is a disposition among later exegetes to admit this. Thus Haupt: "All those questions that come up in the treatment

And if we are unable to form any definite conception of the pre-existent state of Christ so as to state the difference between it and His earthly one, we are as little able to say what relation it bore to His state in Glory. If we know Him now as the Son of God and the embodiment of the power of the Divine Spirit, we believe that He was never less than this; and that if we can speak of His pre-existence at all, we are warranted in holding that the Spirit and Divine Sonship that now characterise Him and that shine through His life express the truth of His eternal pre-existent nature.[1] But, plainly, it is through the humanity now Exalted in His person that these terms have meaning for us; and His present possession of a human nature, with the concrete experience of a human life and history that fell to Him as an Individual Man, has not only added to the fulness of His own being, making Him more than He was before, it has also made Him to us the object of positive knowledge, which He never could have been had He not thus been revealed. For the ideas of Spirit and Sonship, however true they may be of the Eternal Christ, are no more than words to us till they receive meaning by being realised in a Man whose influence upon us is

---

of the dogmatic doctrine of the Kenosis are entirely foreign to the connection of these words. How the earthly existence of Jesus is related to the essential attributes of the Godhead is a matter that does not concern the apostle here. The question here is regarding the contrast between two different forms of life" (*Der Philip. Brief,* p. 82). The one truth regarding the eternal nature of Christ, as discovered in His willingness to pass from the one form of life to the other, is the truth of His self-sacrificing love.

[1] The words of Clement of Rome (πρὸς Κορίνθ. B.) are often quoted as representing most accurately the thought of Paul regarding the pre-existent Christ, ὁ Κύριος ὁ σώσας ἡμᾶς ὢν μὲν τὸ πρῶτον πνεῦμα, ἐγένετο σάρξ (ix. 5), "the Lord, who saved us, being first Spirit, became flesh." The same idea occurs in another passage (xiv. 2) of this most interesting document, which Lightfoot speaks of as the earliest Christian homily extant. It is worthy of mention, also, that in "The Shepherd of Hermas" Christ is more than once referred to as the "Spirit" (S. ix. 1).

recognised as that of the Spirit of God, and whose human Goodness is perceived to be that of God Himself. The difference of metaphysical being between Christ and all others must be acknowledged. But it is in virtue of what He became through the participation of our Humanity and through His Exaltation as Man, victorious over sin and death, that He is the object of our religious faith and love, that He is to us the vehicle of the Spirit of God and the Mirror in whom God's face is seen, that His Person, in short, is invested with the unspeakable importance it possesses for the moral and religious life of the Race.

On the metaphysical or speculative side, then, there is a limit to our understanding of the Person of Christ. On the ethical side, He stands clearly known to us as the revelation of the life of God; but we are baffled when we attempt to penetrate the mystery of that life, and to explain the nature of its Premundane existence and its Transcendent relation to God. What more can we say about it than what St. Paul says in that passage that has engaged our attention, that it is love, love that seeks not its own glory but the good of man, the fountain and original of that love that is seen in the life and work of the historical Christ. Little profit is to be got from the attempt to explain the intellectual mystery by the application to it of our theoretic conceptions of the Divine as differentiated from the human. The Divine is intelligible to us only as the Principle or Causality of that which is highest and most perfect in our notion of the human. And Christ is recognised by us as the union of the two, because He is the producing cause in us, and in all who surrender themselves to Him, of that life of righteousness and love in which we reach the perfection for which we were made. The truth of our Lord's Divinity must rest, as we have seen in this review of Paul's teaching, on the experience that testifies to the Divine life that proceeds from Him.

A distinction is made by theologians between truths that are of primary and others that are of secondary importance. And in regard to the Doctrine of Christ, it has been contended that to the former class belong those truths that express the experiences formed in the life of faith upon Him, while to the latter we must refer those truths that relate to His pre-existence, as being speculative in their nature and unverifiable in experience. There is much to be said for this contention. For the metaphysical distinction between Christ and all others is a mystery that lies beyond our apprehension, except as a fact, and belongs plainly to a different order of truths from those that set forth what He is to us in the experience of the life of faith. These appeal to us with an authority that commands assent. Truth that is in its nature theoretical, whose claim to be accepted rests on its being the presupposition or implicate of truth that shines in its own light, stands on a different footing from truth that is practical in its nature and is borne witness to by the facts of the life of God in our souls. There is a place for the former in the scheme of truth, but it is not that place of pre-eminence which is due to the latter alone. And if this be so, then our faith in the Divinity of Christ is based, not so much on isolated passages in the apostle's writings that teach His Pre-existence and His transcendental relations to God and the universe, as on that practical experience of the Supremacy and All-sufficiency of Christ for the wants of the higher life of man, that finds abundant expression in the Epistles and that forms the burden of the apostolic testimony. The most convincing part of the evidence is by no means that on which there has been a general disposition to place the chief importance—I mean those texts that point to a divinity understood in the metaphysical sense. The Divinity of Christ in the apostolic writings is a truth on which the soul rests from the experience of His Divine Power, and the satisfying character of the Revelation of God that is conveyed in His Person and character. It is defined in terms that are supplied by the experience of the new life of which He is the author. It is the soul's confession of the Supremacy of its Lord in the region of the moral and spiritual life. And inasmuch as there is not a page of the apostle's writings in which this sense of the supreme significance of Christ for the true life of man does not break out in words of affection, trust, devotion, worship, it is a truth that does not depend on single passages, but as an inseparable element in Christian conviction, it is borne witness to in every page of his Epistles. Dr. Dale, a profound student of Paul, truly remarks that the least impressive and conclusive proofs of the Divinity of our Lord are those in which it is definitely asserted. Comparing the latter to the sparkling crystals that appear in the sand after the tide has receded, "these are not," he says, "the strongest, though they may be the most apparent, proofs that the sea is salt; the salt is present in solution in every bucket of sea-water. And so the truth of our Lord's Divinity is present in solution in whole pages of the Epistles, from which not a single text could be quoted that explicitly declares it. It is present in the passionate and unmeasured love and devotion with which the apostles regard our Lord; it is present in their exulting faith in Him; it is present in their profound belief that the very springs of their higher life are in Christ, and that only as they are one with Christ can they hope for righteousness in this world, or for glory in the next.[1]

[1] *Christian Doctrine*, p. 87.

VII

THE CHRIST OF HISTORY AND THE PAULINE INTERPRETATION

LECTURE VII

THE CHRIST OF HISTORY AND THE PAULINE INTERPRETATION

WE have traced in past lectures the main outlines of that conception of Christ that we owe under God to the Christian genius of Paul, and that recognises in so striking a way the Supreme Function of Christ in relation to the moral and religious life of Man. It is based, as we have seen, on the apostle's own personal experience of the power of the Exalted Christ. It is an interpretation of the Person and work of our Lord in the light of the impressions of His Risen Glory. But now we turn to consider how far this magnificent conception agrees with the picture that we have in the pages of the Synoptic Gospels. As I have had occasion to remark, the picture of the historical Christ is, with Paul, in the background. It is of secondary importance, and is seldom referred to by him. The knowledge that possessed saving power for him began with the impressions he received from Christ as Glorified, and was derived from the experience of His benefits; and these benefits he did not regard Christ as qualified to bestow till He had died and risen again. All that preceded His Death in the history of Jesus lay for the apostle in the shade, and contributed little to the conception of the Saviour that was so great a power over his life. But we cannot help asking, In what relation does this Christ of faith and of Christian experience stand to the Jesus of history? Is it in full agreement with the revelation of Him that is given in the words and acts of His historic life? Outwardly, the differences between the two pictures are great; and on a surface view of the matter the one may appear to be irreconcilable with the other. Exception has often been taken to the legitimacy of Paul's representation. The feeling of an antagonism between the two, and of dissatisfaction with the prominence of the Pauline doctrine in the thought of the Church, has found utterance in the cry frequently raised, "not Paul, but Christ"; and the plea, in itself a reasonable one, on behalf of a "return to Christ," means, on the lips at least of some, the entire repudiation of the Pauline Christology, as being a corrupt form of the original doctrine. We can scarcely, then, close our review of the subject without some consideration of the grounds on which the validity of Paul's interpretation of Christ has been questioned, as well as of the grounds on which a different Christology (drawn, in contrast to that of Paul, from the facts of history) is contended for, in preference to his, by many who are one with us in the acknowledgment of Christ as Lord and Master.

One fundamental objection taken to the truth of Paul's conception is that it vastly exaggerates the real significance of the Person of Christ. While, it is said, in the synoptic accounts, Jesus makes little or no reference to Himself, puts forth no claim of personal supremacy, but places the great truths of the Kingdom of God and the Divine Fatherhood and human duty in the foreground, in the Pauline teaching the Person of Christ becomes all in all.

Our first point of inquiry, then, is this, Does Paul assert of the Exalted Christ what is inconsistent with what Jesus claimed for Himself, and what is out of harmony with the facts of His Personal history? Or is there in Christ's recorded thought about Himself that which may be regarded as the germ of the more developed teaching of the apostle? And does the admitted contrast between Christ's own thought of Himself and the circumstances of limitation and obscurity in which He was found in the days of His flesh not lead us to expect, that when death has put the finishing touch on His life-work and disclosed the Divine purpose of His Mission, He will stand forth as He did to the eye of the apostle, clothed with religious functions that exhibit the close relation which He holds to the higher life of man? This, I believe, will be felt to be the case when full justice is done to the picture of the historic Christ in the Gospels.

There is of course a question of criticism behind the settlement of this question. Are the records reliable? Did they not, it may be urged, receive their present form at a time when the higher views of the Person of Christ originating with Paul had already indoctrinated the mind of the Church, and unconsciously influenced those who handled the tradition of the life of Christ? and if so, are we not compelled to regard much that is contained in these Gospels not as pure fact, but rather as fact and doctrinal idea as well,—fact after passing through minds that were already filled with the most exalted conception of the Master, and could not help leaving the impress of that conception on the recorded story? There is much that may with great plausibility be said to this effect, much that cannot be altogether disproved. We find that the Gospels do bear the marks of the individuality of their authors. Traces are discoverable of the influence of dogmatic bias on their composition; and there is nothing *à priori* against the possibility that the Pauline bias may have added to the original Picture touches borrowed from the dogmatic ideal. But that this tendency operated to any considerable extent is exceedingly doubtful. For while Paul's views on the free grace of God and the universal destination of the Gospel quickly gained ground and prevailed, there is no evidence that his Christology made any deep impression at the time, or that it was in favour in those circles from which the Gospels in their present form emanated. That the value of the record as a source of historic truth has been impaired to any extent by theological bias proceeding from the school of Paul, is what scarcely anyone will admit who feels the power of the Life depicted in the Gospels. The harmony of the character of Christ as there delineated, the intermingling of the Divine and human in such a way that "the lowly and human never degrade Him in our eyes, nor His Power and Greatness remove Him out of our sympathies and understanding," is inconsistent with the supposition. That such a picture was or could have been the growth of unconscious theologising is far more incredible than that it is what it professes to be, the record of a sublime reality.[1]

No documents have been subjected to a more unfettered criticism than these Gospels, and to no part of them has a more thorough investigation been directed than to that which relates to the Messianic consciousness, as it has been called, or the conception Christ entertained of Himself and His personal relation to God and man. Most students of the Gospels are agreed that He did claim to be the Messiah, and that His consciousness of Messiahship was rooted in His knowledge of Himself. That He knew Himself to be the Son of God, and inspired with the filial spirit toward God, is beyond all question. Equally beyond question is it that He was conscious that He contained in His own Person the principle of salvation for mankind, and that He regarded it as His mission to bring men into that same relation to God and to one another that was embodied in His own life,—to kindle in them that same spirit

---

[1] "I esteem the Gospels to be thoroughly genuine, for there shines forth from them the reflected splendour of a Divinity, proceeding from the Person of Jesus Christ, of so Divine a kind as only the Divine could ever have manifested on earth" (Goethe).

of trust in and obedience to their Heavenly Father, and of active love to mankind, that was the source of His own blessedness. This was the task of His Messiahship. If He, in accomplishing it, did not at the first plant Himself in the foreground of their thoughts as the object of men's faith, but rather held before their minds the great truths of pure and spiritual religion, there was, as has often been pointed out, good reason for His doing so. The ideas of men at the time were so carnal that the premature disclosure of His Messiahship, before their minds could welcome the religious Good that answered to the true idea of the Messianic salvation, would only have precipitated the crisis that He was anxious as long as possible to avoid.

The reticence of Christ about Himself is indeed remarkable. He told the world nothing, and His disciples exceedingly little,—indeed, so far as the Synoptists report, not a syllable,—of a pre-human life. He made no personal pretensions; He demeaned Himself as the servant of all, and shrank from all personal recognition or compliment. In His teaching He pointed men always to the Father, and refused any allegiance to Himself that did not proceed from loyalty to God. This reserve—this modesty and absence of everything akin to a spirit of egotism, this unfeigned humility—is one of the most beautiful traits in the character of Christ, and not only proved His fitness to be the Sovereign of souls, but marked Him out as the Channel of the highest spiritual communications. For if God is to speak to the world, the fulness and clearness of His message must be in proportion to the humility and self-renunciation of the messenger.[1] But on the other hand, Christ does not speak as a mere prophet. He used language that no one who was a prophet and

---

[1] This point is well brought out by Selby in his *Ministry of the Lord Jesus*, chap. iii.

nothing more could have used. He identified His Person with the message He delivered. He required of men not only belief in the truth of the doctrine, but trust in Himself, loyalty to His own Person. To give up all for the Truth was to give it up for Him; to give it up for Him was to renounce it for the Truth. He did not, like Buddha and other teachers, place the truth above Himself, or bid men take His words to heart and forget about Himself, the speaker. "Jesus knows no more sacred task," says Herrmann, "than to point men to His own Person."[1]

This is the striking fact that meets us when we try to understand Christ's thought about Himself. It points to His having the consciousness of a life that was united to God as no other human life was, in consequence of which He was personally one with the truth He revealed, and the greatness of the truth was the greatness of the Person revealing it. Out of this consciousness He spoke as one who stood in a central relation to mankind, that made their attitude to Him all decisive for their character and destiny. He declared Himself to be the Judge of all. He spoke of men as passing judgment on themselves according as they gave their personal service to, or withheld it from, Him. These claims betrayed a consciousness of oneness with God, an identity of will, mind, purpose with Him; so that while entirely destitute of personal pretensions in the ordinary sense of the word, while the humblest and meekest of men, and subject to the laws of human nature, He was moved at times to adopt a style of self-assertion that no other ever ventured to use. He placed Himself before men's minds as the object of religious trust and obedience, as if He, being the personal embodiment of the truth of human character as well as of the Holiness and Love of God, were more than all the words

[1] *Communion with God*, p. 76.

He spoke, and as if the following and confessing of Him exhausted the whole duty of men to God and to one another.[1]

When we have regard to this element in the Messianic consciousness of Christ, we see that His thought about Himself and Paul's thought of Him are not so far apart as some would have it—that they are indeed in fundamental agreement. If in his Epistles Paul attaches an extraordinary importance to the Person of Christ and to the understanding of what He is, he is simply echoing Christ's own estimate of Himself. As we have seen, it is through the experience of the Risen Christ on his own inner life that the apostle arrived at the understanding of what Christ personally is; and an interpretation of Christ thus arrived at may well embrace elements of truth that were not present to the consciousness of the Person Himself who is thus interpreted. It is no reason for discounting the worth of any aspect of truth which we owe to the apostle, that Christ Himself, as far as appears from the record, did not teach it. It is surely a pointless remark of Cone, in his book on the *Gospel and its Interpretations*, to say that "the Great Teacher of the synoptic tradition would certainly not have recognised Himself in the 'Second Adam.'" Even though it were so, it would prove nothing against the validity of the conception the term expresses, or its suitableness to set forth the truth of Christ's qualification to be the power in us of a new manhood. The view has indeed been held by many that Christ's favourite designation of Himself, "the Son of Man," is an exact equivalent of the Pauline term "the Second Adam," and that in so speaking of Himself Christ had present to

---

[1] The charge of egotism has been brought against Christ's doctrine. But the real question, as Abbot in his *The Spirit on the Waters* has pointed out, is, Was Christ's judgment of Himself true? Did Jesus possess the power to forgive sins, to give rest and peace to weary humanity? "If He did, how could He do otherwise than call the world to accept what He had to give?" (p. 209).

His mind the same idea of His universal significance, as the Pattern Man and Beginner of a new Humanity, that the apostle expresses by the term that he borrowed from the Jewish schools of theology. "Can one," exclaims Gess, "more happily interpret Christ's thought of Himself as the Son of Man than is done by Paul in the contrast he draws between the First and Second Adam?"[1] Singularly enough, the title "Son of Man" that was so often on Christ's lips dropped very early out of the public teaching of the Church. It occurs only once in the New Testament outside of the Gospels (Acts vii. 56). Paul seems to have been entirely ignorant of it, "Son of God" and "Son of David" being the only Messianic titles known to him besides that to which he himself gave currency, the "Second Adam." The oldest Christian literature that we have, the writings of the Apostolic Fathers, make no mention of it. It first occurs in the writings of Marcion and of the obscure Gnostic sect of the Ophites. These striking facts leave room for speculation as to the origin of this Messianic title, the "Son of Man"; and more, perhaps, has been written on the subject than about any other point in N. T. theology.[2]

[1] *Christi Person u. Werk*, ii. 368.
[2] Lietzmann (*Der Menschensohn, ein Beitrag zur N. T. Theologie*, 1896) goes so far as to hold that, as a Messianic title, it was imported into the Gospels by Greek translators influenced by the Pauline idea of the "Second Adam," and that as used by Christ Himself the word meant just what it means in the Aramaic, "Man." It is undeniable, however, that in Christ's mouth the word had a Messianic significance, at least in Mark xiv. 62. There the reference plainly is to the passage in Daniel vii. While the prophet there, in speaking of "one coming in the clouds of heaven like unto the Son of Man" has in his eye the *People* of Israel and its exaltation over the other nations, Jesus applies this prophecy to Himself personally, and thereby makes the strongest possible claim to Messiahship. In His answer to the High Priest He virtually says, "I am He of whom it holds true that God gives Him power and honour and dominion so that all nations and peoples and tongues shall serve Him: His Rule is everlasting and His kingdom shall have no end."

It cannot, however, be said that there is as yet any agreement among scholars regarding it. The very meaning of the title "Son of Man" is still under discussion among students of the Gospels, and the greatest variety of opinion prevails regarding it. On that account I am unwilling to make much of it as a point of contact between the Christ of the Gospels and the Christ of Paul, although I think there can be little doubt that the history of the one phrase has had an influence on that of the other, and that this points to a belief that they mean substantially the same thing.

On the other hand, there is no doubt that in the emphasis Paul places on the Divine Sonship of Christ he reproduces the Lord's own judgment of Himself. The thought that He was the Son of God was indeed the secret of His own heart, being seldom divulged, and for the most part left to men to find out for themselves who had experience of what He was and could do for them.[1] To awaken the life of Sonship in men and to evoke faith in Himself as the Son of God and as able to make them sons of God too, was the very object of His mission. In viewing salvation as consisting in Sonship derived from Christ, the Son of God and the Incarnation of the Filial Spirit, Paul was simply faithful to the teaching of his Master. Again, from his experience of the Spirit's power that came from Christ, Paul apprehended Him as the embodied Spirit of God. And herein, too, He is in full agreement with the representation of the Gospels. It is not only that the historian refers the endowment of Jesus to the Spirit;[2] Christ knows Himself to be dwelt in by the Spirit of God, and His life to be under His continual inspiration.[3] And when we look at that life as set before us in the Gospels,

---

[1] "He waited till He could pluck the discovery of His Sonship as ripe fruit from the lips and from the hearts of those who had gone in and out with Him, and had been the immediate witnesses of His working from the beginning" (*Über den Christl. Glaub. von Jess.*, 1892, p. 73).

[2] Luke iii. 21, 22.   [3] Luke iv. 18; Matt. xii. 28.

and think of the goodness it breathes, its invincible strength, its unwearied self-sacrificing pursuit of the highest ends, its universal sympathies and regards,—when we think of the wonderful union it exhibited of a love to man and a faith in man's redemption that never failed, with a trust in God and assurance of His presence and help that no disaster, trial, or disappointment could shake,—the impression we receive is, that here is a Man who is different from all others in that the Power of the Spirit of God inspires and directs every movement of His soul, is the active principle of His inner life and personality. In apprehending the Exalted Christ as the Man of the Spirit, Paul describes Him not only as He is to experience, but as the known facts of His history reveal Him to us.

If in certain respects Paul's interpretation goes beyond Christ's own thought of Himself, or the thought that the study of His life on earth leads us to form, and includes elements of truth, aspects of His Glory that are peculiar to the apostle's experience, the worth of these is not lessened by this circumstance, since in the estimate Christ formed and encouraged others to form of Himself, there is a judgment of His Supreme place in relation to the spiritual life of men that warrants us in expecting statements of what He is in human experience that surpass what is said of Him as the Christ of history. If He had spoken of Himself as a prophet or preacher of God's truth merely, Paul's conception of Him would have to be regarded as a misinterpretation. But as we have seen, the language of Jesus shows that He regarded Himself as the Revealer of God, and the very Truth of human life and character. And this is the idea of Him that lies at the root of Paul's thinking, that finds expression in the language dictated by human experience in his highest ascriptions of worth to His Exalted Lord.

Is Paul's interpretation of the Death of Christ warranted,

it may now be asked, by anything contained in the Lord's own teaching? According to the apostle, as we have seen, the event on Calvary was a Divine appointment, by which His gracious purpose towards sinful men was accomplished, and salvation for them provided. To view the death of Christ in this light is manifestly to separate it from the death of every other, and to ascribe to it a worth that can be claimed for no other. It had proved itself a power of salvation in this sense in the experience of Paul; and the question naturally occurs, Does Christ in His teaching give any hint that His act in dying was to have this saving virtue—was to be, from the highest point of view, an act of grace on God's part, by which He was to restore the sinful race to fellowship with Himself? We cannot of course expect the doctrine of the saving effects of Christ's suffering and death to be set forth in His own teaching in the same terms that we find it in Paul's; for here again the remark applies, that the apostle's experience of what Christ and His death were must necessarily include elements that were not in Christ's own thought—must include in it reflections on its relation to facts of his inner life that go beyond the vision of Christ; nor are we to pass judgment on the findings of the servant on this subject because they are not confirmed by express words of the Master.

The real question is, Have we any words that show that Christ's own attitude towards His death was the same as that which finds elaborate expression in Paul's writings —that He conceived of it as destined in the providence of God to issue in the redemption of men from sin and death? His reticence on this subject, too, is indeed remarkable; but there is no doubt that the idea was present to His mind that great moral and religious consequences were to follow from His death, and that it lay in the scope of His mission as Messiah, who had come to bring salvation to men, that

He should die. We have only two words recorded by the Synoptists in which this conviction finds expression: that in which He speaks of Himself as dying to ratify and establish the new covenant,[1] in which forgiveness of sin was a principal benefit, and that in which He declares the Son of Man was come to "give His life a ransom for many."[2] We cannot do justice to these words unless we take them in the sense in which the death of Christ is understood by all the writers of the New Testament, who uniformly refer to it as the Divinely arranged means for the execution of a Divine purpose, which contemplated man's recovery from sin and death. And just as little can we account for the universal understanding in the Apostolic Church of the issues of Christ's death, and of the ends served by it, unless we believe that Christ Himself gave His sanction to that view in words that He spoke; and that we have in the utterances I have quoted a true record of what He said. On what principles we are to explain the connection between the death of Christ and the effects of it on man's salvation is a matter on which we have little in Christ's express teaching to guide us; but neither does it furnish, as it seems to me, ground for calling in question the legitimacy of the apostle's reasonings on that aspect of the subject, or for disproving their truth. On this one essential point they are agreed: that the death accomplished at Jerusalem, while brought about by the sin of men, was the means intended by God to work out a gracious purpose of redemption. The emphasis placed by Paul on the Cross as the achievement of salvation is warranted by the importance attached by Christ Himself to His death as an integral part of His mission to save men, and as the condition of the success of that mission.

But the ground of complaint that the modern mind has against Paul and his interpretation of the Historic

[1] Matt. xxvi. 28.   [2] Matt. xx. 28.

Christ appears just at this point. It is objected that his conception of Christ takes account only of His death and resurrection, and ignores the bearing on our salvation of all the activities of His earthly ministry. And that, it may be argued, can be no proper or adequate interpretation of Him that singles out one fact in the history, and passes over, as of no worth for forming a judgment on the whole, the lessons that are to be learnt from the record of those deeds and words in which one personality reveals itself to others. Paul, indeed, it may be said, had a direct knowledge of Christ in His Exalted state, and his interest was naturally concentrated on the impressions that flowed from his immediate fellowship with the Living and Glorified One. Connecting these impressions with their source (the once crucified but now Risen Saviour), he perceived the influence of the death that Jesus died in qualifying Him to be the Source of them, and to be the Author of the moral and religious benefits which the apostle enjoyed: having this understanding of the Cross in its relation to the Heavenly Christ, he did not require to go beyond that one event which closed the earthly history. Hence his silence about the Preceding Life, and his apparent indifference to its lessons. We, however, cannot occupy that ground. We have no such knowledge of Christ as Paul had, to whom He was immediately revealed in His Perfected state as Exalted. In that capacity He is to us unrevealed. For a reliable conception of His worth for us we are thrown back on history—on the knowledge to be gathered from the Gospels. This points to a doctrine of Christ that we are to form for ourselves from a study of His Life and words, for which it may be claimed not only that it is more true to fact, and more real to us, —its standpoint being the Historical and not the Exalted Christ,—but also that it does fuller justice to the riches of Christ's Person, because it draws not from one event, but from the entire revelation that we have in His Life.

What I have said represents fairly enough, I think, the view of very many at the present day; and the questions that are raised by this attitude of mind are very serious and demand consideration. That there is a one-sidedness about the Pauline conception, from the circumstance alluded to, is to be granted. One who believed, as Paul did, that the real significance of Christ for man's salvation belongs to His Heavenly and not to His earthly life, and who, in consequence, goes back on what was transacted in those brief years of the Lord's life on earth only in so far as they bore on the transcendent virtue of His present life for us, must needs omit much that is of the highest importance for us to include in our Picture of Christ. Paul tells us nothing of the revelation of God which we have in the human life of Christ, or of what is to be learnt of the Divine character from all those acts of mercy and grace and sympathy with men in their various circumstances of need, in which the heart of Jesus was displayed.[1] He passes over the work of the Prophet of Nazareth. The unrivalled supremacy of Christ as a Teacher and a Revealer of truths bearing on human conduct, that command conviction and dispel doubt and ignorance regarding human life in its higher aspects and relations, finds no place in that Image of Him that we owe to the apostle. He calls Christ indeed the "wisdom of God,"[2] but he does not thereby mean to exalt the teachings about life and duty that came from His lips and that are

---

[1] According to Paul, the Incarnation is a humiliation to Christ, and the glory of His Personality is hid and concealed, if not curtailed, by His earthly limitations; it is not till He has died and is Risen again that He is revealed in His proper nature. This is not the view of the Apostle John. He regards the Incarnation as the continuous unveiling of the Divine glory of Christ. The glory of His love and goodness is apparent all through His earthly Life. The resurrection is but the consummation of it. Paul's point of view naturally led him to undervalue the instruction to be derived from the Life.

[2] 1 Cor. i. 18–25.

so precious to us, but rather to signalise the truth of the Divine character and purpose which we learn from the death of Christ in its redemptive aspect, and the disclosure of the plan of God for men's salvation that is made to us in the mission and work of Christ as a whole. That there are omissions in Paul's representation of Christ, when we look at it as the portrait of His Personality, is evident. Christ is greater than all the interpretations of Him, and Paul's is but one of these. There is more truth to be learnt from the study of His Person and work than men have yet been able to spell out. But while all this is granted, it must be denied that there is any such inconsistency between the historic Christ and the Christ of faith and experience as some allege, and I must demur to the position that there is such a sufficiency in the revelation of truth contained in the Christ of the Gospels as to make us independent of that contained in the Christ set forth in the Epistles. Each is necessary to the understanding and appreciation of the other. And while it is true that for us the Exalted Christ can be reached only through the Historical, and is a Power over our lives in the measure in which our thought of Him and of His actual relations to us is enriched with the memories of His earthly life,[1] it is equally true that the history as a whole, and His death in particular, must be conceived from the point of view of the apostle who exhibits to us the Exalted Christ as the key to the understanding of the History, if our faith in Him is to be the faith of the apostle, that is, if Christ is to be to us the Power of God for our redemption from sin and death.

Let us at this point go back for a minute to the past and watch the evolution of Christian thought on this subject, that we may see more clearly how the matter stands.

[1] "We need again and again to go back to the consideration of the historical Jesus" (Gore, Bampton Lectures, 1891, p. 144).

It is to be borne in mind that alongside of the faith in the Heavenly Christ, which was everything to Paul, and which, undoubtedly, tends to become separated from its roots in history and experience, and to harden into a dogmatic conception, there was from the beginning at work in the Church an instinct that clung to the historic tradition of the Man of Galilee who in the flesh had revealed God to men. The Gospel of John is regarded by many as having been called forth by that feeling that craved more in the Church's Lord than a Christ who had been exalted to perform redemptive functions, and whose human personality was in danger of being lost sight of in the Divine activities of His Heavenly Life. The Gospel of John is an interpretation as well as a narrative of the Historic Christ; but, unlike that of Paul, which limits itself to the single event of Christ's death, it covers the whole life, and finds the truth it is written to enforce illustrated in historic event and spoken word from the beginning to the end of His earthly career; and this Gospel is of priceless value to the Church, because it takes us back from the Risen Christ to the Historical, and sets before us the manifestation in the Flesh of the Son of God, of that Divine Life which is His Gift to His people. But it cannot be denied that, after all, the view of the Jesus of History it presents is a partial one, for its didactic purpose is to exhibit His Personal glory as the Son of God and the Revealer of the Divine nature, and it selects only such material from His Life as can be made to contribute to the exposition of that idea. Then came the Synoptic Gospels, embodying the tradition of the Life in all its memorable features. The doctrinal bias of the writers is here reduced to a minimum; and the Church has always accepted these histories as presenting a faithful Picture of the Son of Man as He revealed Himself in His goodness and truth in the varying situations of a human life. The patristic period followed, characterised by the speculative discussions regarding the Person of Christ into which the Church was forced in its controversy with error. From these discussions it came forth triumphant, but at a cost; for while the dogma in which it expressed its conviction of the union of Humanity and Divinity in the Person of its Lord grew in definiteness and sharpness of outline, the historic Figure in which the Divine and Human had been in fact so beautifully harmonised receded into the background. The theological definition of Christ contained in the formularies of the Church hid from men's minds the real human Christ who had in His life brought God near to man and raised man up to God.[1] But definitions cannot satisfy the hunger of the soul; and the religious life of men throughout the ages when the Gospels were almost unknown connected itself less with the creed of orthodoxy that had removed Christ so far from human feeling and made Him as inaccessible as God the Father was, than with the worship of the Virgin. To her had been transferred that ideal of a pure and pitiful sympathy with sinning men that had in fact been realised in Jesus;[2] and she was in consequence to many an erring soul the Saviour and Helper it needed. Enthusiasm for Mary, which was at least the worship of pure love, helped no doubt to vitalise the religion of the Middle Ages. But here and there a truer vision came to men, a vision of Christ not as the stern Judge of the world, but as He had been beheld of old in His humility and grace in the pathways of a human life. It was the Image of the Jesus of the Gospels, full of compassion for miserable men, living only to do them good, and finding

[1] See Note A, where Dorner's striking testimony to this is given.
[2] The worship of the Mass must have kept alive the memory of the crucified Christ in the Mediæval Church, and was one point of contact between the worshipper and the historical Christ. See *The Nicene Theology*, by H. M. Scott, D.D., p. 220 (note).

His joy in poverty and loss for their sakes, that touched the heart of Francis of Assisi, inspiring in him and his followers a life fashioned even to the letter to that of Jesus, a life which made men feel that the Son of Man was once more present in the world to heal and bless. Again, it was the Image of the Man of Sorrows, perfected by the discipline of the Cross into patience and untroubled peace, that rose on the vision of Thomas à Kempis and burnt itself into his soul. The power that the words of that old monk still possess to comfort the sad and sorrowful is due to the vividness with which he reproduces before the mind's eye the Jesus who had hung on the ignominious Cross, and the skill with which he transfers from the Gospels and lodges in the heart that Image of patient, uncomplaining, all-enduring sorrow.[1] And surely it is a marvellous tribute to the universal power of the Figure depicted in the Gospels that the men who have been raised up from time to time to reform religious life, and who have represented in each case the spirit and genius of the age in which they lived, have always found in it some new meaning, that which most swayed their hearts and the hearts of their contemporaries, that which best met their peculiar needs and fulfilled their loftiest ideals.

When the Reformation came, a crisis had arisen in the history of religion similar to that in Paul's day; and the Christ whom the apostle had preached once more spoke to men. It is Christ the Exalted Head and Lord, the Vanquisher of sin and guilt, the Mediator of God's gracious love to mankind, whom the Reformers saw and proclaimed. Then, and as often since as He has been held up to faith,

---

[1] Readers of George Eliot will recall the striking scene in the *Mill on the Floss* in which Maggie Tulliver, in trouble of mind, happens to open the pages of the *Imitatio Christi*, and as she reads catches a vision of the "Invisible Teacher, the Pattern of Sorrow, the Source of all Strength," that reveals to her the secret of life, and brings to her peace of soul.

this Christ has proved a Divine power in the experience of all who wrestled in earnest with the questions that arise out of that consciousness of guilt and moral weakness which is an essential element in the self-knowledge of the race.

With the recovery of the Christ of Paul and of the apostles, the quest after the historical Christ did not, however, cease. It may in truth rather be said, that since that time down to the present it has gone on with increasing ardour as well as success; and the enlarged understanding of the character and mind of the Christ of history that has been attained, has fostered in many the belief in its all-sufficiency for the moral and religious life of mankind, to the denial or overclouding of the higher significance attached by the apostles to the Spiritual Heavenly Christ. I need not dwell on the causes of this; but among these may be mentioned the growing indisposition in modern times to admit the supernatural, the impatience of dogma and of an interpretation of Christ that implies dogma, the revived interest in historical study, and the hesitating tone regarding the humanity of Christ that was, and still is, too characteristic even of Protestant theology, and that was bound to bring about a reaction and to lead to a severance in men's thoughts of the Christ of history from the Christ of faith.

These and other causes have quickened a spirit of critical inquiry into the contents of the Gospels that has issued in remarkable results. Learning and imagination have been devoted to the task of revivifying history, so that the Figure of Jesus may glow before our eyes, and His words may sound in our ears as a living voice. One biography of Christ after another has appeared in which the events of the Sacred Life are made to follow one another in accordance with the author's idea in each case of the plan of the whole; and the interest of the reader is sustained by the writer's endeavour to account for the movements of Jesus by an assumed knowledge of the motives that influenced Him. His character has been made again and again the subject of profound study, and has been set in fresh lights that illustrate His commanding claim on the love of men. His words have received similar attention; and justice has been done to the principles of His teaching and the plan or idea of His mission in a way that has not been done hitherto. Witness the reconstruction of His doctrine that has been attempted again and again by means of His own great thought of the Kingdom of God—that reign of God in human lives in which we reach the true end of our being, and which is realised when He awakens in men trust in Himself and love to one another. The gain of all this original research is a knowledge of Christ—of the thoughts of His mind, His aim and purpose, His sympathies, judgments, ideals of life, characteristic excellences, for which it is claimed that it is the only proper understanding of Him and the one basis of a Christology that rests on historic fact. If, it is said, a person is known in the living image and expression of his soul when we know what his aims are, what his mind is, what he did, whom he loved, what judgments he formed on the profoundest and most interesting subjects that can occupy our thought, then Christ is most truly known in an understanding of Him that embraces these matters, and not through any dogma about Him or about His life in a state of Being in which He is really inaccessible to knowledge. The LIFE of Christ, it is urged, contains the revelation we need; let us know how He lived and felt and acted, how He dealt with men, rich and poor, good and bad, needy and prosperous, how He stood in relation to God and the world, what He thought about man and God and duty, about the things of time and the things of Eternity—let us go back to the Gospels and learn the secret of His influence by following Him as He moved about among men, teaching, healing, consoling, blessing them; and when we know Him thus, we may look for Him reasserting His power and renewing His triumph over human hearts.

Now, apart from the exaggerated length to which it is carried and to which I have given expression, this movement of the modern mind back to the historical Christ is to be welcomed on many accounts, not only for the new feeling of reality with which it enables us to contemplate the Christ of the Gospels, but for the aids it furnishes to a deeper understanding of His religious worth as the Exalted Head of His people. At first sight, indeed, it seems to carry us away entirely from the Pauline interpretation; for while, in the latter, the knowledge of the historical Christ is secondary and that of the Heavenly is primary in importance, the reverse holds of the new point of view. Christ is regarded as an object of knowledge proper only as He is revealed in His Life on earth; as Exalted He is declared to be beyond knowledge. There is a sense in which the latter statement is true. We can have no proper idea of the modes of Christ's activity as the Glorified Head of His people except by means of the impressions made upon our minds by His earthly course. In the apostle's view, indeed, the death and resurrection of Jesus seem to mark His entrance on a life that is cut off from the former one—on a life that is new, and whose glory cannot be measured by anything that befell Him in time. But, as I have tried to show in these lectures, the life of the Exalted Son of God is new only in this sense, that it is a liberation of His Personality from all that hindered the perception of His real nature when He was on earth, with the consequent expansion of His distinctive powers for the activities that lay before Him as the Perfected Messiah of the human race.[1] For the real knowledge of what He is and does for His people we most fall back on the records of His earthly life, and fill up, by

[1] See Note B on The Historical and the Exalted Christ.

the impressions we derive from these of His Grace and truth, the content of our conception of His Present state.[1] Paul does not, indeed, refer much to the human history, but there is no doubt that he presupposed in his readers an acquaintance with it. Behind all that he says of the Heavenly activity of the Lord there was in his own mind a vivid impression of the human personality that gave meaning to what he said. "He could not have written as he does of Christ," says Dr. John Ker, "unless he had before him the Christ of the Gospels in word and deed and death and higher life."[2] And we cannot understand his language regarding the Glorified Christ unless we bring with us a knowledge of the Historic Jesus. Were we to obliterate from our minds all impressions of His earthly Life, and to content ourselves with a belief in Him exalted to communicate to us the benefits of His Work, He would be little more to us than an intellectual conception or a theological idea,—a category of thought, without power to touch our hearts. Or, if conceived by us as a Person, He would be to our souls what the spiritual Christ is to a certain class of Mystics, the object of an intercourse in which impressions are referred to Him that really come from their own hearts, and that have no connection with the historical manifestation of the Son of Man.[3]

---

[1] In thinking of Him as Exalted we must not conceive of Him as changed in His humanity or in the nature and range of His human sympathies. "The man who would truly paint Jesus," says Naumann, "must not show Him in pillared aisles or on the steps of altars, but under thatched roofs and by the side of village roads," meaning that in his lowliness and preference for lowly ways He is in glory what He was as seen in the flesh.

[2] *Thoughts for Heart and Life*, p. 96.

[3] "The relation of faith to the Exalted Christ can be thoroughly ethical in its character only by the ethical content of His Personal Life being made intelligible to us in the Exalted One, and presented to us as a direct point of contact for our faith. This is the case, however, only in virtue of the Identity of the Exalted One with the Personality of the earthly Jesus Christ : only in the Saviour Jesus Christ, one with the

The one safeguard against these evils is to draw our conceptions of His present mind and present Activity in and through His people from the material supplied in the record of His life on earth. From His personal characteristics as there revealed, we are able to form a true idea of what He is to us now. If it is His work in Heaven to convey to His people the Good He Himself possessed on earth, and possesses now in perfection, we can partake intelligently of that Good only when we look at Him in the mirror of His earthly life. If we are to share in His Glory as the Archetypal Man, we must learn from His conduct, in the relations in which He stood to God and His brethren, what that Pattern Manhood is that He once realised under earthly conditions, and that He would form in us. The changes on ourselves that we may expect His Indwelling Spirit to accomplish we can understand only when, falling back on the Gospel record, we observe the graces of moral and spiritual character that distinguished His human life, and that came from the personal Indwelling in Him of that very Spirit of God that is His Gift to us. And how could we conceive of that Divine Sovereignty which He now wields over the world if we had not the history of His life to show us that the power by which He overcame the world and subdued the hearts of men was, as it still is, the power of Love and of patient endurance, the majesty of Self-sacrifice, the kingly might of Meekness? It is in the earthly life that we are to discover the nature and effects of that Lordship which the Exalted One now exercises over men. All in that life is indeed humiliation; but were there nothing but humiliation, were there not a hidden glory under it as well that was to be manifested in

Father and living to save sinners, and in His redemptive activity in living personalities, is the ethical character and influence of the Exalted One made intelligible and brought near to us, so as to be, through the impression that He irresistibly makes on the conscience, the object of a spontaneous ethical trust" (Max Reischle).

due time, and to characterise His present and continuous Activity on the lives and experience of His people, we would have no idea at all of His Risen Glory. Any certainty we have that what we now receive from communion with the Ascended Saviour is really due to His influence upon us, and is a part of the Blessing He is exalted to give, is based on the perception of its correspondence with the activity of the historical Christ. The effects of His present working on His people must coincide with the characteristic activities of His personal life on earth. And His Divine Glory and Functions as Exalted are intelligible to us only as the reproduction in His people of the personal attributes of His historic life.

Hence the chief value of the Gospels consists in the light they throw on the religious worth of the Christ of Glory. As material for the construction of a biography they are insufficient. Our so-called lives of Christ must always exhibit lacunæ that demonstrate their failure to realise our idea of the biography of a historical character. But the Gospels were not given us to be put to the use that has become so common since Renan's *Life of Christ* led the way in this department of theological literature. Their value lies in the aid they furnish to the understanding of the Christ of Glory, and of the benefits that flow from present fellowship with Him; and their preciousness in this point of view cannot be exaggerated. The elucidation of this point is one merit of the Christology of Albert Ritschl, and is a service to the cause of truth by that much abused theologian that deserves acknowledgment.[1]

All this must be emphasised against a tendency to depreciate the value of the Historic Picture as compared with that of the Heavenly Christ, which has found expression in the writings of certain authors of the present day.

[1] See Note C on The Christology of Ritschl and his School.

The sifting to which the Gospel history has been subjected in late years, and the doubt that has been cast on the truthfulness of many details, have caused a feeling of uncertainty and distrust in regard to the Historic Picture in many minds. Is it wise to base our faith on the facts of history? Do we not expose it to the danger of being undermined in the course of critical inquiry? This doubt has led the writers to whom I refer, in the interest of truth, to magnify the Christ of Experience at the expense of the Christ of History. Thus in his otherwise admirable work on *Christ and the Four Gospels*, Dr. Dale says: "If Christ does, in answer to faith, redeem us from sin, impart power to vanquish it, cause us to love God and transform us into new creatures, what further or stronger evidence can we have that He is Redeemer and Son of Man? What though we were ignorant of parts of His earthly history, it would still be possible to believe in Him as our Lord, and the experience of the Church throughout the centuries would take the place of the Gospels, and confirm our faith in His power to redeem from sin all who trust in Him." And Weiss, in his *Life of Christ*, puts the case even more strongly: "The Christian faith would remain much the same and would suffer no material loss if it had pleased God to leave us only the apostolic announcement as it lies before us in the Epistles of the New Testament, and with the Gospels to deprive us of all the records from which we may construct a detailed picture of the earthly life of Jesus."[1] One can sympathise with the desire of these writers that the truth of the Gospel, by being made to rest on its own authority, should be seen to be independent of questions of historical criticism. But it appears to me to be a very hazardous position; nor do I see how any lasting results could be accomplished by a faith in the Exalted Christ that knew little or nothing of

[1] *Das Leben Jesu*, i. 15.

the life and walk of Jesus on earth, or of the Spirit that characterised His Earthly Activities. I believe that Weizäcker is nearer the truth when he says: "But for that Gospel which was speeding its way by the apostle's side, rendering immortal the wonderful words of this Jesus, and perpetuating His Image in all its human grandeur and Divine inwardness (Gottinnigkeit), this preaching of the Cross of Christ, the Sent of God, who destroys the flesh and inaugurates the reign of the Spirit, would have remained a message for thinkers, an edifice of conceptions."[1]

But after making the fullest acknowledgment of the value of the history of Christ, we turn now, on the other hand, to emphasise the truth and supreme importance of the principle which such writers as Dale and Weiss only carry to excess: that it is to the Heavenly Christ, to what He is as Exalted, that we must look for the full and proper experience of the salvation that He came to give. Viewing the earthly history of Christ as a whole, and as culminating in His death, Paul interpreted it as a preparation for His entering on His proper Messianic activity in glory, in which He was to manifest Himself in the experience of men as the Author of their restored fellowship with God, the Conqueror of sin and death, the channel to them of the gift of God's Spirit. This higher view is excluded by

[1] *Das Apostolische Zeitalter*, p. 150. In an article in the *Theological Review* on "Christ in Modern Thought," Dr. Bruce sees evidence of the partiality and one-sidedness of Paul's representation in his limited interest in the Historical Christ, and adds, in a strain similar to the quotation from Weizäcker: "While not reflecting on him, one may be thankful that other tendencies were at work in the apostolic age, that within the same Christian community, side by side with Paul's subjectivity and at peace with it, there flourished a simple, healthy objectivity which desired to know the facts about Christ, to ascertain as far as possible what He said and did, to get a clear, vivid picture of His life and human personality —to know Christ, in short, not doctrinally merely but historically, as the Synoptist Gospels in part enable us to know Him."

many in these days, and we have forced upon us the question, Is this Pauline interpretation true or not? Is it in communion with the Spiritual Christ, Supreme, Victorious over sin and its consequences, the Source of new Life to men, that we come into the possession of the real Divinely ordained issues of His Mission? Or, is it in a fellowship with the Jesus of History, whose virtue upon us takes effect, and is exhausted in the enlightenment of our minds by the truths He taught, and in the encouragement of our wills by the Pattern of goodness and nobleness of life He has left us? We know what Paul's answer was. He believed that no idea of the Christ did justice to the prophecies that bore on the Messiah, save that which He saw fulfilled in Him who died for our sins and rose again. He believed that no other met the real need of human nature, the craving for a revelation of God—for a token that God has *done* something by which His Holy Love can find access to human souls so as to destroy the power of sin and bring to an end the reign of death. He believed that this conception of the Divine purpose and aim of Christ's life-work had been communicated to him by the living Lord Himself, who had appeared to him from glory, and had originated in his personal experience great moral and religious changes which pointed directly to saving issues wrought by the death and Resurrection of Jesus. And he preached this Christ to men, and had in the regenerating effects that followed abundant testimony to its truth and power. The Gospel he announced was the Gospel of the Risen and Exalted Lord, in whom, by the grace of the Father, a new life of sonship and holiness was offered to sinful men. There is no evidence that any such saving effects would have followed had he been content to be the expounder of Christ's words, had his preaching been simply the recital of the Sermon on the Mount, or the proclamation of such truths as the Fatherhood of God, and the

Brotherhood of men, and the glory of service. The question that really interested men was, whether God had spoken and made accessible to them a new life, including forgiveness, power over temptation, victory over death; and Paul's declaration that God had raised up His Son from the dead, and that in Him this New Life had been secured, and was offered, met their case, and was welcomed because it did so.

In his brilliant Yale lectures, recently published, on the *Gospel for an Age of Doubt*, Dr. Van Dyke insists that the prophetic work of Christ is the aspect of truth that must now be preached if we are to speak with effect to the age in which we live. "We must get back," he says, "to the unity and integrity of the thoughts of Jesus, the creed of Christ, the broad outline of His vision of things human and Divine, the central verities which appear firm and unchangeable in all the reports of His teaching, the point of view from which he discovered and interpreted the mystery of life, that is what we must seek. And when we find it, we must take our stand there, as men who feel the solid ground beneath their feet. The Rock of certainty is the Mind of Jesus expressed in His living words and in His speaking life. Beyond that we need not, and we cannot, go. Here is the ultimatum. This is the truth we say to men, because Jesus knew it, and said it, and lived it."[1] The author puts into emphatic language an impression that is shared by very many, who feel the incomparable beauty and power of Christ's teaching: that it is from the preaching of His doctrines and example that we are to expect a revival of the Christian faith. That this result would follow were the proclamation of the Gospel to be limited to, and to stop short at, the reiteration of the truths Jesus taught, and the commendation of His character for our imitation, is, I think, exceedingly doubt-

[1] Page 200.

ful. History gives us no encouragement to believe that it would. It was certainly not a presentation of Christianity in this form that won for the Faith the enthusiastic attachment of men at the first. "It is an unpardonable historical blunder," says a recent writer belonging to the Ritschlian party in the Lutheran Church, "to suppose that the faith of primitive Christendom was based on the impression of the earthly image of Christ. A school might have been formed, a hero-worship might have been instituted, had that been all; but a religion could arise only because the ancient Church was conscious that God had revealed Himself in the Resurrection and Exaltation of the Lord. The ancient Church, too, derived inspiration and impulse, comfort and strength, from the living Image of Jesus; but its faith and its hope did not rest upon that, but on the transcendent experiences of the reception of the Spirit, and the testimonies of the working of the Exalted Lord."[1]

Much has happened since then that is bound to have an influence on our apprehension of the Christian truth; but there is no reason to think that the situation is so altered as to call for a presentation of it that would leave out of account the essential elements that were the secret of its success in its original promulgation, or to encourage us to hope that, were we to shift the emphasis of faith from the Exalted to the earthly life of Jesus, and to ignore the higher point of view from which the apostle, regarding the life as a whole, saw in it a revelation of the saving purpose of God, results would follow now that could not have followed such a one-sided view then. If we are left with doctrines and moral truths alone, without the living Christ to breathe into us His Spirit, so as to make these the power of life in us as well as to remove the hindrances within to corresponding action, we are as far from the salvation that

---

[1] *Die Nachfolge Christi und die Predigt des Gegenwart*, von J. Weiss, p. 83.

our nature craves as they of old felt themselves to be, with all the help that philosophy gave them, till they had the assurance that God had interposed on their behalf in great redemptive acts through the instrumentality of His own Son, whom He had raised from the dead.

It is objected, indeed, that it is impossible for us to have intercourse with the Exalted Saviour such as Paul had. He saw the Lord of Glory in a vision, and had thereafter direct fellowship with Him. We cannot have this, and must be shut out from the experience of the benefits that are the fruit of His Exalted Activity. But the apostle nowhere lays any importance on the vision by which he entered on that intercourse, nor does he teach that a supernatural impression of the Risen One is a condition of others exercising the common privilege of communion with the Exalted Christ. All that was necessary was the hearty acceptance of the apostolic testimony of the Christ who had died for men. Christ exercises His sovereignty through the Cross, through the love revealed there. And when men beholding that love were turned in faith and penitence to God, they were made to realise that Christ was indeed exalted and mighty to save; for how could His love prove omnipotent over them, or become the vehicle by which new life was quickened in their souls, if He were not in very deed the living Christ—one with God, Lord over all? Nor are we to limit to the Cross or to the revelation of Divine love on the Cross the power of Christ to draw near to the soul, and by awakening in us a new life of trust and faith in goodness, to bear witness to His activity as the Exalted Son of God. In his beautiful book on *Communion with God*, Herrmann insists that any impression made upon our hearts by the glory of the Inner Life of Christ, such as brings God near to us, and assures us of the love of a God whose will is to redeem us from sin and to make goodness triumphant, is a testimony to the influence upon us of the Risen One. It is through the understanding of what is historically true of His Inner Life and the entire appearance of Christ that we experience His kingly might over our souls, and His function as the instrument by whom God Himself draws near to us, touches us, works upon us. In the intensity of his faith in the power of the love that died for men, Paul exclaimed, " God forbid I should glory, save in the Cross of our Lord Jesus Christ" (Gal. vi. 14); and we may surely attribute to the efficacy of the Risen One every manifestation of the historic Christ, and every discovery of His Personal Life that carries home to our hearts a similar impression of His holy love that shames the bad in us, makes the good better, and turns us to God.

There are many, indeed, who must take a slower and more circuitous way in order to arrive at a faith in Christ as Risen and Exalted. They have no such perception of a Divine power going forth from Christ on the view of His life and death. But one thing must be certain to them if they are true to themselves and to their better nature. There can be no doubt of the justice of the claim of Christ, in virtue of the ideal perfection of His life and character, to the obedience of men. Let them accept in a practical way His Lordship over their lives, and that union with Him that consists in the practical adoption of His leadership, in the cultivation of His moral sympathies, in the active support of the cause of humanity for which He lives, in the regulation of life by His will, in submission to the trials of life in His Spirit, will in due time convey to them the assurance that they are in living fellowship with Him, and that it is only through what He is and is doing for men as their Exalted Head that they are enabled thus to follow Him.[1]

---

[1] I well remember, as a student, being impressed by the emphasis with which Professor J. T. Beck of Tübingen urged upon his student-audi-

All this, of course, goes to exalt the importance to faith of the Christ of history. And had it been the intention of the author, in the sentences I have quoted, to insist on obedience to the precepts and example of Christ as a means by which men may rise to the higher point of view from which Christ is presented in the apostolic testimony, I would have had no controversy with him. For I believe that to many who nowadays have lost faith in the supernatural, the one way open to a recovery of it, if they are sincere in the desire for religious assurance, is to put themselves into the position of the disciples while they had the Lord with them, to attach themselves to Him whose perfection in human goodness and wisdom appeals to all, whatever may be their doubts as to His Higher Nature, and, following Him faithfully, to wait till the silent influence of His Personality upon their souls brings with it the conviction that He is Living and Supreme.[1]

ence, many of whom had been caught in the current of sceptical thought that then ran so strong, to seek religious certainty by beginning with the Christ of the Gospels, and living in fellowship with Him. "Hold fast," he exclaimed in closing his course on Christian ethics, "by the Redeemer, and learn to know Him increasingly in His Original Form. Follow Him as He is and acts and speaks in the Picture furnished by those who were eye and ear witnesses to Him. He lived of a truth; such a picture could not have been drawn by the pencil of man; no one invented it. Get to the heart of the matter, build upon the Christ of the Gospels, and you will have a foundation of rock on which the floods even of this age will dash themselves." As the works of this remarkable man, who in his lifetime was so great a religious power in South Germany, are little known in our country, I have given in the Appendix an extract of some length from his *Gedanken aus und nach Schrift*, to the same effect as the above. See Note D. There is also a striking and impressive passage towards the close of Bishop Temple's Bampton Lecture, in which he shows how the study of the Jesus of the Gospels leads on to a religious certainty (*The Relation between Religion and Science*, pp. 248–252).

[1] The place of the "Historical Christ" in the evangelical system is the subject of an interesting article by Max Reischle in the *Zeitschrift für Theol. u. Kirch.*, 7 Jahrgang, 3 Heft. (1897), pp. 171–284. He points out that the starting-point of the faith of Paul and the first disciples was the *Risen* Christ; it was the view of Christ Risen that made His earthly

But in that case we could not speak of the elementary faith in Him that is sufficient for a starting-point as the ultimatum, or the highest attainable, as Van Dyke has done. Unless we are to regard the apostle as self-deceived in his interpretation of Christ, unless we are to resign ourselves to disappointment of the hope of the human heart for a revelation that will throw light on the dark problems of human life, we must believe there is a higher truth than that mentioned by the author in the passage I have given: we must hold that the real ultimatum of human belief is faith in Christ as Living and Supreme, and as the Founder of a new fellowship between God and man, in which sonship, forgiveness, and eternal life are more than truths to be believed — are Divine blessings to be realised, gifts graciously bestowed by God for His Son's sake, and to be received by us through faith in Him.

Both pictures of the Lord are indispensable to the Church: that which is derived from His earthly ministry, and that which reflects His state as Exalted. Nor is there any real inconsistency between them. There have been times, indeed, when the one has been realised so vividly that the religious life has found it almost impossible to realise the other along with it, or to make a proper use of

life intelligible to them, and the object of their faith. To us, who know only through others that Christ rose from the dead, and have had no vision of Him for ourselves, the Character of the earthly Christ, and the influence of His Spirit on others in the Church, is what faith naturally fixes upon in the first instance, and from this we rise to the conviction of His Resurrection. The conditions of the origin of faith are different in the two cases, but the faith itself must be the same. If ours begins with the apprehension of Him as He is revealed to us in His gracious intercourse with sinners in the days of His flesh, it must go on to the certainty of Him as Risen and Exalted, in order to be one with the faith of the apostles; and the apostolic faith, on the other hand, if it is to be an evangelical faith in Him as the Saviour of sinners, must descend from the vision of His risen glory to the knowledge of the redeeming power of His life and death. "The Exalted Christ to whom their faith clung was, as regards the content of His life, none other save the Crucified One."

the other. In the apostolic age the greatness and glory of the Exalted Christ was so real to believers, that many could not grasp along with it the thought that He who was now in possession of Divine prerogatives could ever have stooped so low as to be born into the world and to share in the humiliating experiences of a human life. They doubted whether His suffering and death had been real—whether, after all, the Son of God had been a man in more than the appearance. Paul did not share that doubt; but we can see from the Epistle to the Hebrews, which was written to those who were familiar with His teaching, that it was shared by some who took his lofty views of the Person of Christ. And his reserve in regard to the earthly life of Jesus, which, as we have seen, is so characteristic of his Epistles, proceeded, one is almost disposed to think, from a lingering feeling in his mind of the incongruity between the two pictures. With our altered conception of things, our difficulty is not where the primitive Christians found theirs. It is in the opposite direction. To us Christ is so manifestly human, our perception of the moral beauty and conformity to the highest standard of human action, of that spirit of self-denial that bore shame and death for us is so keen, and our conviction of His oneness with us in every human experience and in every sympathy that belongs to manhood is so strong, that we are apt to stumble at the idea that One who was so unmistakably a Son of man can have risen to that height of glory in the heavenly places in which He is set before us in the Epistles. The danger is that, in our intense realisation of His human life, we may lose hold of the truth of His present life as the Exalted Son of God.

Christian experience, however, brings these two pictures together and makes them one, or shows us at least that we are dealing simply with two aspects of one and the same Personality. For the life of faith in Him reveals a Power working in us that makes for holiness and is stronger than sin and the flesh and the world, pointing thereby to the Supremacy of Him from whom it comes, and to His identity with God. While the effects of that power on the character and life of believers, the resemblance to Jesus in His lowliness and love and purity and manly strength which it works out in them, points to its identity with the personal life of the Son of Man, who embodied in so distinctive a form these and all other graces of true character. What the spirit of Christ does in the hearts of His people now is seen to be the continuation of that same gracious Activity whose achievements are narrated in the Gospels. The knowledge of Christ that is fruitful is that which is derived at once from history and from faith—history revealing to us the personal grace of the Head of His people, faith disclosing to us the Power by which He reigns still and repeats in us the characteristic qualities of His Life.

In that movement that has riveted the minds of men in these days to the human life of Jesus, and to the memoirs in which the Picture of that human life is preserved, we may surely see the hand of God, the striving of the very Spirit of Christ leading us into a fuller apprehension of what He is and is able to do for us. No doubt it has been needed to correct the tendency to a dogmatic understanding of Christ and of Christianity, that finds itself more at home in the Epistles than in the Gospels, and in consequence apprehends the truth that dogma represents in a form which, however accurate and scientific, is without warmth and conveys no conviction. It is reported of the late Professor J. Ch. K. v. Hofmann of Erlangen, that towards the end of his life he said, " Paul has had his day, it is time the Gospels had theirs."[1] And Hofmann was a devout man, a profound believer in the

---

[1] My authority for this statement is Naumann in his little book, *Was heisst Christlich Social*, p. 47. His words are : " Der selige Professor v.

truth of God's word, and an exegete to whom students owe more for the light he has thrown on Paul's Epistles than to any other modern expositor. We believe that good must come of all the study and labour that are expended on the Gospels in order to bring out into clearness the great thoughts of Jesus, and the revelation of the Divine Will that is given to us in His life and character. We will be made to realise more vividly than before that the great instrument for the moral quickening and elevation of humanity is the personal influence of Jesus Christ on the heart and life, and that we are in possession of that knowledge of Him, of His aims and purposes, of His sympathies and moral judgments, that is indispensable in order that His Personal influence upon us may lead to the highest results. But while the gain from all the inquiry that is directed toward the Christ of history is in this way unquestionable, it cannot make Paul's interpretation superfluous, or lessen its value for the Christian life. Nor are we to understand the words of v. Hofmann as if he meant to suggest this. Paul himself was the most signal instance of a character that reached, we might say, the very pinnacle of human greatness through the influence of Jesus Christ upon his inner life, and the perfect sympathy of mind and feeling with His Lord that flowed from his fellowship with Him. So dominant was this influence, so absorbing the attachment that grew out of it, so assimilating a power did it prove in his conscious experience, that he could say, "I live no more, but Christ lives in me."[1] But this same Paul, who illustrates so strikingly the elevating influence of Christ on the life and character, attributes it all to the living Christ who had laid the human race under an eternal debt of gratitude by His work of atonement for sin and His victory over death, and who is clothed with the power of

Hofmann in Erlangen hat einmal gesagt, 'nach der Zeit des Paulus müsse eine Zeit der Evangelien kommen.'"

[1] Gal. ii. 20.

the Spirit of God to reproduce, in all who surrender themselves to His love, the characteristic qualities of His own perfect manhood. And in order that our knowledge of Jesus Christ in His human manifestation may become vital in our experience, and may prove an influence conforming us to what He was, we must add to it the faith of Paul in a Christ Risen and Exalted. As long as there are those who are burdened with memories that are a continual reproach, and who feel the power of evil appetites they are unable to rise above,—as long as there are those who tremble before that event that seems to mock all their efforts after a higher life, and who crave an assurance that death has not separated them for ever from friends whom they have lost but cannot cease to love,—men will turn with thankfulness to this teacher who shows us what God made Jesus to be when He raised Him from the dead, who announces a Christ who has put away sin, who has vanquished death, who is now by the grace of God the Head of a new Humanity, and able to repeat in as many as believe in Him the wonder of His own Holiness and Immortality.

APPENDIX

APPENDIX

LECTURE I

NOTE A, p. 8.—PAUL AND THE HISTORICAL CHRIST

A GREAT amount of investigation has been directed in modern times to the allusions found in Paul's Epistles to the teaching and incidents recorded in the Gospels. Paret's article on "Paul and Jesus," in the *Jahrbücher für Deutsche Theologie* (iii. B., 1 Heft, 1858), led the way in this inquiry; and that article remains the classic on the subject. All that has been written since is in substance contained in it; and it ought to be read and re-read by those who would understand the relation in which Paul stood to the historic Christ. *The Witness of the Epistles*, by Rev. R. I. Knowling, M.A., 1892, is a mine of information on what has been written since Paret's day; and in the fifth and sixth chapters of that work the reader will find a detailed account of references in the Epistles to our Lord's life and teaching; the fullest acknowledgment is made of the author's indebtedness to Paret. Sabatier's brief statement on the subject (*The Apostle Paul*, p. 70–75, English translation) is worth reading; he emphasises the point that one thing calculated to impress us more powerfully than all the isolated facts mentioned in the Epistles is the general picture Paul draws of the Saviour's life, so "exactly answering to the impression left on us by the Gospel narratives as a whole."

Hausrath (*der Apostel Paulus*) remarks that "if Paul in his letters makes little of the historical, and deduces the Messiahship of Jesus from the Old Testament rather than from the life of Jesus, if the individual incidents of the Lord's life weigh less with him than the significance of His death, the reason was not that his knowledge is defective on these matters, but that the speculative tendency of his spirit thinks in religious postulates and not in facts." The following passage from him may be quoted as presenting a summary of the historical knowledge to be gathered from the Epistles: " That he knew, in a particular case, to give the historical even to detail is proved by his own statement to the Galatians, that he had so set Jesus before their eyes as the Crucified One that he never believed he would have reason to fear that they would turn to another Gospel. His knowledge embraces the whole life of Jesus. He mentions His Davidic descent (Rom. i. 3, ix. 5), and he knows of His baptism, and makes an allegorical use of it in his Epistles (Col. ii. 11; 1 Cor. x. 2; Rom. vi. 3-4). He knows the preaching of the kingdom of God, and the sending forth of the apostles, and their being furnished with power over the devils (2 Cor. xii. 12; 1 Cor. xii. 10, 28, 29; Gal. iii. 5), and he has so accustomed himself to call them the Twelve, as in the time of Jesus, that he uses this expression even when it was no more applicable (1 Cor. xv. 5). The poor life of Jesus (Phil. ii. 4-8), the spirit of meekness and gentleness that animated it, the self-forgetting, humble, serving love—all this is perfectly present to the apostle (2 Cor. v. 15; Gal. ii. 20; Phil. i. 8). He has a more accurate knowledge than the Evangelists themselves had of the history of the Passion. At least his narrative of the Lord's Supper in the night on which he was betrayed corrects the differences of the Synoptists (1 Cor. xi. 23); it is not unknown to him that it was the princes of this world, and not the people, that wished the death of Jesus (1 Cor. ii. 8), and the treachery of Judas (1 Cor. xi. 23). The reproaches of the Crucified One (Rom. xv. 3), His weakness on the cross (2 Cor. xiii. 4), and the nailing to it of the handwriting of the proconsul (Col. ii. 14)—all this stands in so living a way before his soul that he can picture it also before the eyes of others. The narrative of the appearances of the Risen One is, in particular, given by him with great regard to detail (1 Cor. xv. 3)" (pp. 142-3).

Jowett has an interesting note in his Commentary on 1 Thes. iv. 15, on "What did St. Paul know of the life of Jesus?" "In 1 Cor. xv. 3–10," he says, "the apostle describes himself not only as preaching to the Corinthians the doctrine of the resurrection of Christ, but as dwelling on the minute circumstances which attested it." He goes on to ask, "Had he told them in like manner of other events in the life of Christ—had the parables and discourses of Christ interwoven themselves in his teaching, were the miracles of Christ a witness to which he appealed?" These questions, he says, must remain without an answer; "but as far as we can trace, it was not the sayings or events of the life of Christ, but the witness of the Old Testament prophets that formed the larger part of St. Paul's teaching, the external evidence by which he supported in himself and others the inward and living sense of union with Christ, the medium through which he preached 'Christ crucified.'"

NOTE B, p. 12.—PAUL'S IDEA OF THE CHRIST BEFORE HIS CONVERSION

There is every reason to believe that before his conversion Paul shared the carnal notions of his countrymen about the temporal might and dominion that were to belong to the Christ who was to come. These ideas seem to have blinded him to the spirituality of Jesus' claim. His repudiation, after he was converted, of the Jewish idea of a national deliverer is probably referred to in 2 Cor. v. 16, where, speaking of the change that had taken place in his estimate of persons and things from the time he had discerned the love of Christ in dying for all, he says, "Yea, though we have known Christ after the flesh, yet henceforth know we Him no more." Some, indeed, think that these words imply that Paul had had a personal knowledge of Jesus when He lived with men, and that he here declares that he had no longer any interest in that knowledge of the incidents and words of the historic Christ now that he had an understanding of Him as the Lord of Glory. It is difficult, however, to believe that the biography of Jesus was so destitute of interest or of value to the apostle that he could use this language regarding it. Others infer from these words that, for a time after his conversion, Paul attached importance to the Jewish descent and nationality of Jesus as giving his believing fellow-countrymen some advantage over Gentile Christians, and as making obligatory on the latter the observance of the carnal ordinances of the Jews. This is the view of Dr. Matheson in his suggestive book on *The Development of Paul* (p. 101). He regards Paul here as looking back on the first period of his Christian life, before he had stepped into the larger view of Christ he afterwards reached, and as confessing, "there was a time when I made much of what Christ according to the flesh was, but that time is past." When we think, however, of the circumstances of Paul's conversion, and of the complete recoil from the old ideas that had so misled him that was sure to take place in a mind so thorough as his was, it is scarcely credible that any lingering suspicion of the worth of carnal distinctions could have survived the dissolution of his scheme of belief which followed, as soon as he was convinced that Jesus was the Messiah, and that as spirit He now belonged to a state of being where all such outward distinctions were absolutely without meaning. When he speaks, then, of "knowing Christ after the flesh," it is more natural to understand him as using the word "Christ" in its official sense rather than as a proper name, and as saying, "Once, with the rest of my countrymen, I believed in and looked for a Christ who was to come in outward glory, and to raise Israel to a place of supremacy among the nations, but I cast away that notion from the time I knew Jesus to be the Christ, Jesus who died for all men, and has founded a kingdom in which the spirit is everything and the flesh is nothing." This is the view that is taken by Gess, Neander, Schmiedel, and Denney in his "Second Epistle to Corinthians" (*Expositor's Bible*), pp. 204, 205 ; see also a fine sermon on "Knowing Christ after the Flesh," by Rev. F. Mudie, in *Bible Truths and Bible Characters*. Dr. Bruce thinks that the words in 2 Cor. v.

16, must be looked at in the light of Paul's controversy with the Judaistic section of the Church, who made much of external companionship with Jesus as a qualification for apostleship, and questioned Paul's right to call himself an apostle because he had not had this privilege. Paul's reply would then mean that he had known Christ thus, but that he regarded such an acquaintanceship as valueless. Dr. Bruce agrees with those who are opposed to an understanding of the words that would imply on Paul's part a depreciation of the worth of the knowledge of the historic Christ. "To cast a slight on the words and acts spoken and done in that ministry, and on the revelation of a character made thereby, was not, I imagine, in all his thoughts" (*St. Paul's Conception of Christianity*, pp. 255–6).

Note C, p. 28.—The Conception of Christ in the Pastoral Epistles

Since Schleiermacher wrote his treatise calling in question the Pauline authorship of 1 Timothy, the question of the apostolic origin of these Epistles—for all three form one problem—has been eagerly canvassed. Perhaps it is yet too soon to come to a decision as to the final result. Those who deny that they came from Paul's pen refer them to the early part of the second century, and regard them as having issued from a circle where Paulinism prevailed, and as having been intended to meet the practical errors and confusion in Church-life that were produced by the spread of Gnostic ideas. The general conceptions are Pauline, but there is truth in the allegation that they are wanting both in the depth and sharpness of outline that characterise the treatment of doctrine in the undisputed writings of Paul. The aim of these Epistles is strictly practical.

The emphasis is placed less on doctrine than on the "godliness" (εὐσεβεία) that is produced by sound doctrine. And this accounts for the general terms in which Christ is spoken of. There are few references to the historical Christ. He is declared to have come into the world

(1 Tim. i. 15), and to have "appeared" and been "manifested" in the flesh (2 Tim. i. 10; 1 Tim. iii. 16) (where ὅς must now be accepted as the true reading[1])—a form of speech that reminds us of John's apprehension of the Incarnate One as the manifestation of God. It suggests, too, the pre-existence in another state of Him who is "manifested" in time. Christ is also said to have been of the "seed of David" (2 Tim. ii. 8), and to have, "before Pontius Pilate, witnessed a good confession" (1 Tim. vi. 13). We read also of the "wholesome words of the Lord Jesus" (1 Tim. vi. 3) as being the test of true doctrine, which indicates the value that was now set on the historical record of our Lord's teaching. Christ is called the "One Mediator between God and Man, the Man Christ Jesus" (1 Tim. ii. 5). The term Mediator applied to Christ is new, and is a point of affinity between these writings and the Epistle to the Hebrews (xii. 24). As the Man who is distinguished from all other men, inasmuch as, while they need salvation (1 Tim. ii. 4), He is in the position to mediate between them and God to convey salvation to them, He answers closely to the idea of the Second Adam expounded in Rom. v. 12–19. The idea of His Person conveyed in the words (1 Tim. iii. 16), "He was manifested in the flesh and justified in the spirit," is strictly Pauline. The flesh, the seat of His manifestation, is synonymous with human nature on its material side, while the spirit in which He was justified is the higher element of His Personality. By His "justification in the spirit" we are to understand, that in virtue of this higher principle in Him,—the spirit,—He was authenticated as being that which He really was in spite of appearances; the reference, doubtless, is to the Resurrection, where, according to Paul in Rom. i. 3, Christ was "marked out as being the Son of God" (which He had really been in the days of His flesh in a concealed and incomplete form) "according to the spirit of holiness." He became then, according to the teaching of Paul in the undisputed Epistles, "a Life-Giving Spirit": the words "being justified in the Spirit" conveys much the same sense.

[1] See Hort, *The New Testament in Greek*, vol. ii. pp. 132-3.

The Person and work of Christ are declared very emphatically to be a manifestation of the Goodness of God. In Him there was a signal appearing of the "Grace" (2 Tim. i. 9; Tit. ii. 11) of God "bringing salvation to all," of "the kindness and philanthropy of God" (Tit. iii. 4). God is designated throughout as the "Saviour" of men (1 Tim. i. 1, ii. 3, iv. 10, Tit. i. 3, ii. 10), and Jesus' identity in mind and aim with God is implied in the fact that He also is called the "Saviour" (Tit. i. 4; 2 Tim. i. 10). He came to "save sinners" (1 Tim. i. 15). To this end He "gave Himself for us" (Tit. ii. 14), or, as it is expressed more fully in 1 Tim. ii. 6, "He gave Himself a ransom for all."

The effects of His death are moral rather than religious: it is salvation as an ethical good, and not as a mere deliverance from guilt, that is emphasised; salvation from lawlessness and sin (Tit. ii. 14) more than from the curse of the law, or regeneration (Tit. iii. 4). As Risen and Exalted, Christ is called not only our Saviour, but also the "Lord." He is not mentioned in these writings as the "Son of God."

The Spirit is spoken of as the possession of believers, and as the source of moral renewal (2 Tim. i. 7, 14; Tit. iii. 5); but He is not called "the Spirit of Christ." There is no reference to the truth, so characteristic of Paul, of the Indwelling Christ. The phrase "in Christ" does occur several times (2 Tim. iii. 12, i. 9), but it does not seem to have the same force or significance as in the recognised Pauline writings; and one feels, in reading these Epistles, that there is a measure of truth in Schenkel's judgment: "The Christ-Image of the Pastoral Epistles is made up of Pauline formulas, but there is wanting the Pauline mind and spirit, the mystic inwardness, the religious depth and moral power which live in the Christ of Paul" (*Das Christus-Bild der Apostel*, p. 361).

On the other hand, the leading features of the Pauline Christology are here. Christ is a Man, but a Man who stands in a unique relation to God and men, as Mediator. He has for us the religious value of God, for God is manifested in Him, and He is Lord and Saviour, as God is: He is mentioned habitually along with God as of the same importance to us (1 Tim. v. 21, i. 1, 2; 2 Tim. iv. 1; Tit. i. 4, ii. 13), and the language in which His Incarnation is spoken of, as a *manifestation* in the flesh, pointing, as we have seen, to a prior existence with God (whether in person or principle), seems to account for the fact that He who was a Man has been raised to such a practical equality with God in the thought and regard of the Church.

LECTURE II

Note A, p. 39.—St. Paul and the Supernatural Birth of Christ

THE statement that Paul does not in the Epistles teach the doctrine of the supernatural birth of Christ will scarcely be disputed. Allusions to it have been found in Rom. i. 3, 4, and Gal. iv. 4. In the former passage the Divine Sonship of Christ is based on "the Spirit of Holiness"; but there is nothing in this inconsistent with the natural origin of His physical being, any more than there is anything in the words applied to Isaac (Gal. iv. 29), "born after the Spirit," that is inconsistent with his human parentage. The other passage that has been appealed to, Gal. iv. 4, "God sent forth His Son, made of a woman, made under the law," is equally indecisive. The pre-existence of Christ is implied here, but not His supernatural birth; for it is the object of the apostle to point out, not wherein Christ differed from other men, but His identity with them in His human experience and in the manner of His appearing. The words "born of woman" of themselves no more exclude the idea of a human parentage than do the same words when applied to John the Baptist in Matt. xi. 11.

Nor is it at all clear that his conception of Christ as the sinless Second Adam involves as its necessary implicate a miraculous birth. In order to answer to the idea conveyed by that title, indeed, Christ must be regarded as a new Moral Creation. As the Fountain of a new moral life to men He must owe His distinctive Being to a fresh creative act on the part of God. No theory of evolution can account for His unique moral greatness. On the other hand, the miracle of His moral life does not necessarily imply a physical miracle at the beginning of His human existence, although all that we know of the very close connection between the material and the spiritual, the flesh and the spirit, points to such a physical miracle as rendering more credible the wonder of the sinless development of His humanity.

It has been further argued that Paul's idea of Christ as a Central Personality, from whom each member of the human race derives the life that issues in the moral development of his separate individuality, compels us to conceive of Him as possessing our human nature, not as an individual member of the race, but in its collective character, not as the Son of an individual man, but as born of Humanity in virtue of a sovereign act of God. But any view that would rob Christ of His individuality in order to maintain this universal significance that belongs to Him is an erroneous one, and leads to a Doketic denial of His humanity. Nor could He be to us the Perfect Example of a religious life, if the religious life was divorced in Him from any marked individuality of trait and temperament. The Christ of the Gospels is intensely individual, in the true sense of that word.

On the whole, it seems impossible to argue such a matter to a satisfactory conclusion on general considerations. It must be determined by the view we take of the historicity of the chapters in the Gospels that relate to Christ's birth of the Virgin. It is plain, however (if we are to argue from the silence of the apostle), that he did not attach any fundamental importance to it. His Christology was based, not on the fact of the supernatural conception, but on the fact of the Resurrection and Glorification of Christ. The words of Schenkel here express the truth: "The problem of the supernatural birth of Christ did not exist for Paul, because with him the *resurrection* is the real birth-hour of the Heavenly Man, Christ" (*Das Christus-Bild der Apostel*, p. 257). Similarly, Sabatier in his *L'Apôtre Paul* (1886), p. 339: "The part which the fact of the supernatural birth plays in the Church theology is taken in Paul's system by the fact of the Resurrection. The new historical epoch begins with the Resurrection of the Saviour, which was the first appearance of the supernatural life on earth."

It has been pointed out by Abbott (*Spirit of God on the Waters*) that the attitude of John in his Gospel to the question of the supernatural birth of Christ is similar to that of Paul. He, too, represents faith in Christ the Son of God as resting on grounds that are independent of the settlement of that question. Nathanael welcomes Jesus as the Son of God, while he is still under the impression that He was the Son of Joseph and Mary according to report (i. 45–49). Faith is spoken of throughout the Gospel as arrived at without any reference to the circumstances of the beginning of Christ's earthly life. There is no mention in his Gospel of the miraculous conception, and it is doubtful whether the evangelist knew of it. The common understanding among those who figure in the Gospel is that He was a native of Nazareth, and born of Joseph (vi. 42, vii. 41). That was made a pretext by the captious Pharisees for not believing in Him, inasmuch as they inferred from prophecy that Messiah was to be born "in the town of Bethlehem, the city of David" (vii. 42). The design of the evangelist is evidently to show that faith in Christ as "of God" rested on the spiritual perception of the divine glory in Him, and was not affected vitally by knowledge or ignorance of the facts regarding the beginning of His earthly life.

This harmony between Paul and John, the two great interpreters of Christ, in regard to the relative insignificance to religious faith in Christ of our belief on this subject, is to be kept in view in our judgment of those who hesitate to accept the narratives in Matthew and Luke on the infancy of Jesus. The words spoken by Julius Müller, author of the classic work on the *Christian Doctrine of Sin*, before the General Synod in 1847, are memorable: "Wenn jemand wahrhaft verstünde was Busse und glaube ist und so das Evangelium vom Heiland der welt, dem Sohn Gottes und des Menschen aus lebendiger Erfahrung seines Hertzens predige, also auch unfehlbar an der flecklosen Herrlichkeit Christi festhielt und doch dabei verriethe, dass nach seiner Ansicht die göttliche Wirksamkeit in dem Anfang des menschlichen Lebens Jesu das natürliche Medium nicht ausschliesse,—nun, so hoffen wir zu Gott, dass Er die Evangelische Kirche nimmer so tief sinken lassen wird, einen solchen heterodoxen Prediger, der ihr hundertmal mehr nütze ist als ein Amtsgenosse von der reinsten aber seelenlosen Orthodoxie, aus ihrem Dienste entfernen zu wollen."

On the general subject, and especially on the historical question involved, the student may consult with advantage Gore's *Dissertations*, the article on "The Virgin Birth of our Lord." The more speculative aspects of the subject are treated in Rothe's *Ethik*, iii. par. 534–6, and by Gess, *Christi Person u. Werk*, iii. pp. 394–5. Both Rothe and Gess maintain strongly the miraculous origin of Christ's humanity as the postulate of His sinlessness. On the other side, see Lobstein on *Die Lehre von der übernatürlichen Geburt Christi*, and Hering's article in *Zeitschrift für Theologie u. Kirche*, 1895, 1 H., on *Die Dogmatische Bedentung u. der religiöse, Werth der übernatürlichen Geburt Christi*.

NOTE B, p. 62.—ON THE GRADUAL APPREHENSION OF THE CHRISTIAN IDEAL

CANON GORE illustrates the point, that the contents of the Christian ideal have been gradually understood and appropriated, in the following words: "No doubt, for example, many early Christians had an imperfect perception of the obligation of truthfulness, but when Augustine vigorously asserted it to be a part of Christian morality, he asserted what is undoubtedly true. Christ did lift all conversation to the level of absolute truthfulness, to the level formerly held only by statments under oath: 'Let your yea be yea, and your nay, nay.' We in our time, to take only one more example, have learnt to give great prominence to the virtue of considerateness. The rough and summary classifications of men in groups, the equally rough and summary condemnations of them, the inconsiderate treatment of heretics, and even of speculators—these facts in Church history strike us as painful and unworthy. Considerateness, we say, is a Christian virtue. 'Let your considerateness be known unto all men.' We look back to our Lord and are astonished that any can have failed to see His intense respect for individuality, His freedom from fanaticism—in a word, His considerateness. Certainly it is there. Only, lest we should be arrogant, we need to remember that other ages and other races have caught more readily in Him what we ignore,—His antagonism to pride or to the selfish assertion of property,—and that the whole is not yet told" (*Bampton Lecture*, pp. 169, 170).

LECTURE III

NOTE A, p. 76.—THE REVELATION OF GOD'S LOVE IN THE DEATH OF CHRIST AND HIS RESURRECTION

THEODOR HÄRING, in his suggestive little work, *Zur Versöhnungslehre* (1893), shows that without the resurrection of Christ the revelation of God's love furnished by His death would have been incomplete. The point is so important, and is so well put by the author, that I quote his words:—

"Daher wird auch in diesem Zusammenhang besonders deutlich, warum dieser Liebe bis in den Tod der Erweis der Todesüberwindung nicht fehlen darf, wenn sie jenen Glauben hervorzurufen soll im Stande sein: der Todesüberwindung eben nicht nur in dem Sinn, dass sie in der Todesprobe Stand gehalten, mithin sich als eine in diesem Menschen seinem natürlichen Leben überlegene Macht erwiesen hat, sondern als die höchste Macht alles Wirklichen. Mit andern Worten; ohne das Kreuz kein Erweis der höchsten Liebe, wenn man das Wesen der Liebe ins Auge fasst; ohne Auferstehung kein Erweis der höchsten Liebe, wenn man danach fragt, ob sie die alles beherrschende Wirklichkeit ist. In den Worten 'höchst' und 'göttlich,' die wir unwillkürlich gebrauchen, wo vom Tod Jesu die Rede ist, liegt ein Anlass zur Zweideutigkeit. 'Grössere Liebe,' 'göttlichere Liebe' giebt es nicht dem sittlichen Werte nach, als die sich in den Tod opfernde; aber damit ist noch nicht notwendig gesagt, ob sie göttlich ist in dem Sinn, dass sie als das Wesen Gottes unzweideutig sich brundgibt. Eine Wirklichkeit ist sie selbstverständlich, wenn immer sie die Kraft in einem Menschenherzen gewonnen, die von Natur stärkste Kraft unseres inneren Lebens zu überwinden; aber Glaube, Vertrauen auf Gottes Liebe, das jeder Anfechung widerstehen kann, entsteht nur, wächst und vollendet sich nur, wenn die Liebe Gottes als die Wirklichkeit, ohne gleichen, als die schlechthinige, jede andere Wirklichkeit, auch die des Todes überragende, sich offenbart" (pp. 46, 47).

Note B, p. 85.—On Sacrificial Language in Paul's Epistles

There are in all only three passages that can be quoted in this connection. The first is Rom. iii. 25, referred to in the text. The second is Eph. v. 1, "Walk in love, as Christ also has loved us, and hath given Himself for us an offering and sacrifice unto God for a sweet-smelling savour." The death of Christ, however, is here spoken of as a sacrifice in the moral sense, in so far as it was the sublime expression of His Love and self-surrender to the Will of God; and in this respect it reveals a principle for the imitation of believers, who are to act in the same spirit, and so make their lives also an offering and a sacrifice unto God.

The remaining passage is 1 Cor. v. 7: "For Christ our Passover is sacrificed, or slain, for us, wherefore let us keep the feast," etc. The whole passage is an exhortation to believers to live out the Christian life in a spirit of holy gladness. The Passover lamb was not strictly an offering, but a memorial of the death that signalised the deliverance of Israel from Egypt; and when Christ is spoken of as our Passover (lamb), believers are reminded that the means of their redemption from sin is also a death, that calls for the renunciation of all sin on the part of those who are to partake of its benefit. The Passover lamb was slain in order to be eaten at a feast from which all leaven was excluded, and our Passover was put to death in order that, partaken of by us, He might be the author in us of a Life to which everything of the nature of sin was entirely alien. There is not a hint here of Christ's death in the sense of a sin-offering.

Among those who are opposed to the dogmatic understanding of the sacrificial language in Paul's Epistles in reference to the death of Christ may be mentioned R. Schmidt (*Die Paulinische Christologie*), Weiss (*Bibl. Theol. of the N. T.*, i. p. 426, Eng. Trans. (Clark)), Seeberg (*Der Tod Christi*), Jowett (*St. Paul's Epistles*), Essay on Atonement and Satisfaction. It is a striking fact that Paul nowhere teaches that believers were to cease partaking in the sacrificial system then in vogue, which we would have expected him to do had he held and taught, with the author of the Epistle to the Hebrews, that the death of Christ was of the nature of a sin-offering, and made the continued offering of sacrifices under the law an anachronism, if not a sin. Mackintosh thinks this omission accidental (*The Natural History of the Christian Religion*, p. 398).

NOTE C, p. 87.—ON THE MEANING OF 2 COR. V. 21.

This passage bears a strong resemblance to that in Rom. v. considered in the text. The phraseology and point of view are different, but the meaning is much the same. The design of the death of Christ is stated to be " that we might be made the righteousness of God in Him "; while in Rom. v. 19 it is thus put, " that we might be made righteous." The abstract term, " the righteousness of God," is employed in writing to the Corinthians, in order to be in line with the form of speech he uses in reference to the death of Christ, where the abstract term is made use of, being required by the nature of the case: " He hath made Him to be sin " (not a sinner) " for us, that we might be made the righteousness of God in Him " (ver. 21). The effect of His " being made sin for us " is thus precisely the same as that attributed in Rom. v. to His " obedience." In both cases alike it is, that we might be brought into right relations to God, into the enjoyment of His favour.

In writing to the Corinthians, the point emphasised by Paul is God's part in so appointing and arranging the death of Christ as to execute thereby His saving purpose: " Christ *was made* sin for us." His aim is to trace all up to

God (ver. 18), to show that the great reconciliation originated with God, and that *His* grace is conspicuous in the entire transaction. On the other hand, in writing to the Romans his object is to magnify the work of the Second Adam, the Divine instrument for accomplishing the reconciliation. Accordingly, we read, in the former case, that Christ, while sinless and undeserving of death, was "made sin," was made to appear a sinner by being subjected in the providence of God to death, the punishment of sin. By dying the shameful death on the cross, He was placed in the position of a transgressor, and was caused to experience in body and soul sufferings that were in sorrowful contrast to what was proper to Him as the Sinless One; and this, that we might be treated as the opposite of what we really are, and accepted as righteous. He was dealt with as a sinner in the death He endured, that we might be dealt with as righteous in the favour we receive. How His being dealt with as a sinner secured our being dealt with as righteous is not explained in this passage, but is explained, in so far as it admits of explanation, in the passage in Rom. v., where His *obedience* to the will of God, manifested in His consenting to die the death He did not deserve, is declared to possess that moral worth that has efficacy to secure our acceptance in God's sight.

Some have found an explanation in the words "for us"; and taking $\upsilon\pi\epsilon\rho$ in the sense "in our room and stead," they interpret the clause as meaning that in being dealt with as a sinner, Christ took our place, and had laid upon Him the punishment that was due to us, so that God can now deal with us as those who have already in the Person of Christ borne the punishment of sin, and cannot in justice be punished a second time. It is possible to take this meaning out of the words. But they do not of themselves suggest it. The preposition $\upsilon\pi\acute{\epsilon}\rho$ means properly "on our behalf," for our sakes. And there is an awkwardness in taking it in the sense of "in our place" here, because it would make Paul say, God hath made Him who knew no sin to be sin in our place, that is, instead of making us to be sin, but in fact we are sinners already. The more serious difficulty which this interpretation encounters is referred to in the lecture.

On the whole, I am unable to attach to this passage the significance in relation to a theory of the Atonement that Dr. Denney does, who speaks of it as "the keystone of the whole system of apostolic thought" ("Commentary on Second Epistle to the Corinthians," p. 218—*Expositor's Bible*). I am disposed to regard rather the passage in Romans in this light. It is just in a doctrinal Epistle such as Romans is that we might look for a clearly defined statement on the subject.

NOTE D, p. 88.—ON ROM. III. 23-26.

This passage is a crux to the exegete. The thought is compressed, and the construction of the relative clauses difficult. I state what appears to me, after a careful study, to be the meaning. I follow the translation of Weizäcker (New Testament), which is based on what seems to be the most natural understanding of the clauses, and which suggests the sense of the whole. He renders from ver. 21 thus:

"But now the righteousness of God without the law is manifested, even the righteousness of God by faith in Jesus Christ, for all them that believe, for there is no difference; for all men have sinned and come short of the glory of God, but are justified (or accepted) as righteous by an act of His own free favour, by means of the redemption in Christ Jesus, whom God set forth as a Propitiation through faith in His blood, that He might manifest His Righteousness—on account of having overlooked the sins that were formerly committed, because God exercised forbearance, having respect (or, with a view) to the manifestation of His righteousness that has now taken place,—in order, then, that He might be seen to be one who, righteous Himself, accepts as righteous him that is of faith in Jesus."

The leading thought of the whole passage is that the design of the Death of Christ, and of that gracious arrangement under which believers have in His death a means of propitiation, is the exhibition of the Righteousness of God (ver. 25). At this point there is a parenthesis, and not till the end of it is reached have we the words, "that He might be righteous, and the justifier of him that believes in Christ"—words which expand and explain the main thought, that the death of Christ is intended to exhibit the Righteousness of God. These words state the double aspect which the Righteousness of God has; in virtue of it, God is at once Righteous in Himself, the Maintainer of Right, true to His own nature as Holy, and, at the same time, the justifier of those who believe in the revelation of His Grace, in that He places them in a relation to Himself that is conformed to what is right, *i.e.* in that He forgives their sin, and restores them to His favour. There is, then, in the Righteousness of God as exhibited in Christ a gracious element. It is, indeed, a gracious attribute. It is love pursuing its end, which is the recovery of man to God, in a holy way, *i.e.* a way in keeping with His character as holy.

The parenthesis, beginning with "on account of the overlooking of sins that are past," is intended to remind us that this exhibition of righteousness was necessary because of the fact that before Christ came sin had been overlooked or passed over. The reason why God had been so forbearing was hid till the death of Christ took place. Then this forbearance was seen to have its ground in the righteousness of God revealed in that event. It was seen, in other words, to have its ground in the gracious arrangement under which men came to have in Christ a Saviour who has expiated sin. This arrangement proved that the righteousness of God was something far grander than men had deemed it to be, or than it would have been seen to be, had God, instead of exercising forbearance, dealt with men in strict justice, and punished them for their sins. Righteousness was thus manifested as that attribute of the Divine nature that not only maintains a holy order in the universe, but that also provides for the forgiveness of sinners. In what way the Death of Christ exhibits the former aspect of the Divine righteousness is not stated here, except generally that the latter is illustrated in the power of His Death to expiate sin. The intention of the author is simply to show that the gospel way of salvation by faith is the exhibition of the Righteousness of God, understood in this large sense, not as punitive or retributive justice, but as holy love, a will ever faithful and true to its own law, which is the salvation of men in a manner consistent with eternal truth and holiness. Recent theologians of all schools accept this as the idea of Righteousness taught in the passage before us. In their *Commentary on Romans*, iii. 25–26, Sanday and Headlam say: "The words (ver. 26) indicate no opposition between justice and mercy. Rather that which seems to us, and which really is, an act of mercy, is the direct outcome of the 'righteousness,' which is a wider and more adequate name than justice. It is the essential righteousness of God which impels Him to set in motion that sequence of events in the sphere above, and in the sphere below, which leads to the free forgiveness of the believer, and starts him on his way with a clean page to his record" (p. 91). Goebel, in his brief *Commentary on N. T.*, says on this passage: "δικαιοσύνη αὐτοῦ ist hier Eigenschaftsbestimmung, aber nicht die Strafgerechtigkeit Gottes, sondern allgemeiner diejenige ethische Unwandelbarkeit Gottes, vermöge deren er das Böse niemals gut heisst, also die Sünde nicht vergiebt ohne Sühne." This scarcely does justice to the gracious element in the conception. Ritschl's account of the matter is truer to the thought of Paul here: "God has manifested His righteousness in the death of Christ, inasmuch as it is in keeping with His nature both to justify him who believes and to require an expiation of sin in entering into fellowship with sinners" (*Altkath. Kirche*, p. 86).

NOTE E, p. 89.—WHETHER CHRIST SUFFERED SPIRITUAL DEATH.

The theory referred to in the text has been held in another and more consistent form by those who have maintained that what Jesus suffered in the place of sinners was the torments of hell, the proper punishment of sin, or the sense of the Wrath of God, spiritual death. This logically is the position we are shut up to if we hold that the essence of the work lay in His having borne the punishment of sin in our room and stead. But surely to speak of Christ's having endured the wrath of God that is directed towards sinners is only to confuse the mind. It is inconceivable that He can have borne our sin in the sense that the guilt or proper punishment of it was transferred to Him, and that He had experience of the pains of remorse. There is a sense, of course, in which we may speak of Christ having borne the wrath of God, if we mean by that expression that He had experience of those evils in the world that indicate the displeasure of God at sin, and of which He would naturally participate as incorporated with the life of man, and liable to share in the evils of man's disordered life. And viewing death as the culmination of this penal element in the world, we may regard His Death as charged with the power to express to Him the wrath of God against sin. But if it be meant that He was Himself in any sense the object of God's displeasure, or that He exhausted, by Himself personally enduring it as it enters into the experience of the sinner, or that the wrath of God broke upon His head, we must repudiate such an idea as altogether unwarranted. It is time that such an expression, so liable to be misunderstood and to confuse our thoughts of God, should be discarded. I entirely sympathise with the remarks of Gess on this subject. "What tact," he says, "is shown by the apostles in their never speaking of Jesus as bearing the Divine wrath! Our sins He has borne on the tree. God has made Him to be sin. He became a curse. The punishment lay upon Him. He is set forth for a manifestation of the righteousness of God in His blood. That the apostles, using such strong expressions, yet never make mention of the Divine wrath towards the Atoner, has its root in the feeling that anger signifies a state of indignant feeling that we dare never attribute to the mind of the holy God towards the holy Jesus. One may say, indeed, that this silence of the apostles is a proof of apostolic inspiration, and that the language even of respectable theologians about Jesus bearing the Divine wrath is a proof how far below the apostles theologians stand. Punishment may fall upon the innocent along with the guilty, anger can be directed only against the guilty. The innocent children of a murderer must, in accordance with the Divine order of the world, bear a portion of the punishment of their father; that God is angry with them no intelligent man would dream of saying. And the idea of the Father being angry with the Son, who drinks the bitter cup in obedience to the Father! Angry at His deed of self-sanctification, John xvii. 19! At the deed which the Father recompensed with the exaltation described in Philippians ii. 9! Not only the language of science but also that of edification ought once for all to free itself from such ineptitudes of expression, which have an effect the opposite of edification in the case of thinking persons, especially of those who think in accordance with Scripture" (*Christi Person und Werk*, iii. 442).

An instructive note will be found in Dr. Bruce's *Humiliation of Christ* on the doctrine that Christ suffered spiritual death in the place of sinners, as held by the Lutheran and by the Reformed Dogmatists—Note C to his sixth lecture.

NOTE F, p. 90.—OWEN ON THE ATONING ELEMENT IN THE DEATH OF CHRIST

It was a pleasant surprise to me to find such emphasis laid on the spiritual elements in Christ's offering by the great Puritan, as his authority is often adduced for a narrow view of the atonement that ignores these elements. In his work on *The Holy Spirit* he devotes a chapter (iv.) to "the work of the Holy Spirit in and on the Human nature of Christ." And here he insists on the presence in His death of those actings of the grace of the Holy Spirit by which He was distinguished all through His life. "And these," he says, "are diligently to be considered, because on them depends the efficacy of the Death of Christ as to atonement and merit; for it is not the death of Christ, merely as it was *penal* and undergone by the way of suffering, that is the means of our deliverance, but the *obedience* of Christ therein, which consisted in His offering of Himself through the Eternal Spirit unto God, that gave efficacy and success to it." He then proceeds to inquire into those "principal graces of the Spirit which He acted in this offering of Himself unto God." They are (I leave out his exposition under each head): (1) Love to mankind and compassion towards sinners. (2) His unspeakable zeal for, and ardency of affection unto, the glory of God. And with respect to the latter, two things were aimed at by Him: (1) The manifestation of God's righteousness, holiness, and severity against sin. (2) The exercise of His grace and love. "His zeal and affection unto the glory of God's righteousness, faithfulness, and grace, which was wrought in the heart of Christ by the Eternal Spirit, was that wherein principally He offered up Himself unto God." (3) His holy submission and obedience unto the Will of God. "His death was the highest act of obedience unto God which ever was or ever will be to all eternity, and therefore doth God so express His satisfaction therein, and acceptance of it." (4) His faith and trust in God, which, with fervent prayers, cries, and supplications, He now rested on God and His promises. He concludes thus, "Now, concerning those instances, we may observe three things to our present purpose:

"1. These and the like gracious actings of the Holy Christ were the ways and means whereby, in His death and blood-shedding,—which was violent and by force inflicted upon Him as to the outward instruments, and was penal as to the sentence of the law,—He voluntarily and freely offered up Himself a sacrifice unto God to make atonement; and these were the things which, from the dignity of His Person, became *efficacious* and *victorious*. Without those His death and blood-shedding had been no oblation.

"2. These were the things that rendered His offering of Himself 'a sacrifice to God of a sweet-smelling savour' (Eph. v. 2). God was so absolutely delighted and pleased with these high and glorious acts of grace and obedience in Jesus Christ, that He smelled, as it were, a savour of rest towards mankind, or those for whom He offered Himself, so that He would be angry with them no more. It was not by the outward suffering of an outward and bloody death, which was inflicted on Him by the most horrible wickedness that ever human nature broke forth into, that God was atoned; nor yet was it merely His enduring the penalty of the law that was the means of our deliverance; but the voluntary giving up of Himself to be a sacrifice in these holy acts of obedience was that upon which, in an especial manner, God was reconciled to us.

" 3. All these things being wrought in the human nature by the Holy Ghost, who in the time of His offering acted all His graces unto the utmost, He is said thereon to ' offer Himself unto God through the Eternal Spirit,' by whom, as our High Priest, He was consecrated, spirited, and acted thereunto."

Note G, p. 91.—Häring on the Death of Christ as a Demonstration of the Evil of Sin

It is a peculiarity of Häring's treatment of the subject, that he apprehends Christ as aiming, by what He did and suffered, at awakening in His Church a consciousness of guilt that answers to its greatness. For without this forgiveness is ethically impossible. There are two ways in which, he says, we may conceive Christ as having accomplished this. Either by His death on the cross, regarded as the supreme manifestation of the wickedness of man. We can conceive Christ as willing to submit to such a death at the hands of men, because He recognised it to be the object of God, in allowing the sin of man thus to exhaust itself on His Son, to convince men of their great guilt, and awaken the consciousness of their demerit. Or, by enduring the death of the Cross in obedience to the Will of the Father, we may think of Him as having practically acknowledged the divinely ordained connection between sin and evil, and thereby the inviolability of God's law; and the Church as led by Him to the same knowledge and recognition. "The fact that the Father surrenders the Son to death — and to this death — forces on us, as it did on the early Church, the thought that Jesus Himself saw in this death of His a direct manifestation for the condemnation of sin, the most powerful sermon on the inviolable earnestness of the Divine love 'which made Him to be sin who knew no sin.'" Häring contends for this interpretation as fitted directly to awaken that consciousness of guilt which is a condition of forgiveness. But he admits also the efficacy for this object of the Death of Christ when apprehended simply as the manifestation of the sin of men, and without the higher meaning attributed to it, when it is regarded as an act of submission on Christ's part to the majesty of the inviolable order of God.

NOTE H, p. 96.—ON THE DOCTRINE OF THE FALL IN JEWISH LITERATURE

The prevailing view in the Talmud is that Adam was not originally destined to die, and that it was his sin that is the cause of the mortality of the race. How far his sin also involved the *moral* ruin of mankind, as Paul teaches, is a point that is not quite so clear. Weber sums up the general result in these words: "Free will, even in reference to our disposition toward God, remained even after the Fall. There is hereditary guilt, but not hereditary sin. The fall of Adam has occasioned death to the whole human race, but not sinfulness in the sense of a necessity to sin. Sin is the result of the decision of every individual, as experience shows, but the Fall has not made it necessary" (*Lehren d. Talmud*, 217).

In the *Apocalypse of Esdras* we have express statements that Adam's sin has involved the human race both in sin and death: "O Adam, what hast thou done? for though it was thou that sinned, the evil has not fallen on thee alone, but on all of us that come of thee" (viii. 48); "the first Adam, being a wicked heart, transgressed and was overcome; and not he only, but all that are born of him" (iii. 20); "for a grain of wickedness was sown in the heart of Adam from the beginning, and how much wickedness hath it brought forth unto this time" (iv. 30). This is identical with the Pauline view, but great uncertainty prevails among scholars as to the date of the composition of Esdras, or at least of those portions of it from which these words are taken. We cannot positively affirm that the apostle borrowed his doctrine from this book, as it is possible that those who refer its composition to the latter years of the first century may be right. In this case, it would be nearer the truth to say that Esdras was dependent on Paul, and not Paul on Esdras.

In his *Book of Baruch* (1896), Mr. Charles insists that the author of the *Book of Esdras*, though a Jew, and writing in the interests of Judaism, was strongly influenced by Christian writings. In the *Book of Baruch*, which in its earlier portions is referred by him to the year 55–70 A.D., there are two different ideas on the subject in different constituents of the book. The one is that Adam's sin brought in physical death; but the responsibility for sin is fastened on each individual. "Each one of us has been the Adam of his own soul" (54, 19) (chap. xxiii. 4). The other refers the universality of sin as well as of death to Adam's sin. "O Adam, what hast thou done to all those who were born from thee, for all this multitude are going to corruption? nor is there any numbering of those whom the fire devours" (48, 42). In another passage (54, 15) Adam's sin is declared to have brought premature death on all. Mr. Charles thinks the more pessimistic passages betray the influence of the darker views of Esdras on the mind of the writer. He regards the *Book of Baruch* as reflecting more faithfully than *Esdras*, except in that one passage, the views of the synagogue. It is then at present impossible to say with certainty that the view of transmitted sin and death that Paul teaches was taken from the Rabbinical teaching of his day. It was a common tenet that physical death had come with Adam's sin; but there is no direct evidence that it was the opinion of the age that spiritual death had also followed: the likelier view is that it was his deeper apprehension of sin and the bondage of human nature to sin, that led him to believe in original sin, and in its proceeding from the same centre as that from which physical death had come.

NOTE I, p. 104.—ST. PAUL AND THE IMITATIO CHRISTI

The apostle's doctrine of the Imitation of Christ is very different from the view of those who have held that the earthly life of Jesus is intended to be copied by His followers. It is the Inner Spirit of that Life that remains for him the principle of true character and the law for all. He is the Indwelling life of those who are united in the roots of their being to Him, and He works in them, freely reproducing in them His mind and disposition; but being now released from the conditions of the flesh, He does not manifest Himself in them in the same forms of action or exhibit the same concrete features that His earthly course presents. "As the way," says Hort, "He is meant to transform us; but the transformation is not into the fashion of Jesus of Nazareth, but into a fashion shaped out of our own materials."[1] There are only four passages in which the historical Christ is referred to by Paul as an Example. The first is Rom. xv. 2-7, where he inculcates the duty of the strong to bear with the infirmities of the weak, and not to please themselves by following a course of action that would be an offence to others. "For even Christ pleased not Himself," he adds, "but bore the reproaches of others." And then, in bringing his argument to a close, he says, "receive ye one another as Christ also received you." The mind of Christ, seen in His gracious fellowship with all men irrespective of what they were, is to be manifested by Christians extending fellowship to those from whom they may differ on points of belief or practice. The love of Christ is commended to their imitation in its unselfishness and indiscriminate bestowal of His fellowship. Again, Eph. v. 2, "Walk in love, as Christ loved us, and gave Himself

[1] *The Way, the Truth, and the Life*, p. 205.

for us," where the *generosity* of His love to man is the point singled out (" He gave Himself for us ") as the characteristic of the love which Christians are to exhibit to one another. Once more, we have the great passage in Phil. ii. 5, etc., where the mind of Christ, who descended from a Heavenly Life to a life on earth for our sakes, is enjoined on us for imitation in a passage where it is Paul's object to exalt the grace of *humility*; and it is as a wonderful example of the spirit of condescending love that Christ is thus brought before us. Now, in all these instances it is one and the same spirit of love that is spoken of under a variety of aspects. Christ is held up to us as the Supreme Example and illustration of Love to Man. And in the way in which the apostle brings Christ before us in this character there is a studied absence of reference to historical instances in the life of Christ; it is that life as a whole that is present to the mind of the apostle as the incarnation and embodiment of the principle of love. When Paul speaks of himself as *under law to Christ* (1 Cor. ix. 21), and bids us *bear one another's burdens, and so fulfil the law of Christ* (Gal. vi. 3), he means the law of love that Christ our Life illustrates. He himself, he tells us, is an imitator of Christ in this subordination of self to the good of others (1 Cor. x. 33), and he does not hesitate to bid the Corinthians to imitate him, as he himself imitated Christ. Recognising the supremacy of Christ as the Perfect Exemplar of human love, he is conscious of himself as acting habitually from the same principle and worthy of being followed by others, in so far as he had successfully patterned his own life on that of his Master.

To Paul, then, the historical Christ was the Ideal of Love, and as such the object of his imitation if not in the particulars of His earthly life, yet most certainly in the spirit that ruled that life from first to last. If it was to that Ideal as realised in Christ who had died and had risen again that he habitually looked, rather than to its historical setting in the earthly Life of Jesus, the reason was that the Risen One alone, he knew well, through the Spirit proceeding from Him, enabled His followers to die to self and live that higher life of love which the Master had once lived on earth. The *Risen* Christ, victorious over sin and death, was therefore the proper object of imitation to the believer; to be conformed to Him in His Dying and Rising again was his ambition and aim. Paul craved in a perfect Example one who was not only in the graces of human character all that man should be, but who had attained to that destiny for which man was made. This he found in the Christ in whom Man had overcome death, and been crowned with everlasting life. He set the once Crucified and now Risen Christ accordingly before him, that he might not only by His Spirit fulfil love in its essential requirement, but might attain to the " resurrection from the dead," and to that perfection which consists in the complete supremacy of the Spiritual over the material.

LECTURE IV

NOTE A, p. 119.—DIFFERENCE BETWEEN PAUL'S DOCTRINE OF THE SPIRIT AND THAT OF THE BOOK OF WISDOM

THIS difference has been well put by Gloel in his suggestive little book on *Die Wirkungen des heiligen Geistes nach der Lehre des Ap. Paulus.* The following quotation sums up the points of difference:—

"Paulus glaubt an den göttlichen Geist, weil er ihn erfahren hat; das apokryphische Buch spekuliert über die Weisheit und kombiniert dieselbe mit der ganz abgeblassten, aus der Tradition entnommenen, Vorstellung vom Geiste Gottes. Für jenen ist der Geist die Gotteskraft, die ihn im innersten Wesen umwandelt; für dieses ist die Weisheit die Lehrerin, die über Gottes Wege unterweist 7, 22; 8, 9; 9, 10 f.; 10, 10. Weisheit lernt der Mensch; der Geist ergreift ihn.—Alle Ausagen beider, so ähnlich sie scheinen mögen, haben also einen ganz verschiedenen Sinn.

"Die Weisheit stattet mit allen Tugenden aus, denn aus ihrer Belehrung entspringen sie (6, 17 ff.; 8, 7). Auch der Geist verleiht alle Tugenden, aber weil er sie als eine Kraft Gottes im Menschen wirkt.

"Die Weisheit bewahrt durch ihre Belehrung den Gerechten unsträflich (10, 5. 13); der Geist wirkt in dem früheren Sünder einen Kampf gegen das Fleisch.

"Die Weisheit macht zu Freunden Gottes, 'denn nichts liebet Gott als den, der mit der Weisheit vertraut ist' (7, 28 cf. 4, 10; 7, 14; 9, 12); der Geist aber wird dem geschenkt, der die erwählende Liebe Gottes im Glauben aufnimmt.

"Die 'Unsterblichkeit' ist der Lohn für ein in Weisheit

geführtes Leben, 'denn gute Bestrebungen bringen gute
Früchte hervor' (3, 15 cf. 1, 15; 2, 22; 3, 5; 3, 14;
5, 15 f.; 8, 13, 17; 10, 17); der Geist ist die Kraft eines
neuen ewigen Lebens.

"Woher die Verschiedenheit? Paulus ist der Apostel
Jesu Christi, der bezeugt, was er erfahren; der Verfasser
des Weisheitsbuches dagegen ein Religionsphilosoph, nicht
unberükt von griechischer Philosophie, dessen Spekulation
im wesentlichen auf moralistischer Grundlage ruht und
nur wenig durch eine aus ernster Frommigkeit hervor-
gehende religiöse Betrachtungsweise altiriert ist (z.B. 7, 7;
bes. 8, 21: Gott verleiht die Weisheit; 9, 9–18); also
eine Lehrweise, welche etwa derjenigen der Patr. Apost.
kongenial ist, von letzterer nur unterschieden durch eine
spekulative Haltung" (pp. 86, 87).

NOTE B, p. 121.—RECENT LITERATURE ON THE
PAULINE PHRASE ἐν Χριστῷ

The Pauline phrase ἐν Χριστῷ has been made the subject of an interesting monograph by Deissmann, 1892 (*Die
N. Tliche. Formel "in Christo Jesu"*). Paul, he maintains,
is the creator of it, and it expresses a truth characteristic
of his theology. It is an instance of the formative power
of Christian thoughts to create forms of language that
express them. It does not occur in the Synoptic Gospels:
there, μετα, "with," not ἐν, "in," is used to describe the
relation of men to Christ, *e.g.* Matt. xii. 30; Mark iii. 14;
Luke xxiii. 43, etc. Paul never uses μετα to set forth relation to Christ: the Synoptic Gospels never use ἐν. Deissmann conceives that it must be taken in a local sense, as
declaring Christ to be the element in which the Christian
lives. It is the technical expression for the Pauline central
thought of the κοινωνια, or fellowship with Christ. The
underlying idea is that Christians somehow live *in* the
element *Christ*, as birds live in the air, and fishes in the
sea, and the roots of plants in the earth (p. 84). It is as
Pneuma that Christ sustains this relation to His people. The
Christian lives in the Pneumatic being, Christ. In regard to

the idea Χριστός, or πνεῦμα ἐν τίνι, which corresponds to ἐν Χριστῷ εἶναι, he says: "As one may, without being guilty of absurdity, say, The man is in the air, and the air is in the man, so may an author, who has represented the manner of existence after the analogy of the air, speak at once both of τὶς ἐν Χριστῷ, and Χριστὸς ἐν τινι" (p. 92). "The same idea underlies both forms of representation; only, the way of looking at it is in the one case *e specie Christi*, in the other, *e specie hominis*. They do not exclude one another, but together complete the *local* mode of apprehending the relation of the individual to the Pneumatic Christ"[1] (p. 93). Even although they could not be perfectly harmonised, the author adds, one has no right, in the case of a man like Paul, who was no systematic theologian, to speak of contradiction here. A religious ethical genius emancipates himself from all theological methods. His expressions are wont to reflect the events of the moment with absolute honesty. "The question whether we must apprehend the *local* ground-thought of the formula in the proper sense, or as a rhetorical expedient (Hülfsmittel), cannot with certainty be determined, but the former view is the more likely." The formula is the proper Pauline expression for the closest conceivable communion of the Christian with the Living Christ (p. 98).

Holding Paul to be the originator of the phrase, he views the Johannine use of it as betraying the Pauline influence on the later writings of John—the εἶναι ἐν Χριστῷ becomes in his vocabulary μείνατε ἔν ἐμοί.

These results have not passed unchallenged. Karl, in his *Beiträge zum Verständniss der Soter. Erfahr. u. Specul. des Ap. Paulus*, 1896, accepts the general position of Deissmann as to the Pauline originality of the phrase, but thinks that he has missed the exact sense of it. Taking for his parallel the expression ἐν Βεελζβούλ, Matt. xii. 27-28, where the idea of a possession of the believer by a personal

---

[1] Abbott (*The Spirit on the Waters*) thinks that we have here a double metaphor,—the *Spirit in the man* representing man as a machine moved by internal springs, the *man in the Spirit* representing man as an organism influenced by an external atmosphere.—P. 311.

spiritual Being is conveyed, he understands the phrase as meaning that the man who is ἐν πνεύματι, or ἐν Χριστῷ, is *within the sphere* of the influence or operation of the Spirit, or Christ (the two being the same thing). On this view, Karl differs from Deissmann in emphasising, more than the latter in his interpretation of the phrase, the personal influence of a spiritual Being to which that man is subject whose state is described by the phrase under discussion.

In an article in the *Stud. u. Kritiken*, 1896, 1 Heft, on *Paulinische Probleme II.*, Prof. Weiss also reviews the conclusions of Deissmann. He agrees with him that in the mass of characteristic passages, ἐν Χριστῷ εἶναι means an "abiding within the exalted Christ." But he thinks that Deissmann has pushed his theory too far; and he finds, after a searching examination and comparison of passages, that Paul often uses the phrase where no such out-of-the-way meaning attaches to it; ἐν, conveying the idea of limitation, often describes the sphere within which the action takes place, *e.g.* Rom. xvi. 3, 9; Col. iv. 7; 1 Thess. iii. 2. The formula, he thinks, must have been in common use in Paul's day, and applied in a general sense, though the specific sense attached to it when it describes the Pneumatic relation of believers to Christ is Pauline. The influence of the Septuagint, where the use of ἐν is used in reference to God, had probably to do with the combination *in Christ*, 2 Sam. xxii. 30; Ps. xvii. 30; Zech. xii. 5.

NOTE C, p. 144.—ON THE USE OF THE TERM Κύριος IN THE SEPTUAGINT

The term Κύριος is the common rendering of Jehovah in the Septuagint. If there was anything originally distinctive in the use of "Jehovah" as the name of God in contrast with other names, this distinctive idea was not present to the Greek translators, who render Jehovah Adonai, when it occurs, either by a double Κύριος (*e.g.* Ps. cviii. 21; Ezek. xiv. 6), or by Κύριος alone (Isa. lxi. 1; Jer. ii. 22). Κύριος and Θεός are used indiscriminately as translations of the Hebrew name for God. Accustomed to this usage,

Paul, however, confines the term Κύριος to Christ, and reserves Θεός for the Father God. With him Κύριος is not strictly identical with the Old Testament Jehovah. "Κύριος, applied to Christ, answers to the Hebrew Adonai, never to Jehovah. While Christ is often termed Κύριος τίνος ἐμοῦ, ἡμῶν, Jehovah as proper name has no suffix. A frequent Divine name in the Old Testament is also Jehovah Elohim, which the LXX. translate by Κύριος ὁ Θεός. But this expression is never used in the New Testament of Christ, a surprising fact if Jehovah in the eye of the apostle was a name suitable to be applied to the Son of Man." So far Cremer.

At the same time, the fact remains that Paul applies to Christ the term Κύριος, which was so freely applied to God in the Old Testament, and this plainly points to the belief that He whom he called Lord was in some sense God as well as He who was termed Θεός. The designation Κύριος implied divinity. It is strictly descriptive of His mediatorial office in glory, for Christ was not Κύριος till He was exalted. At the same time, the κυριότης is a form of the activity of one who in nature is Divine. He possessed in Himself the conditions that must be found in one who is to occupy so central a relation to mankind. This seems to have been the motive at work in the application to Him of a term which in the religious consciousness of the time was equivalent to that of God.

LECTURE V

NOTE A, p. 166.—THE ANGELOLOGY OF ST. PAUL

A STUDY of Paul's angelology would make plain to how great an extent he shared the conceptions of the age in which he lived, and what noble service he did in freeing men's minds from the tyranny of these conceptions. For while he believed with all the world at that time in the existence of angels, he succeeded in exposing the baselessness of their right to the religious regards of men, a right that had been accorded to them in the popular belief. The apocryphal and pseudepigraphic writings, and especially the Book of Enoch, which is full of the angels, must be studied in connection with, and for the understanding of, the allusions to angels in the New Testament. Everling, in his suggestive little work, *Die Paulinische Angelologie u. Daemonologie*, 1888, has thrown much light on such difficult passages as 1 Cor. xi. 10, viii. 4–6; 2 Cor. xi. 2, 3, etc., by quotations from these books that illustrate the notions commonly entertained at that time on this subject. Much instructive matter bearing on Paul's doctrine will be found scattered throughout Klöpper's great *Commentary on the Epistle to the Colossians*, especially pp. 227–236.

Paul shared the general view, set forth in the Epistle to Hebrews as well, that angelic agency was a distinguishing feature of God's government of the world under the Old Testament Dispensation, and that it had ceased with the abolition of the latter. The world of Judaism and heathendom, the old world as distinguished from the new that had come with Christ, the $αἰών\ μέλλων$, was under the angels. They were the intermediaries in its administration and government, and in the communication of God's will to men. Through their instrumentality the law was given (Gal. iii.

19); and this is mentioned by the apostle in the course of an argument meant to prove the temporary character of the law, as a mark of the inferiority of the legal system, compared with the Dispensation of promise, which had come direct from God to men. The "elements" of this world, which he represents the Galatians as having been subject to before they became Christians (Gal. iv. 3, 9), and whose functions, as regards their religious training, he compares to the office of tutors and governors to the son under age, are understood by many to refer to angelic agencies; for these were associated in the common mind with the phenomena of the material universe, and were supposed to animate the world, and to guide the movements of its forces. The heathen religions were ceremonial, and abounded in festivals and rites that were fixed by the movements of the heavenly bodies; and through these the will and activity of the angels were thought to be communicated. The stars moving across the heavens were identified with the heavenly host; many hold that the apostle, sharing this belief, viewed the stars as bodies animated by spiritual beings (1 Cor. xv. 40). The dependence of pre-Christian religions on the movements of sun, moon, and stars, regulating the observance of their rites, might well be regarded as equivalent to the subjection of men to the angels under that old world. But the abolition of legal ceremonial systems by Christianity, meant for the apostle the displacement, once for all, of the angels from the position they had formerly held in relation to man under God's government. In the economy of the spirit, which had succeeded to that of law, men had direct access to God as "sons," and the function and religious significance of angels ceased. Not to angels has He subjected the "world to come" which has already entered, but to Christ and to Mankind in Christ (Heb. ii. 5).

This, in brief, is Paul's view in the earlier Epistles. Angels, for him, exist even under Christ. They are also sources of temptation to men, if we are to take what he says in 1 Cor. xi. 10 as in earnest, and more than a pleasantry. But their power is broken, their office is ended, and they have no influence of one sort or another on the religious life.

It was not till the necessity arose for dealing with the Colossian heresy that he had occasion to speak of the bearing of the work of Christ on the angels, and their altered relation to men in consequence of the Cross. The legalism of the Colossians had its real root in their angel-worship; for, sharing the belief that the angels had given the law and were its guardians, and had power to inflict punishment on those who transgressed it, these false teachers represented obedience to its commandments as being a direct service to the angels, and an acknowledgment of their rights over men; and they aimed, through the outward discipline of the law, at effecting a likeness to angelic intelligences. Accordingly, while formerly he had taught that Christ had delivered men from the law, he now changed his voice, and presented Christ to their faith as having, in the act of setting men free from the law, freed them at the same time from the angelic powers which had tyrannised over them through the law. The question arises, How did Paul conceive of these angelic powers, as evil? or as good? or as neither the one nor the other? Much may be said in favour of the first view. For their hold of men through the law, that is, through the occasion that the transgression of the law had given to them, amounted practically to a power that was exercised by them in inciting men to sin.

The matter was thus looked at. Sin, having through man's own act entered into humanity, has become in conscious experience a power that would naturally appear to the religious imagination as a power wielded by personal evil agency behind consciousness; and it was equally natural to conceive of this personal agency of angels, or demons, as clothed with a certain legal right, as the instrument of God's justice, thus to rule men, making fresh sin necessary and holiness impossible.

Many find, in his early Epistles, indications of the apostle's belief that there is the personal working of unseen powers behind all the manifestations of evil in the human race, and that it is the real cause of these manifestations. So they explain 1 Cor. ii. 6–8, where the princes of this world are spoken of as the authors of the Deed on Calvary, and their wisdom is declared to have been brought to nought there,—as really referring to evil intelligences representing the powers of the unseen world. And similarly, the personal language used by the apostle (Rom. vii. 17) in reference to "sin in the flesh" of human nature is explained by the idea that the ἁμαρτια of the flesh is "not properly the sin of man, but a personal power of sin to be distinguished from man's sin, the kingdom of demons that is hostile to man, and would subject man to itself" (See *Die Psych. des Paulus von Simon*, pp. 54–60). If there is truth in this view of the connection, in the apostle's mind, between sin and the law on the one hand, and the power of demons on the other, man's deliverance from sin would be conceived of as really a deliverance from the power of evil agencies, and their being deprived of the right to have dominion over human souls. And Christ would be viewed as the Agent in this deliverance, and effecting it either by having given Himself as, in a manner, the ransom by which their right was acknowledged and satisfied, as in the old view of Irenæus and Origines, who founded on the passage in Col. ii. 18 their doctrine that the purchase of souls from sin by God was accomplished by the surrender of Christ as a compensation to the devil; or, the death of Christ might be regarded as having stripped these powers of their rights over humanity, inasmuch as His being slain of them was a gross abuse of these rights, He being without sin, and therefore not amenable to the death which they had power to inflict upon sinners. By their violence toward the Champion of Humanity they may be viewed as having outwitted themselves, and deprived themselves of their former rights over the race he represented. This opinion has also been held. But it is plain, I think, that till we know more of the demonology upon which these Epistles proceed, certain aspects of the soteriology of the apostle will remain a problem to us.

One thing certainly that makes us hesitate to regard these "principalities and powers," of which God "divested Himself" in the death of Christ, as malignant powers, is that in this Epistle the angels, who were thus set aside by Christ from the authority they formerly had, are represented as within the sweep of Christ's reconciling love as now dependent on Christ, in order to be brought within that harmony of all things with God which is the end of His Son's work.

On these two points, then, we notice an advance in the later Epistles with regard to Paul's teaching about the angels, first, in his apprehension of the death of Christ as having displaced them from the rule they once exercised over men; and second, in his inclusion of them in the Divine plan of redemption. But it is significant that Paul's interest in the angels is exhausted when he has made good his point that they are powerless, and have no real relation to the religious life of men. He does indeed, in Eph. vi. 12, speak of the Christian warfare as being with principalities and powers,—by which he intimates his belief in spiritual agencies that are in active opposition to the Divine will. But of angels as concerned in the administration of religious influence to men we hear no more after he has shown that the Christian dispensation has abolished the function they once discharged in the Divine Economy.

There is nothing in Paul of that prying curiosity into the secret administration of Providence which we find in Jewish literature, and which revelled in speculations about the ranks and orders of angels. The Romish Church has here served itself heir to the fantastic imaginations of Jewish theology on this subject. But Paul had too much practical good sense to trouble himself much about these matters.

We cannot, indeed, say much regarding the nature of the spiritual Force that is the cause of the phenomena of the material world. It is more consonant with our modern ideas to conceive of God as directly and immediately acting on nature, and according to that regularity of action that we speak of as law. Ancient thought, on the other hand, conceived of God as effecting His purposes through subordinate spiritual agencies. Cardinal Newman is perhaps the only great writer in modern times who is true to the spirit of ancient thought in this particular, for he holds very strongly the belief that all movement in nature is caused by angelic intelligences. In his sermon on the Feast of St. Michael, or the powers of Nature, he says: "Proceeding on such passages as John v. 4; Ex. xix. 16–18; Acts vii. 53; Rev. vii. 1; Gen. xix. 13; 2 Kings xix. 35; 2 Sam. xxiv. 15–17, as far as scriptural communications go we learn that the course of nature, which is so wonderful, so beautiful, and so fearful, is effected by the ministry of these unseen beings. Nature is not inanimate: its daily toil is intelligent; its works are duties. . . . Whenever we look abroad we are reminded of those most gracious and holy beings, the servants of the Holiest, who deign to minister to the heirs of salvation. Every breath of air and ray of light and heat, every beautiful prospect, is, as it were, the skirts of their garments, the waving of the robes of those whose faces see God in heaven."[1]

There may be nothing irrational in all this, however alien to our ways of thinking. It is a form of expression for the faith, that nature is living, or rather, that spirit, spiritual intelligence, is the real cause of all power and energy in the world; and that faith is welcome in whatever form it clothes itself; in its most fantastic dress it is preferable to the idea that nature is dead, and that there is nothing more than mechanical force at work in its phenomena.[2]

To the apostle the religious interest at stake in the question about the angels was secured when he had made good his point that Jesus was supreme over all, and that no intermediate intelligence had power to come between him and God, or to subject our life to the thraldom of that material world which was supposed to be the seat of their

---

[1] Newman's Sermons, vol. ii. pp. 360-362.

[2] R. Rothe was a firm believer in angels. It is said that when dying he bade his friends stand aside, smiling as he added: "It is not good that there should be too many people around a deathbed; then there is no room for the angels."

power. And if the truth of Christ's supremacy over "all principalities and powers" is to have value for us as a religious truth, we must translate it into the form I have set forth in the text, and regard it as the expression of the truth that through Christ, the Second Adam, and faith in His love, we are able to make all things in the natural world, even those that would otherwise work adversely to us, to minister to our Highest Good.

For a full statement of the Old Testament doctrine of angels there is nothing better than Prof. A. B. Davidson's article on "Angels" in the forthcoming *Bible Dictionary* edited by Dr. Hastings, by whose kindness I have been permitted to read it in proof.

NOTE B, p. 180.—BECK ON TRUTH AND LIFE

The following is from the opening lecture of his course on the Doctrine of the Christian Faith. I extract it from his *Gedanken aus u. nach der Schrift.* Neue Folge, 1878.

"Ich weiss es, . . . wie wogenartig auch edlere Gemüther umhergeworfen werden von Zweifeln und mancherlei Lehrmeinungen, und eben desshalb lege ich Ihnen die Bitte aus Herz: Fassen Sie Ihre Seelen in Ruhe und Geduld während des Vortrags, und seien Sie nicht schnell zu innerem Murren, wenn manches Sie eine harte Rede dünkt, auch nicht schnell zum hoffnungslosen Verzagen, wenn nicht in Bälde alles denk und mundgerecht für Sie ist, und die Frucht nicht vom Baume Ihnen in den Mund fällt. Das ist nicht wesenhafte Wahrheit, sondern Schein und Wahn, was sich bequem und rasch macht, was nicht enge Pforte und schmalen Weg hat, nicht Kraft und Ernst des ganzen Menschen in Anspruch nimmt, sondern nur eine vereinzelte Operation, die Denkoperation. Die Wahrheit besteht nicht aus blos formalen Gedanken, sondern ist reales Leben. Die Mittheilung der Wahrheit kann nur als Lebenseinpflanzung stattfinden und diese erfordert Offenheit, Stille und Ausdauer, dass Anwurzelung und Entwickelung zu Stande komme. Die Wahrheit muss Anstössiges und Fremdartiges für uns haben, so lange und so weit wir selbst ihr noch fremd sind; die Zubildung zu ihr und die Ausbildung in ihr geschieht nach festen Gesetzen eines Lebensprocesses, und nicht nach blossen Gesetzen eines Denkprocesses. Darum kann die Wahrheit, die höher ist als wir selbst, auch nur allmälig und stückweise von uns erkannt werden, kann auf der Entwicklungsstufe, auf der wir gerade stehen, nicht in allen Theilen und Beziehungen uns zugänglich und verständlich werden. Wer ausharrt und das festhält, was er schon als innerlich versiegelte Wahrheit hat und dabei das noch Befremdliche nicht wegwirft, sondern für weitere Prüfung sich reservirt, der gewinnt Boden und Samen, woraus ihm immer reichere Ernte erwächst; wer abspringt, so oft ihn ein Zweifel juckt, statt seinen Zweifel selbst zu bezweifeln, wer abbricht, wo sichs seiner angelernten Manipulation nicht fügen und biegen will—der mag ein fahrender Schüler werden oder ein versessener Antithesenmeister, aber zur Wahrheit, die ihn trägt und über sich selbst hinausführt, die ihm Lebenssubstanz gibt und Capital für eine Ewigkeit—zu der Wahrheit kommt er nie."

LECTURE VI

NOTE, p. 210.—DIFFERENT FORMS OF THE THEORY OF THE PRE-EXISTENT GOD-MANHOOD OF CHRIST

MOST of those who have believed in the Pre-existent God-manhood of Christ have represented it as an eternal determination of the Godhead, or of the Logos. But the opinion has also been held by some that the Pre-existent Humanity of the Son of God is not eternal, but was assumed by Him in an act prior to creation, in order that through It all things might be created, and that it is this taking of our nature into union with His own Eternal Nature that constitutes Him the First-Born of creation. This is the doctrine of Isaac Watts and others, and it has been recently revived, although without any apparent dependence on previous writers, in a work entitled *The Nature of Christ*, by William Marshall, 1896, in which, with great earnestness and confidence in the scripturalness of his view, the writer, in opposition to previous Christologies, advocates the position that the Son of God, before creation and for mediatorial ends, became the Divine Man in order to represent God to men and men to God: and that it was this Divine Humanity that He laid aside when He became Incarnate, in order that in our flesh and blood He might work out our salvation. He thus distinguishes between a twofold incarnation, that which took place before and for the ends of creation, consisting in the assumption of our nature in its spiritual essence, and that which took place when He descended to this world, consisting in the assumption of a flesh and blood humanity subject to temptation and disease and death.

The point of sameness in this view and the ordinary form in which the doctrine of the Pre-existent Divine Humanity of Christ has been held is that in both there is posited a pre-existent humanity, which in its Divine or Heavenly form is laid aside at the Incarnation in order that a flesh and blood form of it may be assumed; but while, on the one view it is regarded in its Heavenly form as Eternal and essential to the Son of God, on the other view, that advocated by the author I have mentioned, it is represented as brought into existence in time and for mediatorial ends. I confess I am not able to appreciate, as the author himself does, the advantage that his view possesses over the other, or the importance he attributes to its adoption as likely to bring about a reform in our religious thinking. The whole subject belongs to a region of pure speculation, into which we may venture with our theories, if we choose, but where we are not likely to make discoveries that will approve themselves as such to any others besides ourselves.

LECTURE VII

NOTE A, p. 239.—DORNER ON THE "IDEA OF CHRIST IN THE MIDDLE AGES" (*from History of the Doctrine of the Person of Christ*, Div. ii. vol. i., pp. 273–275)

"BUT when, in opposition to Adoptionism, it had been established that Christ was the Son of God even as to His humanity, the long-repressed torrent burst irresistibly forth; then was the humanity of Christ robbed of its proper significance, and the image of His own Person was so sublimated into the pure transcendence of the deity, that to the eye of simple faith He only bore the aspect of 'our Lord God.' Thus, whilst apparently heightened, Christology was brought to a point at which the God-man, the sympathising High Priest, who belongs to our race, practically ceased to exist; and there remained only the unapproachable holy God, as He was conceived and feared by men previous to the appearance of Christ. All that was now expected with regard to Christ was that He should come again to judgment. No marvel, then, that an Antichristian horror of death and Hades fell on Christendom,—that it sought a compensation for the loss of the sympathy of the God-man in human intercessors, whose post it was, forming as they did the ideal Church, to preserve sinful humanity from the devouring fire of the holy Judge, into whom Christ had been transformed. The loss of the historical God-man, of the Son of man full of grace and truth, thus reawakened, in the religious nature of humanity, impulses similar to those out of which had grown, prior to the coming of Christ, the myths and Christological preludes of heathendom.

. . . .

"The first result of this loss of the living, divine-human

Mediatorship of Christ, was that the piety of the Middle Ages created for itself, in the exercise of a phantastic imagination, by way of compensation, a host of mediators, amongst whom the Queen of Heaven occupied the foremost place. By this procedure another tendency of the natural heart found a kind of satisfaction,—the tendency, namely, to the deification of nature, that is, to the deification of humanity and its powers, apart even from Christian grace; a tendency in which are combined at once timidity and defiance, indifference and haughtiness. For Mary, the mother of the Lord, was held not to have needed redemption; and was not, therefore, on an equality with the other members of her race: she was raised above them by her freedom from original and actual sin; she was absolutely pure and holy from her very birth; and on the ground of this, her perfection, which she possessed prior to the birth of Christ, she was fitted and worthy to be the mother of God. She sets before us, therefore,—she who stood, to the piety of the Middle Ages, in a relation of such prime importance,—what human nature is capable of producing out of itself even apart from the redemption by the God-man."

Note B, p. 243.—On the Historical and Exalted Christ

We distinguish between the Historic and the Exalted Christ, but we are apt in doing so to forget the essential sameness of the two. On this Deissmann has some good remarks, that call attention to the fact that to the apostle the distinction had not the significance we sometimes attach to it.

"The Exalted Christ is the centre of his Christian thinking. This Christ is to him indeed the same as He who, after a life of poverty, had died on the cross and had been raised again; but this Risen and Exalted Christ is to him a historic Greatness in the eminent sense of the word. When we speak to-day of the 'Historic' and the 'Exalted' Christ we are influenced by the modern view of the nature of historical science, for which, as is self-evident, only that life of man that lies between birth and death can be viewed as historic reality. To the man of antiquity, however, everything is history that takes place in heaven and on earth and under the earth, in time and eternity, among Gods, heroes, and men. The man of antiquity in this respect resembles the giants in battle who εἰς γῆν ἐξ οὐρανοῦ καὶ τοῦ ἀοράτου πάντα ἕλκουσι, ταῖς χερσὶν ἀτεχνῶς πέτρας καὶ δρῦς περιλαμβάνοντες.[1] The men of the N. T. are no exception. The statement ἐν ἀρχῃ ἦν ὁ λόγος is meant for a historical statement, as much so as is that other, καὶ τῇ ἡμέρᾳ τῇ τρίτῃ γάμος ἐγένετο ἐν Κᾶνα τῆς Γαλιλαίας. To expect from the Apostle Paul, a nature so completely dominated by ethical religious interests, a consciousness of the modern conception of history would be a gross anachronism. He thought ἀτεχνῶς: when he spoke of the Risen Christ he did not reflect, Now I have left the ground of history and am venturing into another sphere,—on the contrary, what made him great, the remarkable energy of his faith in Christ, was rooted in this, that he was as immovably convinced of the Historic Reality of the Risen, Living Christ as he was of the historic fact that Jesus had died on the Cross, or that he himself had had a vision of Christ" (*Die N. Tliche. Formel " in Christo Jesu "*), p. 81.

NOTE C, p. 246.—THE CHRISTOLOGY OF RITSCHL AND HIS SCHOOL[2]

The Christology of the school of Ritschl is one of the most interesting features of the remarkable movement of theological thought initiated by that theologian. The leading outlines of the master's mode of apprehension of the subject are reproduced with striking fidelity in the teaching of his

[1] Plato, *Soph.*, 246 A.
[2] The edition of Ritschl's *Rechtfertigung u. Versöhnung*, vol. iii., to which reference is made in the following account, is the 3rd, 1888. I have also consulted Ritschl's *Leben*, vol. ii., p. 208–220. There is a brief account of his system by Thikötter (*Darst. u. Beurth. der Theol.* A. Ritschl, 1887) which will be found useful. Students will

disciples, though there are divergences from Ritschl amongst them as well as differences from one another on points that are not unimportant. Complaint is sometimes made that Ritschlianism is one thing in one case and a different in another. And there is an element of truth in this, for it is a method common to all who have come under his influence, rather than a system that is adopted by them in its various parts. But the impulse that he has given to Christological study follows in all cases much the same lines. I must content myself with a very general account of his teaching on this subject. Ritschl's quarrel with the ecclesiastical Christology is that it proceeds on a wrong method. It defines the Divinity it attributes to Christ before it has taken account of the actual effects of the working of that Divinity in history and human experience. Not till after it has thus defined the nature of Christ and His transcendent relation to God does it inquire into the forms of activity in which it manifests itself to us. In other words, instead of proceeding on the inductive method, starting from experience and asking what the confession of Christ's Divinity means for those who make it, and what that religious experience is which originates the confession, it follows the deductive method, and begins with a so-called intellectual or scientific knowledge. We must, however, be satisfied with a *religious* knowledge of the subject—with one, that is to say, that is based on the experience of the religious benefits that we owe to Christ. We thus return to the position of Melanchthon in the first period of his theological activity, that the knowledge of the benefits of Christ is the starting-point for the understanding of His Godhead. The knowledge of the Divinity of Christ is inaccessible to those who come to the study of the subject with ideas of the Divine borrowed from natural religion. The true knowledge of Him flows from faith.

receive much help from the instructive work of G. Ecke, which has just appeared (1897), *Die Theologische Schule A. Ritschl.* It may be recommended as by far the fullest in information, as well as the fairest in tone, that has been published on the questions at issue between Ritschl and his opponents.

The judgment of Christ's Divinity at which we thus arrive is, it is true, a "Werturteil," or a judgment *of value*, to use the well-known Ritschlian phrase; that is, it affirms a truth that expresses the sense of His religious worth to us. It does not follow from this, as some say, that it is a merely subjective judgment, or that it does not state that which is true of Christ in Himself. All religious judgments, Ritschl holds, are "Werturteile." "We can know God and what is Divine," to use his words (p. 376), "only through the apprehension of His value for the satisfaction of our nature." "The 'Werturteil,'" as one of his disciples says, "declares whether the thing is for us of importance or is indifferent, whether it affects us with pleasure or the reverse. Applied to religion, it means that what we can know of God is to be gathered from the effects of His working upon us." There is no contrast between the thing as it is in itself and the thing as apprehended by us; the "Werturteil" is contrasted merely with a theoretic judgment, which necessarily excludes the personal factor. "He who does not understand this through sheer intellectual prejudice," says Ritschl's son and biographer, "might with as good ground say that Ritschl denies the existence of God and teaches atheism, as that he denies the reality of the Godhead of Christ in the full sense of the word" (*Leben*, p. 212).

The Godhead of Christ is thus the confession of the religious estimate of its Founder by His believing Church. It is the outgrowth of their experience of Christ. On the one hand, He is "Lord," a term by which His people confess His sovereignty over all, His dominion over the world, a confession that has its root in the experience of His present activity in saving them from sin and overmastering the hindrances to their well-being. And, on the other hand, He is the Revealer to them of the grace and truth of God. The disciples recognising what the Exalted Christ was to them, viz. the Revealer of the loving God and their personal Lord, expressed their convictions of what He was by calling Him Lord, and speaking of Him as Divine; "for an authority," says Ritschl, "that either excludes all other standards or subordinates them to itself, and that commands in an exhaustive way all the trust of the soul that is due to God, has the value of Godhead" (p. 383).

But this knowledge of Christ, derived from experience, must be authenticated by the history of Christ: " If the Divinity of Christ, or His Sovereignty over the world in the form of the Exalted One, is to be apprehended as necessary knowledge, or as a part of the Christian religious view of the world, it must be borne witness to by the operation of Christ upon us. But every operation of Christ upon us must have its standard (by which we judge its claim to be an effect of Christ) in the historical Form of His Life. Accordingly, the Divinity or the Sovereignty of Christ must be discoverable in definite features of His historic life as attributes of His temporal existence. For what Christ is in His Eternal Life, and what He, as Exalted, effects on our experience, would be utterly unthinkable if we did not see it exemplified first in His historical existence in time. If the conception of His present Sovereignty cannot be filled up with definite characteristics derived from His working in His Historic form of Being, it is either a worthless scheme of thought, or an occasion for every possible sort of fanaticism. On the other hand, holding fast the conviction that Christ now rules over the Church of the Kingdom of God, and is working towards the object of gradually bringing the world under the Divine rule, we must then be able to recognise this Sovereignty over the world as a prominent characteristic of the historical life of Christ" (pp. 383, 384).

Accordingly, the real interest is transferred to the historical Christ, which is the exclusive ground of, and the one norm for all representations we may form of Christ's extra-historic Being and Activity. We may not attribute to Christ Exalted any feature of material importance which cannot be shown to hold first of His historic life and to be part of the picture given to us in the Gospels. The historical Christ is the source of our Christological affirmations. And, accordingly, Ritschl takes us to the Gospels, and emphasises the study of the Christ of history and the features of His personal life. Christ comes before us, there, in the capacity of the Founder of the Kingdom of God. It was the task of His life and teaching and activity to establish the Kingdom, and this He does, on the one hand, by revealing the love of God to men. This is one aspect of His Divinity as a historical Person—He is one with God in His love, His will, His mind. And the other is, His Sovereignty over the world; for God is Sovereign, and Christ attests His claim to this Divine position by His power over the world. This power was evinced in His independence and spiritual mastery of the world, and His superiority to all the hindrances it presented to the prosecution of His mission, as well as in His patience under the suffering it inflicted upon Him—for in bearing its evil and the bitter consequences of falling under its displeasure, Christ conquered it, broke its power. It is not in any private display of power of a material, palpable sort, either in His historical life in the world or in His supernatural life in His Exalted State, that the Sovereign Might of Christ is displayed, but in the sphere of His spiritual life, through the victory of good over evil, by His patience and meekness under wrong, and the unflinching fidelity with which He bore the sufferings to which He was exposed (pp. 428–436).[1]

According to the suggestions of the N. T., then, the elements in the historical appearing of Christ that are comprehended in the attribute of His Godhead are His Grace and Truth in the execution of the calling of His Life, and the superiority of His spiritual self-determination to the particularistic and natural motives that the world offered (p. 436).

The Divinity thus predicated of Christ is purely ethical. There is no contrast between the human and the Divine natures, as in the orthodox doctrine. For Christ as man is not apprehended as in possession of an abstract human nature, but as the individual man Jesus, who was faithful to His special vocation, and by His perfect love and patience

---

[1] There is a fine passage in the Ep. to Diognetus in the spirit of Ritschl's Christology, in which the author shows that man may imitate God even in respect of His Lordship, inasmuch as the latter consists not in using force to inferiors, but in one taking upon him the burden of others (chap. x.)

furnished the self-manifestation of God (*Leben*, p. 216). This identification of God, whose nature is love, with man in the one Person, while a paradox to reason, is religious truth and the intuition of faith.

It follows also that the Divinity predicated of Christ is transferable to His people, and is thus predicable of His Church in so far as it is viewed as the sphere of His continued influence. The Church is the organ by which God manifests Himself and exercises sovereignty over the world; it exhibits the operation of Him who in the historical Form of His Being revealed God and exercised dominion over the world. "It is included," says Ritschl, "in the full idea of the Godhead of Christ, that His Grace and Truth and world-subduing Patience should reach their proper effect in the existence of a Church of the Kingdom of God that should be invested in the same attributes. For one must combine together in idea Him who exercises Divine lordship, and is, to use Lutheran language, my Lord, and those who experience this sovereignty in themselves. The Church, the Kingdom of God, must be viewed in this light, since its members, acting from the motive of universal love of man, and wielding a power over the world that renders them independent of it, thereby manifest the effect upon them of the peculiar working of Christ.[1] Hence we explain the fact that the idea of the Divinity of Christ, or the application of the Old Testament name of God to Him, first proceeded from the Church. Christ was not in the position to designate Himself so. Accordingly, we can form a right theological judgment regarding this attri-

---

[1] Ritschl is careful to define the power that he ascribes to the Sovereignty of Christ. It is not a fact of sense-experience. "The phenomena in which many seek the proper proof of the power of Christianity, political influence, legal authority of persons and Church institutions, are suspiciously like a falsification of Christ's purpose, and there is needed a very strong faith in the Invisible, in order, under the the confusions and atrocities as well as pitiful things in Church history, to keep in view the growing might of Christ over the world" (pp. 433, 434). Then he explains that the Power over the world which he attributes to Christ's people falls within the sphere of the spiritual life, as in the case of the Master.

bute only when we think of Christ as Efficient Head of the Church of the Kingdom of God. For it is not till we thus combine Christ and His Church that we recognise that He is in *His order unique*" (dass er in Seiner Art der Einzige ist) (pp. 437, 438).

The further question with which ecclesiastical Christology busies itself, How the Person of Christ comes to have such a value for the religious life of man? is, according to Ritschl, "no proper object of theological inquiry, because the problem lies outside of inquiry of every kind. What the Church tradition offers us in this connection is in itself obscure, and not fitted on that account to explain anything. Christ is given to us as the Bearer of the perfected Revelation, that we may believe on Him. But the union between Him and God the Father admits of no explanation of a scientific sort. And as a theologian, anyone may know that useless inquiry after such explanation only leads to the obscuring of the recognition of Christ as the perfected Revelation of God" (p. 426).

The general idea of the Christology here sketched is shared by all who acknowledge Ritschl as their master. All are agreed as to the importance of the principle that the historical life of Jesus, and the experience of His continued activity in the Church which accepts Him as its Founder, are the sources of true Christology, and that the religious estimate of Him that is drawn from these sources is final for the faith. His Divinity is a judgment of His religious value. The confession of it is an expression of the experience of salvation that we owe to His person. The words of Gottschick, one of the earliest of Ritschl's disciples, have the genuine Ritschlian ring: "If the faith in the Godhead of Christ is really religious faith, and no speculation of the understanding; if it expresses the fact that Christ, as we have experience of Him, calls forth our absolute reverence, our full thankfulness, our unreserved surrender to love, that He secures us in the blessed and eternal life that is the specific gift of Godhead,—then His Godhead, being the correlate of this experience and personal surrender, must be recognised by us in those very characteristics that call forth the determination of our personal life. But these are the marks of His *manifested* historical human life, not of a hidden background of it which we may postulate to explain them. The Godhead of Christ, therefore, expresses the value which the historical reality of this Personal life possesses, as the power that produces the new humanity of regenerate and reconciled children of God."

There are disciples of Ritschl, indeed, who emphasise the understanding of the *historical* Christ as the basis of religious faith and certainty almost, as it may seem, to the exclusion of the other aspect of His activity as *Risen* and *Exalted*; while another section, more faithful to the apostolic representation, which reserves the application of Divine honour and prerogatives to Christ as Glorified, accentuate the experience that is formed by faith in Him under the latter aspect. With Herrmann the historical Christ is everything. The one dominating thought in His "Communion with God" is the experience of the Divine that is formed by spiritual contact with the Christ of history. Kaftan, on the other hand, more Pauline in his sympathies than Herrmann, insists on communion with the *Risen* Christ, and on the experience of the *summum bonum* that the Glorified Christ confers (see his *Wesen der Christl. Religion*, pp. 337–342).[1] But Kaftan holds as firmly as Herrmann does, that the true idea of the Divinity of Christ is derived from the Picture of Jesus contained in the Gospels, and that we cannot receive from the Exalted

[1] Rade, another of Ritschl's disciples, emphasises even more than Kaftan this point. "The worship of the Glorified Christ," he says, "is what we mean when we speak of faith in the Godhead of Christ. This is what the early Church meant; and by this worship they exalted Him to a position of oneness with God. This worship of Christ grew out of their impression of His Person and the experience of His work upon them. It still holds that no one can call Christ God who has not found in Him a Redeemer. But he who has experienced Christ's power cannot regard Him as a mere man. For a man cannot redeem us from what is the universal fate of man. If Jesus was a mere man, then He was indeed the Genius in the religious sphere, as others are geniuses in other spheres. But then we could not speak of His being a Redeemer in the Christian sense."

Lord "revelations that are new, that complete or surpass what is given to us in the historical Jesus." And in spite of the occasional obscurity of Herrmann's language, it is evident, I think, that the power he attributes to the historical Christ to reveal God and to make God a power in our lives, belongs to Him as living and exalted and using the Gospel picture of His Personal life-work as the medium of His present activity in human hearts. "The Exalted Christ," he says, "is really present to the Christian." "The Lord who has overcome is near us with His human sympathy." "Faith at its height is in a position to apprehend the working upon us of the Exalted Christ."

Herrmann and Kaftan and the disciples of Ritschl generally recognise that the historic Figure of the Gospel shows no trace of the possession of omnipotence, omniscience, omnipresence, and maintain that these are inconsistent with the being of the historical man, and that it is the holy love of God that constitutes the proper nature of God, and is revealed in the human life of Jesus.

When we inquire as to the views of the school of Ritschl with respect to the Transcendent Being of Christ, or His hyper-historical relation to God and man, the answer is more difficult to give. Ritschl himself held a somewhat extreme opinion on this subject, in which he is not followed by the majority of his followers. The predicate of Godhead applied to Christ is exhausted, he held, when we have recognised Him as the Revealer of God and the Archetype of spiritual sovereignty over the world. The question of how He stands, in that relation, to God and to us is set aside as an idle one, as lying outside the limits of knowledge; conceived of under the attribute of Pre-existence, Christ is not revealed but hidden, and has no religious value in that capacity because it suggests a relation of Christ in which He is separated from, and is inimitable by us. H. Schultz, Harnack, and Wendt occupy the same position as Ritschl here, insisting that that which constitutes the inmost essence of Christ's Godhead is not anything that separates Christ from His own, but a something that connects them with Him, and which they receive from Him.

But most of his disciples refuse to go the length of limiting the application of the predicate of Godhead to what is recognised as characterising His earthly historical life, and is participated in by His people. Kaftan, Kattenbusch, Loofs, and others, while hesitating to assert the personal pre-existence of Christ, go a long way in claiming for Him an essential Godhead that makes it possible for Him to be to us what He proves Himself to be in our spiritual consciousness. Kaftan recognises truth in the doctrine of the Pre-existence of Christ in so far as it ascribes to Him, the Personal Bearer of the Perfect Revelation, a relation to the Father that is unique and incommunicable. Again, he speaks of the Incarnation as an "event in the Divine life." Kattenbusch speaks of Him as the "Messianic King in virtue of His unfathomable but personal-essential relation to God the Father." Loofs, referring to Thomas' confession, says that he who makes it "must know that the mystery before which he bows in worship must be on God's side conditioned in a way that completely surpasses our understanding"; and Bornemann, in speaking of Christ as distinguished from others, says: "while we other men are all created by God and are His creatures, His work, Jesus alone is born of God, that is, is like Him in His proper nature. Between us and Him there is all the difference that exists between the works of an artist, that reflect the spirit, mind, and character of the artist, and the only son of the same artist, who alone can be the peculiar, real, and perfect image of his father in nature and character."

Herrmann regards the thought of Christ's personal pre-existence as a self-contradictory expression, but still the only one at our command to set forth an important truth, "that the Person of Christ is independent of the world which represents the dependent sphere of His rule. The contradiction would be removed if the problem of time in which we now behold our existence were solved. The supposition of an ideal pre-existence seems to surrender what was originally intended, as much as the ecclesiastical Christology does when it thinks of the pre-existent One, not as the Lord of the Church, but as the

Logos-subject, destitute of content." He forbears all speculation concerning the personal pre-existence of Christ, holding that we have here a final and conclusive thought of faith, and will have nothing to do with attempts to explain the mystery of the personal life of Christ by definitions of the relation of His essential Godhead to His true Humanity.

The fresh point of view from which the whole subject is regarded under the scheme of thought that I have sketched, has beyond all doubt given a new impulse not only to the theology of Germany, but to the popular teaching and preaching of the Church. Unbiassed witnesses speak of the earnest evangelical tone it has imparted to the pulpit in many parts of the Church, and the fresh interest in the practical work of the Church that has been awakened; and as an instance of the use of its leading ideas in the popular exposition of New Testament truths, I shall give two or three quotations from a little work on the Christian Faith by the late Theodor Jess[1] of Kiel. The work is prefaced by a notice of Jess by Prof. Nitsch, who tells us it is but a fragment of a larger work which it was the intention of the author, had he lived, to publish. Jess was cut off prematurely, and is spoken of by Nitsch as a man of singular power as a preacher. The work consists of five lectures. I quote from the last, in which he treats of Christ as God, Mediator of the New Covenant, the Archetype of Humanity, and the Image of God: "The place where Jesus Christ lived on earth, suffered, died, and was buried, is now empty: we look up to the glorified Lord. But inasmuch as He who is exalted to the Right Hand of God is one and the same with the historical Christ who walked this earth, His earthly life is of as great importance to us as His heavenly. A perverted picture of Christ is always the result when we take account of either the exalted or the historical Christ to the exclusion of the other. The purely historical handling of the life of Jesus that is indifferent to the recognition of Him as the Eternal Head of the Church is far from doing justice to Him—the evidence

[1] *Über den Christl. Glauben Vorträge*, von M. Jess, 1892.

of this is not wanting. It is an equally defective treatment that He has sometimes received in Christianity when the life and work of Christ are ignored, and one inquires into the special manner of His existence and rule in heaven. We learn to know Him as He is and lives in eternity, only as 'clothed with His word,' that is, in His historical words and works in this world. In these He is intelligible to us; and hence all depends on our combining the historical with the religious estimate of His Person. This object is not attained when one forms thoughts of His heavenly glory that ignore the manner of His appearing in the state of humiliation; we as certainly fail to attain it when we do not succeed in discovering in His earthly appearing the marks of the glory that is now peculiar to Him. If we found in His life on earth nothing but humiliation, His eternal glory would be concealed from us and be a mystery. But He makes it manifest in His life and death in the flesh, and we must learn thus to apprehend it" (p. 68).

Again, in speaking of Christ as the Lord of the Church, and of the Church as the organ of Christ's Rule, by which He is subjecting all things to Himself: "Christ works on no one without means: personal as must be the relation between Him and those who are brought by Him to God, the relation is not unmediated. If Scripture attributes such importance to the fact that Christ is come in the flesh, that God has revealed Himself in this appointed Man, then the maintenance and diffusion and deepening of the Christian Church is bound up with its connection with the historical Christ. The Personal continuance (Bestand) of His human life is regulative for the religious life of all. In this respect He occupies an entirely Unique Position among all who are born and die in the world, and He continues to occupy this position notwithstanding all who come to God by Him and obtain Eternal Life. What we become, how high soever we rise, is all through Him. That is the permanent difference between Him and all perfected righteous ones. Christendom is held together by the fact that it hangs on Him who is the Head, and that it is His Body. For us, this Man, who was crucified in Jerusalem, and

God, who helps us in our need and calls us to Eternal Life, are bound up together inseparably. We know God only in Christ, we know about God only in Him. God's final aim is revealed to us in the life-aim of Christ. God's purposes are disclosed to us in the Mind of Christ. From Him we learn that God's aim is to receive human beings into His Kingdom, that His motive is Love, that He has the same aim as Christ. The latter is in the world free and supreme over it, as God is: these are the marks of His Godhead. And in all these relations that hang so closely together, He is unique among His brethren, as God is, the only Begotten of the Father in the great company of God's children. However many there be who enjoy the Christian Good and realise its Ideal of life, they are unlike Him in their dependence upon Him. And not only in this respect, but He is the unapproachable Ideal by whom the impulse is stirred in us to walk in His footsteps. This unlikeness remains to all Eternity, because Christ is unique.

"Experience shows that the Good and the Ideal of Christianity suffer in their distinctiveness as soon as the connection with the historical Christ is undervalued and neglected. The character of our whole life is to-day, in every movement, conditioned by that of this Man; therefore we must realise Him as continually present. What His Will is we can learn from His historical working, and from the words recorded by the Evangelists. But the manifestations of His Spirit mediated by the word of the Gospel are certain and of universal validity. Luther was aware also of the claims to a so-called direct relation to Christ, but He condemned them as fanaticism. The Living and Risen Lord has intercourse with us only as clothed with His word: it is phantastic to speak of influences that go beyond His word. Only then are we really in contact with Him, when the movements of our own minds die away before His purpose made plain and intelligible in the word of His Gospel. The Mediator between us and God is hence the Historical Christ.

"But for us He is not to be separated from God—to separate between Him and God is unbelief. To believe in

Him means to find God in Him, my Lord and my God. All men must honour the Son of God, who, like the Father, summons into life with creative power, even as they honour the Father. He is the Perfect Revealer of God, and the Original of Humanity. What is to be brought together through Him, God and Humanity, is united in Him" (pp. 104, 105).

"Christ is then really the Mediator of the Covenant between God and man, for He belongs to both—God's perfect image and man's antitype, Jesus Christ, the historical Christ, He of whom the Gospels tell us. Does reason object? do these things appear perfectly irreconcilable? let us be assured *that* is due to the representations of so-called reason about God and man. If we hold by the notion of God (coming to us from heathenism) as Infinite Being in antithesis with man, who is mere finitude and limitation, we cannot indeed see how they can be reconciled. But the fact that we see in Christ the God-man should lead us to form and shape our thoughts of God and man according to Him. We seek to learn to know God and human nature nowhere else save in Jesus Christ. That is the way by which one really finds God.

"No man hath seen Him at any time: He dwells in light that no man can approach unto. Therefore one learns really to know Him only through the Revelation which we have in Christ. To know and possess God, that is, to trust in Him, and to know that we may leave ourselves with Him, that He cares for us, that we are of value in His eye, —*that* conflicts with what Hellenic heathendom regards as His majesty. Even learned men among Christians are afraid to confess that human beings can be of value to God. Such assertions, they think, touch too closely the sublimity of the Creator; it accords better with His Greatness to regard human beings as something He could do as easily without, had He chosen not to create them. But such thoughts are not born of Christ. The proper view of the world is not got by means of scientific proof, but is a contribution of the Christian religion. The Christian view of God is the solution of the problem of life, how we are to bear ourselves as Christians in relation to nature. Under the influence of Christianity one has learnt to view nature with new eyes. If we abandon our Christian faith in God, there is found in the many tendencies that are at work in the universe absolute aimlessness; Nature appears to be irrational alike in destroying and bringing into being: the dice seem to fall without aim. We trace powerful and destructive forces as well as benevolent ones. There is retribution, but it is not nicely adjusted. Without Christ one sees not whither it all tends. The history of the Hellenic religion shows that men began with the honest intention to believe in the righteousness of their gods; but they ended with the feeling that human beings were nothing to the Immortals, and they despaired of faith in the gods. It is a mistake to wish to go back to a natural and universal knowledge of God that embraces all matters about Him and His omnipotence and retribution, adding more precise and definite information from Christianity. No, the trust in God that comes of faith, that enables us to comfort ourselves in Him, the confidence it begets that we are really of some value to Him—this is not to be got till God is seen in Christ. How often does Dr. Luther insist on this: 'To look at the majesty of God leads to terror and despair, and may take a man to Hell itself, but to cherish confidence in God is possible when one seeks Him in the face and in the walk of Jesus Christ'" (p. 107).

NOTE D, p. 254.—BECK ON "INTERCOURSE WITH THE CHRIST OF THE GOSPELS" (*from Gedanken aus und nach der Schrift*. Neue Folge).

Der Hauptmangel bei uns studirten Leuten ist allerdings der, der Ihnen klar geworden, dass alles für uns mehr Begriffsleben ist, wenn es uns auch erfasst hat, und sich immer wieder zersplittert in Reflexion. Entscheidend ist für uns wie für andere Menschen, dass die Wahrheit in persönlicher Gestalt an uns herantritt und in uns persönliche Gestalt gewinnt, und dazu ist eben der Sohn Gottes Mensch geworden, hat die uns rettende Wahrheit gerade in den

Knotenpunkten und Krisen unseres äusseren und inneren Lebens so persönlich durchgebildet und uns vor Augen gestellt, dass er täglich vor uns treten und bei uns sein kann mit den Worten: ich bin der Weg, die Wahrheit und das Leben. Er hat dabei so herzgewinnend mit Wort und That und mit den äussersten Opfern sich uns nahe gebracht, dass er eben damit als persönlichster Magnet die persönlichste Regung der Liebe in uns hervorrufen und so eine Person-Verkettung zwischen ihm und uns bewirken will. Eben desshalb muss es von Aufang bis zu Ende unsere Hauptbeschäftigung bleiben, dass wir die Evangelien lesen, und da täglich zu ihm kommen, so schlicht als möglich, ihn hören und beschauen, und so die unmittelbarsten Eindrücke seiner eigensten Person empfangen, im Gebete sie vertiefen, unter dem Tagleben erneuern, und so einen persönlichen Verkehr mit Jesu einüben. So führt er uns wie seine Jünger nach und nach dahin, dass wir nicht nur durch ihn zu Gott Kommen, um seinetwillen ihn als Vater glauben, sondern in ihm Gott als den Vater finden und haben. Diess ist eben der Mangel der menschlichen Darstellungen, dass sie Gott und Jesum Christum zu sehr ausser einander halten, dass sich Gott über dem Christus wie verliert für uns und überflüssig erscheint, oder wie ein schreckendes, immer zur Strafe bereites Wesen im Hintergrund bleibt. Dagegen der Christus der Evangelien zeigt uns von Aufang an des Vaters Güte in der Natur und seine erbarmende Liebe in der Sendung des Sohnes als das, wodurch er eben die, die ihn fürchten, aufsucht und an sich zieht, um ihnen zu helfen, damit wir dann am Ende (und so in den Episteln) nicht einen zu versöhnenden oder nur versöhnten Gott neben dem Sühnopfer haben sondern im Sohne selbst den versöhnenden und mit der Versöhnung alles Weitere nach seiner weisen Ordnung uns mittheilenden Vater (Röm. viii. 31 ff.). Werfen Sie nur das Vertrauen nicht weg, dass, wenn Sie die vom Herrn selbst uns aufgegebenen Grundfunctionen, wie Bitten, Suchen, Anklopfen, Ringen, nicht lassen, Sie auf dem von Gott versiegelten Weg zum Ziel sind.

INDEX OF NAMES AND SUBJECTS

Abbott, *The Spirit on the Waters* quoted, 96, 229, 273, 294.
Amiel, Journal, 214.
Angels, worship of, in Jewish theology, 157; Christ's work in relation to, 165, 172, 297, 299.
Angelology of St. Paul, 296.
Antichrist in St. Paul's teaching, 137.
Apollinaris' Christology, 211.
Archetypal Man, Christ the, 50, 160.
Arnold, M., on Paul's doctrine of faith, 104.
Atonement, nature of Paul's statements concerning, 80; theories of, 81, 84, 89 (see under *Reconciliation*).

Baldensperger, on the Messiahship of Jesus, 13; the angelology of the Jews, 157; on pre-existence, 195.
Barnabas, Epistle of, its characterisation of Christians, 61.
Baruch, Book of, on Adam's sin, 288.
Baur (*N. T. Theologie*) on the Person of Christ, 26.
Beck, J. T., on truth and life, 180, 303; on the Christ of the Gospels, 254, 323.
Beyschlag, on the pre-existence of Christ, 185, 193; on Phil. iii. 5–11, 191.
Biederman, view of, on pre-existence of Christ, 198.
Biographies of Christ in modern times, 241, 246.
Bornemann on the Person of Christ, 318.
Bruce, Dr. A. B., on 2 Cor. v. 16, 267; Davidic descent of Jesus, 42; the Kenosis of Christ, 206; the historical Christ, 248.

Calvin on the humanity of Christ, 49.
Candlish, Dr., on Sonship of Christ and of believers, 44.
Catholic Church, its conception of the God-man, 205.
Chalcedon, formula of Council of, 22, 204.

Christ the natural Head of all men, 192; the Son of God, 41; the Spiritual Man, 35, 232; His prophetic work ignored by Paul, 236; the mystical Christ, 122; indwelling of Christ, 123, 128, 130; His lordship, 134; Vicegerent of God, 142; the "end" of creation, 176; His historic life and His religious significance for us, 245; continuity of His life in pre- and post-incarnate state, 199; Paul's idea of, before his conversion, 266; conception of, in Middle Ages, 239; prayer to, 144.
Christology, Greek Church, 21; uses of study of, 208; modern view of, 242.
Church, the Body of Christ, 127; idea of, in later Epistles, 162, 164.
Church, Dean, on the example of Christ, 62.
Clement of Rome on Person of Christ, 217.
Colossians, Epistle to, general character of, 152; authorship, 154; its Christology, 156, 159, 165, 170.
Cone: The Gospel and its Interpretations, on the term "Second Adam," 229.

Dale, Dr., on the death of Christ as a revelation of God's love, 77; eternal humanity of Christ, 210; the proofs of Christ's divinity, 146, 220; the Christ of history, 247.
Death, its causal connection with sin the presupposition of Paul's doctrine of the Atonement, 88.
Death of Christ, its supreme significance with Paul, 16, 233; its connection with his life, 87; virtue of, in relation to redemption from sin, 87, 98.
Deissman on the Pneumatic Christ, 119; the phrase "in Christ," 293.
Denney on 2 Cor. v. 21, 280;

the historical and Exalted Christ, 308.
Diognetus, Epistle to, reference to, 313.
Divine and human in Person of Christ not in antithesis, 47, 203, 213.
Dogmatic idea of Christ, 21.
Dorner on the Person of Christ, 208; the idea of Christ in the Middle Ages, 307.
Drummond on Messiahship of Jesus, 13.
Dual consciousness of Christ, theory of, 207.
Dualism removed by Christ (see under *Reconciliation*).
Dyke, Dr. van, the *Gospel for an Age of Doubt*, 250.

ECKE on the theology of Ritschl, 310.
Edwards (*The God-man*) on Person of Christ, 210.
Emerson on the exalted terms applied in New Testament to Christ, 179.
Enoch, the *Book of*, its Christology, 194.
Ephesians, Epistle to, its leading ideas, 151, 162, 163.
Equal with God, the being, meaning of, 189.
Esdras, Apocalypse of, on the sin of Adam, 287.
Essenes, their doctrines, 156; references to, in Epistle to Colossians, 153.
Everling on angelology of St. Paul, 297.
Evil in the world, problem of, 173.
Ewald on Paul's Epistles, 34.
Experience, Christian, the source of Paul's Christology, 14; what his experience of Christ was, 34.

FAIRBAIRN, *Dr.*, on the Death of Christ, 83.
Faith, in Paul's religious system, 94.
Fall of Man, Jewish opinion on, 83, 287; view of modern science on, 96.
Fatherhood of God, Paul's doctrine of, 45.
Final cause of creation, Christ the, 177.
Flesh, the, in Christ, 38.
Forgiveness of sin, connection of with the Death of Christ, 78.
"*Form* of God," meaning of, 189.
"*Fulness* of God," Christ the, 156.

GESS on terms "Son of Man" and "Second Adam," 230; his Christology, 212; his *Person and Work of Christ*, 26; the love of God in the Death of Christ, 76; wrath of God and Death of Christ, 283.
Gifford on Phil. iii. 5-11, 189.

Gladstone, W. E., on Christianity and Theism, 136.
Gloel on the Holy Spirit in the natural man, 36; the Pauline pneumatology, 113.
"*Glory*," meaning of, in Paul's Epistles, 41.
God-man eternal, theory of, 209.
Goethe on the Person of Christ, 226.
Gordon, General, on the Indwelling Christ, 131.
Gore, on the Church as the extension of the Incarnation, 127; the Catholicity of the Church, 162; the Inward Christ, 131; the Humanity of Christ, 23; the Kenosis, 25, 207; on the historical Christ, 237; on gradual apprehension of the Christian ideal, 274.
Gordon, G. A., the *Christ of To-day* quoted, 211.
Gospels, Picture of Christ in the, how far affected by Pauline bias, 225.
Gottschick on the divinity of Christ, 315.
Grafe, E., on Paul and the *Book of Wisdom*, 118.
Grau quoted, 17.
Greek Philosophy, influence of, on Christian ideas, 195.
Green, T. H., on the Immanent Christ, 131.
Gunkel on the Holy Spirit in Paul's teaching, 115.

HÄRING, on forgiveness and penitence, 90; the love of God in the Death of Christ, 278; on Death of Christ as demonstration of evil of sin, 286.
Harless on phrase ἐν Χριστῷ, 121.
Harnack on resemblance between Apollinarian and Pauline Christology, 212.
Haupt on Phil. ii. 5-8, 200, 216.
Hausrath on references to the historical Christ in Paul's letters, 263.
Headship of Christ over Church, 167; over principalities and powers, 170.
Heavenly Man, Christ the, 51; idea of in Jewish theology, 201.
Hebrews, Epistle to: its Christology, 18; echoes in it of Paul's doctrine of the Archetypal Man, 63, 172.
Herrmann on Paul's faith, 29; Jesus' self-assertion in Gospels, 228; God in the historical Christ, 252; Person of Christ, 316, 318.
Historical Christ, the, 6, 238.
Hofmann, von, on Sonship of Christ 43; 1 Cor. x. 4, 187; the Gospels and Epistles, 257.

INDEX OF NAMES AND SUBJECTS 327

Holiness of God revealed in the Death of Christ, 88 ; of Christ, 37.
Holy Spirit, Paul's doctrine of, 113.
Holtzmann on difficult passages in Paul, 29 ; on the doctrine of the pre-existent Heavenly Man, 201.
Hort on worship of angels in later Judaism, 157 ; on imitation of Christ, 289.
Hutton on Paul's teaching on the pre-existent life of Jesus, 187; on the Kenosis, 207.

IDEAL, Christ the, of humanity, 60.
Idealism of Paul, 105.
Image of God, Christ the, 48, 159; in what sense shared by believers, 160.
Imitatio Christi, Christ's doctrine of, 103, 286.
Immanence of Christ, 112.
Immortality, Paul's hope of, 130.
Incarnation, without a Fall, 54; different views of, by John and Paul, 236.
Intercession of Christ not a Pauline doctrine, 142.

JESS quoted, 231, 319.
Jesus, frequency of name in Epistles, 10 ; relation of the Jesus of history to the Christ of experience, 223, 236.
John, St., Christology of, 19.
Jowett, B., on the ethic of Christianity, 103; Paul's knowledge of the historical Christ, 265.
Judaism, belief in angels in later, 166, 171.
"*Judgments* of value" in Ritschl's theology, 311.
Jülicher on the Epistles of the imprisonment, 28.

KÄHLER, on the sinlessness of Christ, 38; on the pre-existence of Christ, 197.
Kaftan on the Person of Christ, 316, 318.
Karl on phrase "in Christ," 294.
Kattenbusch on Person of Christ, 318.
Kenosis, doctrine of, 24, 205.
Ker, Dr. J., on the Christ of the Gospels, 244.
Klöpper, his *Commentary to Epistle to Colossians* referred to, 153.
Knowling on *Witness of the Apostles* to the history of Jesus, 263.
Κύριος use in Septuagint, 295.

LATHAM'S Pastor Pastorum quoted, 42.
Law, the bearing of, on the Death of Christ, 82.

Law, William, on the Second Adam in us, 111.
Lietzmann on the "Son of Man," 230.
Lightfoot, Bishop, on Phil. ii. 5–11, 189.
Lipsius on the pre-existence of Christ, 198.
Logos, incarnation of, in the Lutheran and Reformed systems, 207.
Loofs on Person of Christ, 318.
Lordship of Christ, 134 ; over His people, 138 ; over the world, 139 ; in relation to God, 140.
Love of God, how viewed by Paul, 75.
Luther on the Immanent Christ, 123 ; Christ's lordship, 138 ; the man Christ Jesus, 147 ; Phil. ii. 5–11, 191.
Lutheran doctrine of the Person of Christ, 205.

MARSHALL, W., on the *Nature of Christ*, 305.
Mary, Virgin, substituted for Christ in the Middle Ages, 239.
Matheson, Dr., on the historical Christ, 6 ; on the spiritual development of Paul, 266.
Max Reischle on relation of Exalted Christ to the Christ of history, 244, 254.
Messianic consciousness of Jesus, 226.
Monothelite controversy, 22.
Mudie, Rev. F., on "knowing Christ after the flesh," 266.
Müller, Dr. J., on the supernatural birth of Christ, 273.
Mysticism, dangers of, 132, 244.

NATURAL laws and faith in Christ, 173.
Nösgen on the term "Second Adam," 52.
"*Not Paul* but Christ," 224.
Newman, Cardinal, on angels, 302.

OWEN, Dr. John, on the atoning elements in the death of Christ, 90, 284.

PARET, his article on *Paul and Jesus*, 263 ; source of Paul's doctrinal conceptions, 16 ; the Indwelling Christ, 128.
Pastoral Epistles, Christology of, 267.
Person of Christ as known to us, 25 ; mystery of, 218.
Pfleiderer on the Pauline doctrine of the Holy Spirit, 115.
Pharisaic theology, bearing on forgiveness, 81 ; on origin of sin, 288.
Phil. ii. 6 explained, 215.

INDEX OF NAMES AND SUBJECTS

Philo on the heavenly and earthly man, 51.
Powell on the principle of the Incarnation, 203.
Prayer to Christ, 144.
Pre-existence of Christ, explanations of, 194, 197, 317.

RADE on the Divinity of Christ, 316.
Rainy, Principal, origin of Christian doctrine, 152; the pre-existence of Christ, 199.
Reconciliation, Christ's work of, between God and man, 78; between man and man, 163; between man and angelic powers, 165.
Recapitulation of all things in Christ, 176.
Redemption not an afterthought of creation, 177.
Reformation, the Christ then preached, 240.
Reformed Church, doctrine of Person of Christ, 206.
Resurrection of Christ, its significance in the Christology of Paul, 17; connection with His Function as Second Adam, 55, 65; relation to His Death, 101.
Return to Christ, the, 1.
Ritschl, A., on Christian perfection, 125; justification and its consequences, 78; Phil. ii. 6, 202; service to Christology, 246; his Christology, 309.
Rothe, R., on the holiness of Christ, 38; humanity the medium of a Divine revelation, 49; his doctrine of the Second Adam, 65; on angels, 302.

SABATIER, 18; on Christ and the Spirit, 119; on the historical Christ, 263; on supernatural birth of Christ, 272.
Sacramental acts in reference to the benefit of Christ, 102.
Sacrifice and the Atonement, 84, 277.
Sanday and Headlam, Commentary on Romans, 41, 143, 282.
Schleiermacher's doctrine of the Second Adam, 64.
Schmidt, R., on the Death of Christ, 99; Christology, 26.
Schenkel, on the Christology of Pastoral Epistles, 269; on Phil. ii. 5, 191; on the supernatural birth of Christ in Paul, 272.
Schneckenburger quoted, 205.
Schweizer, on relation of Christ's Death to Law, 83; on Sonship of Christ, 46.

Second Adam, Christ the, 52; threefold function of, 111; idea of, in later Epistles, 161; relation to the representation of Christ in Gospels, 230.
Seeberg on Death of Christ, 79.
Shorter Catechism, its Christology, 22, 47.
Self-emptying of Christ, 191.
Simon (*Die Psych. des P.*), 36, 300.
Sin in believers, 129.
Solidarity of mankind, 86, 97.
Son of God, Christ the, 41, 140, 217.
Son of Man: meaning, 229; history of term, 230.
Sonship to God: Christ's Sonship and believers', 45; stages of, 46; Christ's teaching regarding Sonship, 232.
Sovereignty of Christ in Ritschl's teaching, 314.
Spirit, Holy, Paul's doctrine of, 120; absence of mention of, in later Epistles, 158; Sonship and flesh, 35, 123.
Stanton on the idea of a suffering Messiah, 13.
Strong (*Christian Ethics*) on the teaching of Christ, 10.
Supernatural birth of Christ in Paul's Epistles, 271.
Supremacy of Christ, grander view of, in later Epistles, 152.

TEICHMAN on the Pauline faith in Christ, 130.
Thikotter on Ritschlianism, 309.
Transcendence of Christ, the, 112.
Type, Christ, new t. of manhood, 57, 58, 61.

UNION of the natures in the Person of Christ, 205.
Universalism of Paul, its connection with his idea of Christ as Second Adam, 56.

WEISS, J. (Göttingen), on the preaching of the Risen Christ in primitive Church, 251; Paul's doctrine of the Spirit, 119.
Weiss, B., on the Gospels, and the permanence of the Christian faith, 247.
Weizäcker, on Death of Christ, 98; his translation of New Testament quoted, 41, 135, 280; on the importance of the Christ of history, 248.
Westcott on Incarnation without a Fall, 54.
Wisdom, Apocryphal Book of, its doctrine of the Spirit of God, 118, 292.
Wrath of God and Death of Christ, 282.

INDEX OF TEXTS

Figures in heavy type signify that the text is discussed at length

MATTHEW.	PAGE
x. 10	7
xii. 28	231
xii. 27, 28	294
xvi. 25	101
xx. 28	234
xxii. 43, 44	43
xxvi. 28	234

MARK.	
ix. 4	7
x. 12	7
xii. 35, 37	43

LUKE.	
iii. 21, 22	231
iv. 18	231
xx. 41	43

JOHN.	
i. 45, 49	273
vi. 42	273
vii. 41	273

ACTS.	
ii. 36	134
vii. 56	230
xx. 35	8

ROMANS.	
i. 3	264, 268
i. 4	**41, 46**
i. 5	141
ii. 16	141
iii. 23–26	75, **84**, 88, **280**
iv. 25	95
v. 1	141
v. 6	37
v. 8	76
v. 12	29
v. 14	**86**
v. 16	86

	PAGE
v. 19	**87**
v. 20	107
vi. 3	125
vi. 3–6	99, 264
vi. 10	**100**, 102
vi. 23	141
vii. 17	300
vii. 21–25	125
vii. 25	141
viii. 1–5	125
viii. 2	125, 126
viii. 3	29, 39, 75, 100, 185
viii. 9	116, 126
viii. 10, 11	130
viii. 12	41
viii. 13	126
viii. 14	116
viii. 18–25	125
viii. 23	46
viii. 29, 30	139
viii. 34	143
viii. 38, 39	171
ix. 1	124
ix. 5	29, 42, **143**
x. 5	264
x. 9	95, 135
x. 13	144
xii. 4, 5	168
xiv. 4	135
xiv. 8	139
xiv. 9	135
xiv. 14	124
xv. 2–7	**289**
xv. 3	264
xv. 6	140
xv. 18–29	114
xvi. 20	141

1 CORINTHIANS.	
i. 2	144
i. 3	141
i. 4	141

	PAGE
i. 9	141
i. 13–17	103
i. 18–25	**236**
i. 31	139
ii. 8	41, 264
ii. 6–8	300
ii. 16	124
iii. 1, 4	126
iii. 5	114, 135
iii. 23	140
iv. 2–5	125
iv. 5	138
iv. 16	125
iv. 17	124
iv. 19	135
v. 7	**277**
vi. 17	117, 126
vi. 19	127, 129
vii. 10	7
vii. 17	135, 141
viii. 5, 6	**185**
viii. 6	142, 186, 192
ix. 1	9
ix. 15	125
ix. 21	290
ix. 27	125
x. 2	264
x. 4	186
x. 33	290
xi. 1	125, 133, 139
xi. 3	140
xi. 10	298
xi. 23	7, 264
xii. 3	13, 137
xii. 5	135
xii. 10	264
xii. 12	127, 168
xii. 28	264
xii. 29	264
xii. 31	115
xiii.	61
xiv. 1	115
xv. 3	79, 264
xv. 5	264

330 INDEX OF TEXTS

	PAGE
xv. 22	55
xv. 24-28	136, **178**
xv. 28	139
xv. 40	298
xv. 45-47	51-53
xv. 45	29, 41, 50, 117
xv. 47	50, 186, **201**
xv. 49	41, 50
xv. 57	141

2 CORINTHIANS.

	PAGE
i. 2	141
i. 3	140
i. 12	125
ii. 12-14	124
iii. 3	127
iii. 17	40, 117
iii. 18	41, 117, 127, 139
iv. 6	49
iv. 7	124
iv. 10	101, 124
iv. 11	125
v. 3	29
v. 10	138, 141
v. 14	124
v. 15	94, 264
v. 16	**265**
v. 19	75
v. 19-21	95
v. 21	39, **278**
vi. 3	125
viii. 9	186
x. 7	125
xi. 10	124
xii. 8	144
xii. 12	264
xiii. 3	114
xiii. 4	124, 264
xiii. 14	145

GALATIANS.

	PAGE
i. 1	114
i. 3	141
i. 12	15
ii. 20	258, 264
iii. 5	264
iii. 13, 14	83
iii. 19	297
iii. 20	29
iii. 22	60
iii. 26, 27	103
iii. 28	56, 128
iii.	298
iv. 4	75, 185, 271
iv. 5	45
iv. 6, 7	46
iv. 6	116
iv. 19	126
v. 10	124

	PAGE
v. 16	129
v. 17	125
v. 18	126
v. 22	128
v. 24	99, 126
vi. 3	290
vi. 8	129
vi. 14	76, 253

EPHESIANS.

	PAGE
i. 3	140
i. 10	176
i. 10, 11	152
i. 18-20	41
i. 23	162
ii. 5	163
ii. 13	163
ii. 13-18	152
ii. 14-16	164
iii. 17	168
iii. 19	158, 162
iv. 5	135
iv. 13	**161**
iv. 15	167
v. 1	277
v. 2	289
vi. 8	138

PHILIPPIANS.

	PAGE
i. 8	124, 264
i. 21	139
ii. 3-10	29, 136, **188**, 202, 215, 216, 264, 290
iii. 8	33
iii. 13	125
iii. 21	40, 41
iv. 10	124
iv. 13	124

COLOSSIANS.

	PAGE
i. 3	140
i. 8	158
i. 10	139
i. 14	163
i. 15	155, **159**, 172
i. 15-18	**191**
i. 16	176, 177
i. 18	167, 169
i. 19	**155**, 157
i. 20	177
i. 19, 20	163
i. 24	124
ii. 9	155, 157
ii. 10	**170**
ii. 11, 12	163
ii. 11	264
ii. 13-15	163, **165**, 264
ii. 15-18	172

	PAGE
ii. 16	166
ii. 18	166, 300
ii. 20-23	166
iii. 3	163
iii. iv.	168

1 THESSALONIANS.

	PAGE
i. 6	125
ii. 1, 12	125
ii. 12	141
iii. 11, 12	142
iii. 12	138
iv. 15	7, 265
iv. 16	138
v. 9	141

2 THESSALONIANS.

	PAGE
i. 9	138
ii. 14	139
iii. 3	138
iii. 7, 8	125

1 TIMOTHY.

	PAGE
i. 1	267, 271
i. 5	268
ii. 3	269
ii. 4	268
ii. 5	268
ii. 8	268
iii. 16	268
iv. 10	269
v. 21	270
vi. 3	268
vi. 13	268

2 TIMOTHY.

	PAGE
i. 7	269
i. 9	269
i. 10	268
i. 18	142
ii. 8	268
iii. 12	269
iv. 1	270

TITUS.

	PAGE
i. 3	269
i. 4	269, 270
ii. 11	269
ii. 13	270
ii. 14	269
iii. 4	269
iii. 5	102

HEBREWS.

	PAGE
ii. 5-10	63, 172, 298

REVELATION.

	PAGE
iii. 1	159
xii. 24	268

ERRATA

Page 17, note, *for* "σαρξ" *read* "σάρξ"; *for* "auferstehung" *read* "Auferstehung"; *for* "Schrifthums" *read* "Schriftthums."

,, 23, 11th line from foot, *delete* "that," also "they" in 5th line from foot.

,, 29, 2nd note, *for* "Intercourse" *read* "Communion."

,, 39, 3rd line from foot, *for* "he" *read* "He."

,, 41, note 3, and wherever it occurs, *for* "Weizäcker" *read* "Weizsäcker"; also *delete* hyphen in "mit-Macht."

,, 45, 11th line from foot, *for* "distinction" *read* "distinctions."

,, 48, line 5, *for* "than" *read* "that."

,, 51, 13th line from foot, *before* "it" *insert* "but."

,, 66, 5th line from top, *for* "affecting" *read* "effecting."

,, 81, 3rd line from foot, *for* "Gal. iii. 12" *read* "Gal. iii. 13."

,, 94, 4th line from top, *for* "penetential" *read* "penitential."

,, 98, note 2, *for* "Paulinsche" *read* "Paulinische."

,, 120, 8th line from foot, *after* "same" *insert* comma.

,, 123, 8th line from top, *for* "Gal. ii. 10" *read* "Gal. ii. 20."

,, 125, 9th note, *for* "Ueberzengung" *read* "Ueberzeugung"; *for* "Bewusstein" *read* "Bewusstsein"; and *for* "anstrengungen" *read* "Anstrengungen."

,, 135, 1st note, *for* "Väter" *read* "Vater."

,, 138, 7th note, *for* "Gesicht" *read* "Gericht."

,, 142, 8th line from top, *delete* comma *after* "other."

,, 188, 8th line from top, *for* "Phil. iii." *read* "Phil. ii."; and in note, *for* "vol. t," *read* "vol. i."

,, 195, 4th line from top, *for* "Baldensberger" *read* "Baldensperger."

,, 202, 1st note, *for* "μορφή" *read* "μορφή."

,, 229, note, *for* "Abbot" *read* "Abbott."

,, 257, 4th line from top, *for* "effects" *read* "effect."

,, 273, 1st line, *delete* "of God"; in 7th and 6th lines from foot, *for* "glaube" and "welt" *read* "Glaube" and "Welt."

,, 274, 17th line from top, *for* "Bedentung" *read* "Bedeutung," and *delete* comma between religiöse and Werth.

,, 276, 4th line from foot, *for* "brundgibt" *read* "Kundgiebt."

,, 277, 1st line, *for* "Aufechung" *read* Aufechtung."

,, 300, 5th line from foot, *for* "he" *read* "He."

,, 309, 8th line from top, *for* "ἕλκονσι" *read* "ἕλκουσι"; 16th line from top, *for* "ἀτεχνῶs" *read* "ἀτεχνῶς."

,, 313, 16th line from foot, *delete* "displayed" and *read* "exhibited."

,, 325, *for* "Deissman" *read* "Deissmann."

www.ingramcontent.com/pod-product-compliance
Lightning Source LLC
Chambersburg PA
CBHW071228230426
43668CB00011B/1356